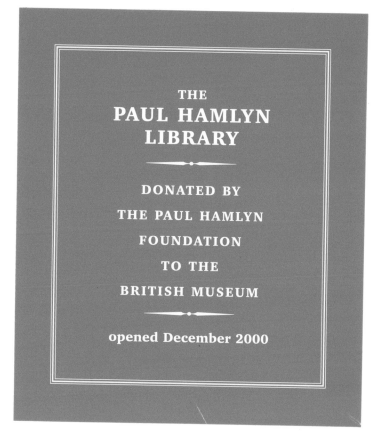

NARRATIVE-BASED PRACTICE

To Alison and Jenny

Once upon a time....

Narrative-based Practice

PETER BROPHY

ASHGATE

Published by
Ashgate Publishing Limited
Wey Court East
Union Road
Farnham
Surrey, GU9 7PT
England

Ashgate Publishing Company
Suite 420
101 Cherry Street
Burlington
VT 05401-4405
USA

www.ashgate.com

British Library Cataloguing in Publication Data
Brophy, Peter, 1950-
   Narrative-based practice
   1. Narrative inquiry (Research method)
   I. Title
   001.4'2

Library of Congress Cataloging-in-Publication Data
Brophy, Peter, 1950-
   Narrative-based practice / by Peter Brophy.
      p. cm.
   Includes bibliographical references and index.
   ISBN 978-0-7546-7159-6
  1. Discourse analysis, Narrative--Social aspects. 2. Narration (Rhetoric)--Social aspects. 3. Storytelling. I. Title.

   P302.84.B76 2009
   306.44--dc22

2008030728

ISBN 978 0 7546 7159 6
eISBN 978 0 7546 8072 7

Mixed Sources
Product group from well-managed forests and other controlled sources
www.fsc.org Cert no. SA-COC-1565
© 1996 Forest Stewardship Council
FSC

Printed and bound in Great Britain by
MPG Books Ltd, Bodmin, Cornwall.

Contents

List of Figures

Preface

Narrative knowing is able to structure information ... The temporal, schematic
linking of events as narrative is the kind of knowing that is used to understand
personal action and autobiography. It is the format people use to organize their
understandings of each other.

(Polkinghorne 1988: 111)

The telling of stories lies at the heart of human communication and underpins the
development and cohesion of all societies and cultures. If we go back to the earliest
human civilisations, we find that it is through story that knowledge, information,
meaning and wisdom are passed from generation to generation. Take as an example
the Hebrew Bible, texts of critical importance to Judaism, Islam and Christianity.
It opens with stories: the creation of the world in six 'days' (with the important, if
now neglected, seventh day of rest!) and the story of the Garden of Eden, used to
provide an explanation of why there is evil in the world, setting out a belief that
this was not how things were meant to be. Continue through the narrative and we
find story piled on story, from Noah and the flood, through Abraham's journey to
the Negev, the slavery of the chosen people in Egypt, their wanderings in the desert
and their eventual establishment in the Promised Land. All of these are stories and
all are stories with a point. They are certainly not presented for mere entertainment
and neither are they intended as a straightforward record of historical events.

Stories, quite simply, are one way of depicting reality and of revealing what
lies beneath the surface of events. They are interested in meaning rather than the
recitation of 'facts'. They help us to explore what is significant. They take full
account of the human dimension. They are concerned with the interpretation of
experience. They invite empathy and participation.

In everyday life stories are used to offer a more graphic description of unfamiliar
scenes than a straightforward factual report might provide. Take, for instance, this
description of medical practice among the ancient Babylonians:

They have no physicians, but when a man is ill, they lay him in the public
square, and the passers-by come up to him, and if they have ever had his disease
themselves or have known any one who has suffered from it, they give him
advice, recommending him to do whatever they found good in their own case, or
in the case known to them; and no one is allowed to pass the sick man in silence
without asking him what his ailment is. (Herodotus)

The story of how medicine was practised gives a much better insight into the society of those times than would a table of mortality rates – and itself recommends the use of personal narrative ('whatever they found good in their own case') as a means of communicating advice. The invitation to storytelling is a means of social cohesion. It acknowledges commonality of experience as well as mutual responsibility.

Throughout mediaeval Europe, the art of storytelling, in prose and verse, was much practised. In England, we had Chaucer's *Canterbury Tales* and Malory's enduring fable *Le Morte d'Arthur*. In Wales, there was the *Mabinogion*; in Italy, Boccacio enthralled his readers with *The Decameron*; in Poland, Jan Kochanowski is credited with writing the first Polish drama, *The Dismissal of the Greek Envoys* and so we could go on. At this distance in time, beset as we are by narrative on all sides, it is hard for us to realise just how powerful such narratives could be.

In Britain, the world's first industrial nation, almost unbelievable poverty flourished during the nineteenth century. Peter Ackroyd described the situation graphically:

> London was indeed becoming what *The Lancet* described as a 'doomed city'. The average age of mortality in the capital was 27, while that for the working classes was 22, and in 1839 almost half the funerals in London were of children under the age of ten. (Ackroyd 2002: 218)

Yet many would argue that it was Charles Dickens' stories of the poor and destitute of London, in novels like *Oliver Twist* and *Little Dorrit*, which did more to change public opinion than any number of fact-laden official reports. Charles Kingsley's *The Water Babies* and George Macdonald's *At the Back of the North Wind* served a similar purpose, coupling the attraction of a well-told fairy story with moral insights into the world as it really was. Of course, those stories had to be supported by hard, quantitative evidence if they were to lead to purposive action. So, alongside Dickens and the others, we had reports such as that by B. Seebohm Rowntree (1901: 119–45) who calculated that of those living in 'primary' poverty (defined as 'families whose total earnings are insufficient to obtain the minimum necessaries for the maintenance of merely physical efficiency'), 16 per cent had suffered the loss by death of the chief wage-earner, 22 per cent had families with more than four children and 52 per cent simply did not earn enough to feed and house themselves properly. It was the coincidence of story and hard data which led to action. Neither would have been as effective on its own.

A story contains meanings which are absent from statistical analysis of the same phenomenon. It is situated in a culture and mores in which, if its central message is to be heard and shared, its reader must participate. So it is that the fascination of stories lies in their connectedness to our own lives. They appeal to experience. Furthermore, they offer an holistic analysis – they consider not just the 'simple' fact, but draw in context and culture and unashamedly offer a point of view. The narrative is much richer than the analysis in its real-life application.

Yet its ability to convey complexity is also its weakness. Stories are powerful because they contain hidden depths of meaning – but therein also lies their danger. Stories can be misused. Hitler, Stalin, Pol Pot and many other demagogues stand as an awful warning to us of the need to discover the truth beneath the veneer of stories.

However, to turn away from narrative to focus solely on 'hard' numbers also misses the point. As it happens, most of my career has been spent in and around libraries, whether physical or virtual. Early in my career, I developed an interest in performance measurement – intrigued by the question, 'Just what is a good library?' Over the years, I have been involved in a long series of research projects which have sought to find answers to that question – and we're by no means there yet. Libraries attract widespread public support as 'a good thing'. People regard the physical library, especially if an architectural statement like the British Library at St Pancras or the Library of Congress in Washington, as a symbol of civilisation. By and large, the value of preserving recorded knowledge on the shelves of the world's great libraries is regarded as a given. Researchers regard the library as fundamental to their work, leading to the widespread claim that it is 'the heart of the university'.

But when those who fund libraries start to ask incisive questions about their value, things become rather more difficult. When I was a young researcher at the University of Lancaster in the early 1970s, I recall serious conversations about the possibility of finding a single numerical 'index' which would indicate a library's worth. After a career both at the sharp end of running university libraries and then in full-time university research, I can look back on those days with a wry smile. Of course such a simplistic measure could not possibly represent the extraordinary range of activity in which any library worth the name engages.

Yet those who provide the funding are right to ask the question. In the public sector, they are accountable for the wise expenditure of money raised through taxation. In the private sector, they are responsible to shareholders for providing maximum value for investment. They rightly require those who manage and provide services to produce evidence which demonstrates the value of the investment. However, after a period when numerical measurement – whether of inputs, outputs, or user satisfaction – was dominant, it is increasingly accepted that meaningful substantiation of decisions must blend 'hard' numerical measures with 'softer' qualitative appraisals; that without an appreciation of the whole context, decision making is flawed.

This requirement for multifaceted evidence is also apparent in many professional disciplines where regulatory bodies may demand to see justifications for decisions that have been made. Financial advisers must show that they offered fair and impartial advice which takes into account all the circumstances of their clients. Medical practitioners must demonstrate that the procedures they selected were backed by rigorous research results – but were also appropriate to the individual patient's needs. All around there is a demand for evidence and for evidence that is more than mere numbers.

This is the context in which this book has been written. It is an attempt to redress a balance which shifted decisively towards quantitative, 'scientific' evidence and is only just beginning to rebalance itself. It draws on a very wide range of theoretical and practical studies to arrive at its central thesis: that professionals must rediscover the value of narrative if their services are to meet the needs of real people in real, and hugely complex, situations. Because the book ranges far and wide it of necessity glosses over some key areas which undoubtedly deserve deeper treatment. If, however, it persuades readers to explore these cases in greater depth and the possibilities that a narrative-based practice presents, then it will have met its intention.

While author acknowledgements are a fraught field of endeavour and sometimes produce more authorial perspiration that the rest of the book, it would be remiss of me not to recognise the help I have received from very many people, colleagues, friends and family, experts in different fields, in developing my understanding of this complex area. While it would be impossible to list everyone – and of course some influential storytellers are encountered accidentally, or perhaps fortuitously, without ever being known by name – this does not signify any lack of gratitude. I hasten to add that in preserving the anonymity of my sources I am not trying to follow in the footsteps of Bob Woodward, who thanked 250 people for helping him write *The Secret Wards of the CIA* – but refused to name them for security reasons! I am also, I hope, justified in avoiding the approach taken by Alice Walker in *Living by the Word*, where she thanked the flowers and the trees, an inscription characterised by the humorist Henry Alford as one that 'can only prompt a reader to check the cover of his book for evidence of gnawing!'. I trust that my readers will find more palatable fare to accompany their perusal of the pages which follow.

Peter Brophy
Lancaster, 2008

To contact the author please email nbp@limc.co.uk

Chapter 1
Evidence-based Practice

One exhibition was doing ear candling for $30. The people selling this said that the suction created by the candle 'cleared your mind and sinuses.' I questioned them enough to establish that they meant this literally and believed the ear was an opening from the brain and sinuses. The woman running the booth stated, 'It cleans the whole head, brains and all – they're all connected you know.' The candling was performed on a table at the front of the booth, so the curious sight of a person lying there with a burning candle sticking out of his ear drew many spectators. During the procedure, a gray mixture of soot and wax drippings collected on a pie plate under the candle. It did not look like melted candle wax, but was quite foul in appearance. Customers were told that these were the 'impurities' of which they had been cleansed, and many went around proudly showing them off, comparing their debris to that of others, and making knowing comments.

Two investigators tested candles to see whether the wax accumulated after burning came entirely from the candle or included wax that came from the ear. To do this they burned candles with the tip (a) inside the ear, (b) outside the ear, so the wax dripped into a bowl of water, and (c) inside the ear but with a tube in place that would permit ear wax to move into the tube but would block candle wax from moving downward. They demonstrated that all residue originated from the candle and that no ear wax was removed from the ear. (Roazen, 2007)

Introduction

Evidence has of course been collected and used by medical practitioners and others for a very long time, but it has not always been applied systematically. Sometimes tradition and personal experience have become a dead weight, stultifying alterations to practice even when the evidence indicates strongly that change is needed. Gambrill remarks:

Consider the experience of Ignaz Semmelweiss who, around 1840, discovered that the death rate of mothers from childbed fever markedly decreased if surgeons washed their hands before delivering babies. [Yet] cleanliness was not taken seriously by the medical profession until the end of the century. (Gambrill 1999: 2)

However, it is perhaps not surprising that when 'evidence-based practice' (EBP) did emerge, it was in medicine and that that remains its core locus. It is generally accepted that the concept of evidence-based practice was first developed at McMaster University in Canada in the early 1990s, broadening out in the mid-1990s to 'evidence-based healthcare'. There are various definitions, although a widely accepted one is:

> Evidence-based practice (EBP) is an approach to health care wherein health professionals use the best evidence possible, i.e. the most appropriate information available, to make clinical decisions for individual patients. EBP values, enhances and builds on clinical expertise, knowledge of disease mechanisms, and pathophysiology. It involves complex and conscientious decision-making based not only on the available evidence but also on patient characteristics, situations, and preferences. It recognizes that health care is individualized and ever changing and involves uncertainties and probabilities. Ultimately EBP is the formalization of the care process that the best clinicians have practiced for generations. (McKibbon 1998: 396)

EBP is now accepted in medicine and healthcare world-wide. In a number of countries, it forms a mandatory basis for practice. It is backed up by a wide range of services, like the Cochrane Collaboration (http://www.cochrane.org/) which provides access to systematic reviews of the medical literature. These reviews search the literature for relevant papers on any particular medical intervention (for example, an operation, a course of treatment, screening for the early stages of a disease or advice on a particular problem), consider each study carefully against predefined criteria, aggregate data (where possible) on outcomes into a meta-analysis, summarise the findings and provide a discussion of the implications by experts. Healthcare practitioners world-wide use these reviews to ensure that they are up to date with latest best practice.

The 'gold standard' for research studies is the Randomised Controlled Trial (RCT), which uses a process designed to exclude, as far as possible, sources of bias and thus to establish a clear cause-and-effect relationship between the intervention and the outcome – for example, between the taking of a drug and the change in a medical condition. In an RCT there is, first of all, a control group. Trials, say of a new medicine, involve giving one set of patients the drug while another set is given a placebo. As far as possible, the two groups need to be identical in their characteristics, so the sample is randomly split between the two groups. The trials are also *double-blind*, that is, a researcher who knows which is the real drug and which is the placebo numbers each dose randomly, maintaining a list of which is which. A different researcher or doctor, who administers the drug to a patient, only has the numbered doses and records the patient's name or other details against each number but has no way of knowing which are the drugs and which are the placebos, and cannot therefore tell the patient or even reveal this information unwittingly, say by facial expression or gesture. The outcomes are monitored and the data passed back to the first researcher, who can assign them to drug or placebo from the master list. The results should be free of bias introduced by knowledge of which procedure has been used.

Controlled trials are not a modern invention. Indeed one is recorded in the Book of Daniel, which was written no later than the mid-second century BCE:

> Daniel resolved not to defile himself with the royal food and wine, and he asked the chief official for permission not to defile himself this way. Now God had caused the official to show favour and sympathy to Daniel, but the official told Daniel, 'I am afraid of my lord the king, who has assigned your food and drink. Why should he see you looking worse than the other young men your age? The king would then have my head because of you.' Daniel then said to the guard whom the chief official had appointed over Daniel, Hananiah, Mishael and Azariah, 'Please test your servants for ten days: Give us nothing but vegetables to eat and water to drink. Then compare our appearance with that of the young men who eat the royal food, and treat your servants in accordance with what you see.' So he agreed to this and tested them for ten days. At the end of the ten days they looked healthier and better nourished than any of the young men who ate the royal food. So the guard took away their choice food and the wine they were to drink and gave them vegetables instead.
> (Daniel 1:8–16, New International Version)

While that experiment would not meet modern standards (the participants knew which group they were in for a start!), it does illustrate that the idea behind RCTs is an ancient one. In modern times, credit for the widespread acceptance of the technique belongs to Sir Austin Bradford Hill, who published a landmark paper in 1952. More recently, there has been acknowledgement that while RCTs remain critical, the most important issue is that the most appropriate method should be selected for the intended experiment and a wider range of techniques can be quite properly applied. For example, ethical considerations will dictate that patients should not be given a placebo where it is known that their condition is likely to worsen if they are denied the drug itself.

EBP as Process

It is important to recognise that EBP is not just about the evidence itself, but also encompasses the process by which the evidence is gathered and applied. Five steps have been identified as necessary if it is to be effective in terms of patient outcomes (Straus et al. 2005):

1. translation of uncertainty, which may be about a wide range of problems,

into an answerable question,
2. systematic retrieval of the best available evidence,
3. critical appraisal of that evidence for validity, relevance, and applicability,
4. application of the results in practice (here EBP practitioners have recognised the importance of integrating the 'hard' evidence gathered with clinical judgement and patient values), and
5. evaluation of performance – the effectiveness and efficiency of the process undertaken.

Thus it is the framing of the question and the search for relevant, valid, reliable and applicable evidence to illuminate it which are critical, as is the review of the performance of the application to practice once it has been completed. EBP would therefore expect an iterative approach where practitioners reflect on and learn from their experience.

Beyond Medicine

It is hardly surprising that a paradigm which has proved so popular and become so widespread in medicine should be taken up by other professional disciplines. Some of these are allied to medicine, such as nursing and physiotherapy. Some are associated with it, as with librarianship where information practitioners in health services were charged with locating the medical literature and started to apply the concept of EBP to their own discipline, spawning evidence-based librarianship (EBL) and evidence-based information practice (EBIP). Some are professional disciplines within the social sciences, such as education and social work, which were seeking more systematic ways to address pressing issues of professional practice. Others are of a more general nature, as when EBP is applied to management. Others again are specialised fields. Ray, for example, writes:

> It is too easy for professionals to use their specialist knowledge as a means of control. Architecture has been particularly bad at setting out the evidence from which a decision can be taken and at continuing to build that body of evidence from experience in use. [But] the move towards research-based design and evidence-based practice is beginning to be accepted by sections of the profession. (Ray, 2005: xvi)

The growing interest in EBP outside healthcare has not, however, seen the overwhelming take-up that it achieved in its original home. It is not that the idea of basing decisions on reliable evidence is rejected – far from it. But often the complexity of the social setting and the intricacies of contextual factors make it much harder to evaluate the usefulness of a particular piece of evidence in a particular setting. As Coe (1999) remarks in a manifesto for evidence-based education:

Education is so complex that slight and subtle differences in context may make all the difference to the effects of some change in policy or practice. One of the things that makes teaching so interesting is that what works for me may not work for you, and even may not work for me the next time I try it. This makes it seem unlikely that the kinds of simple, universal strategies much beloved by governments will produce the improvements intended, although only by trying them can we really be sure. However, this complexity does not mean that there can never be any worthwhile evidence about anything. A more useful kind of evidence would be that which seeks to throw light on exactly which features of the context are important, to find the conditions on which the outcome depends. When we have this kind of evidence we will understand better which strategies are likely to be most effective in each situation.

Before exploring in more detail the kinds of evidence which are needed to make sense of complexity and context, it is useful to examine just why EBP has succeeded in becoming so popular in its home discipline of medicine. It is curious that what was a major change in the dominant paradigm of medical practice occurred so quickly and spread so rapidly. Why should this have happened? In seeking to answer this question we need to look far and wide, at broad societal trends as well as to the subject itself. Ten areas of exploration suggest themselves.

EBP and Professional Status

Over many years, medical practitioners had elevated the status of their profession until the doctor had become among the most important members of the community. This reminiscence would be typical:

> When I was young, we were poor as church mice and we were living in a country town. And there was a sort of holy trinity: there was the headmaster of the school and the bank manager and the local GP (general practitioner) – God-almighty, you know! And it would not matter what sort of clod he was, he was 'Doctor'. When I was a very small child, if my grandparents, for example, had cause to call 'Doctor', the thing to do was to put out a fresh cake of soap and a basin and bring in water for 'Doctor'. (quoted in Lupton, 1997: 480)

However, by the final quarter of the twentieth century, this societal respect was beginning to break down. In large part this came about through broader changes in society, with shifting attitudes to authority and a much-increased willingness to question accepted norms. In the case of doctors, however, it was also influenced by some well-publicised cases which demonstrated that 'Doctor' certainly didn't always know best. As a result we have at times returned to a more medieval characterisation of doctors, typified by Ben Franklin's cynical observation, 'God heals and the Doctors take the Fee.' Or in Matthew Prior's lines,

You tell your doctor, that y'are ill
And what does he, but write a bill. (Porter 1994: 1714)

To counter such cynicism, the medical profession has gone to great lengths to protect its reputation by creating robust mechanisms to ensure that only the 'best' evidence is used – and that where medical practitioners fail in this requirement they are challenged, if necessary admonished and in extreme cases struck off the medical register. Thus public respect for the medical profession is reinforced by the public's perception that in cases where they have not acted in patients' best interests, and particularly where they have neglected available evidence as to the most efficacious procedure, there are mechanisms for admonishing them and in extreme cases preventing them from practising. Even though the public may not be familiar with the concepts of RCTs and EBP, there is an appreciation that in general, even though there are always perceived exceptions, professional standards are applied. EBP underpins the assurances which the public can be given and thus acts to reinforce the notion of the professionalism of the medical practitioner.

The Scientific Research Base

Medicine has developed, and continues to expand, a highly sophisticated and extensive body of scientific research with extensive quality-assurance processes, based on peer review and on mechanisms like the RCT. Comparison between the results of different studies through the process of systematic review has enabled the development of a number of authoritative sources of advice, such as the Cochrane Collaboration referred to above.

It is important to stress that the modern dominance of scientific evidence over folk wisdom, tradition, divine revelation and individual experience is part of a process which has been in place since the Enlightenment of the eighteenth century. The period between the Glorious Revolution in England and the French Revolution (and including the American Revolution), with its emphasis on the role of reason as the basis for authority, found in the West a ferment of new ideas and attitudes. This revolutionary movement, which built its foundations on Immanuel Kant's motto, *sapere aude* (dare to know), built a new meta-narrative which privileged scientific knowledge. It mixed classical learning with a willingness to challenge accepted wisdom and formed the dominant values for Western society for the next two hundred years – indeed, we still live with it. As Gay puts it graphically in his major work, *The Enlightenment: an Interpretation*:

> The Enlightenment, then, was a single army with a single banner, with a large central corps, a right and a left wing, daring scouts, and lame stragglers. And it enlisted soldiers who did not call themselves philosophes but who were their teachers, intimates, or disciples … The Enlightenment was a volatile mixture of classicism, impiety, and science. (Gay, 1966: 6)

This is the context within which EBP has risen to prominence. The Enlightenment value of reason has resulted in huge scientific advances that have benefited all of humankind, albeit with many unintended consequences which we now must face, among them climate change and global warming. However, few suggest that such problems mean that we should turn our backs on the scientific endeavour. Rather, the consensus is that we need to redouble our efforts to gather the evidence needed to make wise and far-sighted decisions for the benefit of all. EBP is one manifestation of this imperative.

Information and Communications Technologies

The ability which information and communications technologies (ICTs) have provided to generate huge amounts of information, to process it and to deliver it selectively to a world-wide audience has clearly made a big difference to the practice of medicine. Not only are findings from across the world more widely available but new discoveries can be communicated rapidly to virtually every medical practitioner on the planet. There can be little doubt that the combination of different ICTs (for example, software for data capture and analysis, pre-print and post-print archives, Web publishing, alerting services) has resulted in a much bigger, and more rapidly changing, literature. Purely in quantitative terms, it is reported that

> ... between 1978 to 1985 and 1994 to 2001, the annual number of MEDLINE articles increased 46%, from an average of 272,344 to 442,756 per year, and the total number of pages increased from 1.88 million pages per year during 1978 to 1985 to 2.79 million pages per year between 1994 to 2001. (Druss and Marcus 2005: 500)

ICTs also enable individual practitioners to manage their access to, and thus use of, evidence. Where in the past medical practitioners might subscribe to a small selection of journals, such as the *British Medical Journal* or *The Lancet*, they can now access selected papers from any of tens of thousands of different journals with near-instantaneous delivery (always allowing, of course, for the vagaries of subscription deals). Systematic reviews are similarly available so that the best available evidence for the appropriate diagnosis or intervention can be identified readily, even when the symptoms are unfamiliar. Furthermore, the aggregation of data on interventions and its analysis is greatly facilitated by ICTs, especially when the basic data – patient records – are available in electronic form. All of these advantages lead to greater use of recorded information, which becomes the content on which EBP can be based. The fact that EBP rose to prominence at exactly the same time as end-user computer systems became commonplace is surely no accident.

Information Overload

The increase in the amount of information published, together with developments in ICTs, has led to the commonly experienced phenomenon of information overload. Not only is an almost limitless range of information available for access on the Web, but much information is pushed to the individual through email, instant messaging, SMS text, voicemail, RSS feeds, aggregators and, of course, paper. It is not only the amount of such information which causes problems, but the independence of different systems means that it can be very difficult to sequence messages. For example, is the latest information to be found in the voicemail I just listened to or the email that has just appeared on my screen? How can I sensibly store all these different messages in ways which create meaningful order from them? Why is this message labelled 'urgent' and is it really more pressing than any other? Will I be able to retrieve the one I want when it is needed? Is it safe to discard this data, or is it better to keep it 'just in case'?

The psychological problems created by information overload are well known. Over fifty years ago, Miller (1956) suggested that it occurs when human cognitive capacity is exceeded, his proposition being that individuals cannot process more than five to nine 'chunks' of information simultaneously. Others (for example, Driver et al. 1993; Marcusohn 1995) have suggested that information overload is connected to the complexity of the environment in which the individual is working, with factors such as deadlines, bureaucratic requirements, perceptions of risk and unpredictable events increasing the likelihood of overload being experienced.

The mechanisms put in place to support EBP, most notably the availability of systematic reviews which take the load from the individual enquirer by undertaking detailed analysis of different sources, have clear benefits in managing information volumes, controlling complexity and providing efficient and logical data structures. In this way, espousal of EBP brings with it the advantage of shared information handling and thus reduction in the weight of responsibility on the individual. For medical practitioners, this is a critical issue since it enables them to maximise the time spent with each patient rather than on keeping up to date with the ever-expanding literature. It also makes it less likely that they will miss a particular, vital piece of information.

Universality of Practice

By and large, good medical practice is universal, in the sense that what works in one geographical location will work in another. For example, laser treatment to correct myopia is as effective in Europe as in China or South America. This is also why medical screening programmes can be operated successfully on a huge scale, and lies behind the defeat of diseases like smallpox where massive vaccination programmes led to the declaration by the World Health Organization (WHO) in 1979 that the disease had been eradicated.

There are limits to this universality, of course. For example, genetic makeup, including variations based on ancestral population differences, can affect the success of some treatments (although this area remains controversial, since environmental factors cannot be discounted). However, these are relatively minor issues compared with the universal applicability of the vast majority of treatments. This universality enables medicine to promote its claims based on evidence gathered anywhere in the world. Indeed, comparisons between regions and countries are often used to highlight deficiencies in health care and to underpin campaigns for changes in priorities and spending.

Again, then, EBP offers considerable advantages to medicine and suggests that other professions which can legitimately claim world-wide applicability could gain similar benefits. Even where this is not the case – law would be the obvious example since countries have different legal systems – commonality of practice across a more restricted area can offer clear advantages to the individual practitioner. Where professionals have greater autonomy the advantages of the EBP approach may not be so clear-cut.

In laying claims to universality or commonality, however, we need to be careful. Clarke has pointed out that very often it is the framing of the question which dictates the method of enquiry and thus the results, while hiding underlying assumptions. She offers the following example:

> Sheldon (1994) reports that systematic review offers strong evidence that prophylactic antibiotics reduce the frequency of infection following caesarean section. Therefore the recommendation is that all women be given antibiotics following caesarean section. However, a patients' representative, on examining the original studies, commented, 'Why is there a variation in infection rates amongst obstetric units in the first place?'. The positing of this question (and the answers it suggests) was preferable to the administering of antibiotics. (Clarke 1999: 91)

Here we have an example where universality, derived from the aggregation of large numbers of cases from disparate locations, masks the even more effective local solution which finds its focus in the context of the individual problem, itself often revealed only by listening carefully to the personal narrative.

Accountability

There has been a very clear trend in recent years to much greater explicit accountability of all professionals, including doctors. With the propensity for apportioning blame and the associated tendency to pursue litigation at any opportunity (epitomised by 'ambulance-chasing' lawyers waiting in the wings) both practising professionals and the public at large are very aware that a poor decision can have far-reaching consequences beyond the immediate effect on the patient. Not that this is a new phenomenon – in 1936, Robert Monaghan wrote:

> The liability claim racket is an American institution, costing Americans tens of millions of dollars annually, corrupting, together with a number of sound social principles, the American courts, the bar, the jury system, the police, and in general threatening the decent progress of honest litigation … with ultimate extinction … There is nothing new about the claim racket except its size … [it] stems from the development of ambulance chasing which, according to its most notorious exponents, came to prominence about 1920. (Monaghan 1936: 491)

It is not surprising that, faced with this situation, medical practitioners have become very careful to marshal the evidence which they can use in their defence. Often there is a requirement for an explicit audit trail and professional indemnity insurers will require that the written evidence which led to a particular course of action is available. Again, this is facilitated if working in an EBP environment, even if the outcomes of treatment prove, in the event, not to be optimal for the patient.

It is also worth noting that in a number of areas the ability to link between evidence and action is critical, even if this is not termed EBP. For example, in materials science, engineers select appropriate substances based on rigorous scientific analyses of their properties and experience of them in use. In aircraft design, for instance, it is mandatory for all of this evidence to be collected and stored in case questions are raised, perhaps years later, about the performance of the materials chosen. This kind of requirement has become a focus of interest in grid computing where vast amounts of quantitative data are processed, yet it is necessary to be able to track the provenance of information products. Here the requirement is not simply to know where the data originated but also the processes of transformation to which it has been subjected over time. This information often needs to be compared with similar provenance data for related datasets. In effect, an audit trail is being built up which demonstrates in a rigorous fashion why conclusions have been reached. Thus the basic tenets of EBP are observed, even if the terminology differs.

Risk Management

Associated with the issue of accountability and audit, but also gaining strength from a genuine concern not to do harm (the *primum non nocere* principle taught to all medical students), there has been a marked increase in explicit approaches to risk management (the more cynical may of course put this down to the alternative Latin injunction, *cura te ipsum*, roughly translated as 'heal yourself first'!).

Trinder regards the notion of risk as 'perhaps the most important consequence of the shift to post-industrial societies [in the] discussion of evidence-based practice'. She draws on the work of Anthony Giddens, pointing out that 'in post-traditional times there is a heightened sense of risk, coupled with a sense that contingencies are generally human created as well as inescapable.' She continues:

> Even the relatively simple task of driving to work requires the lay person to trust numerous unknown others, including other drivers, as well as car manufacturers and repairers, traffic planners and driving test examiners. It is impossible for either individuals or organisations to avoid externally generated risks, ranging from food additives and genetically modified food to stock market crashes and political upheaval. The results are unsettling. (Trinder 2000: 5)

The consequence of this heightened perception of risk may be that there is a greater propensity to gather together evidence before deciding on a particular course of action. However, we also need to recognise that perception of risk is often socially conditioned (the so-called 'cultural theory of risk') and highly dependent on the degree of control which individuals can exercise. In a classic study, Starr (1969) demonstrated that people will generally accept far greater risks if their activity is voluntary and under their own control (such as driving a car) than when they are passive 'victims' (a nuclear reactor exploding in the vicinity of their home, for example).

The argument, then, is that people need evidence with which to manage the risks they face and evidence-based practice will provide this. However, there are plenty of examples where lay people simply will not accept such evidence, a good example being the siting of mobile phone masts. As one doctor complained in *The Lancet* in 2003:

> Looking out of our surgery window it is possible to see the tips of a mobile-phone mast situated on the roof of the block of flats on the opposite side of the road. During the past 3 years, this mast has become the target of a militant local campaign by residents who claim that the mast may be a health risk. Meetings and protests have brought together the residents of this depressed estate in an unprecedented display of community cohesion. It is a sign of our anxious times that fears shown to be groundless in many scientific investigations now provide the focus for public engagement. (Fitzpatrick, 2003: 1484).

From this perspective, it can be seen that while the evidence-based approach has become accepted in much professional decision making, it is not an approach which is always convincing to the population at large. There is a paradox here. A heightened sense of risk is engendered, at least in part, by wider availability of evidence as to causes and effects, yet this same evidence is less than wholly convincing when individuals are called upon to make decisions affecting their own lives. This is one reason that a re-evaluation of the kinds of evidence which EBP typically presents is needed.

Process Convergence

Faced with ever-increasing complexity in the delivery of services and heightened awareness of risk, there is always a temptation to adopt uniformity of process, borrowing from or copying what happens elsewhere when 'elsewhere' is seen as successful. Because something works well in one context, there is a temptation to assume that it is the process used to deliver the product or service which has produced successful outcomes rather than a combination of the people, the context and the methods, perhaps without always giving the matter a great deal of critical thought. Many of the fads which sweep through management – management by objectives, total quality management, business process re-engineering and so on – can be seen in this context. Sometimes industries or professions mandate standards like ISO9000, which requires a particular approach to quality management including extensive documentation of processes, problems and solutions, without any real evidence that the benefits found in other industries are transferable.

In the public sector, process convergence is encouraged, albeit unwittingly, by centrally imposed accountability and audit. Faced with an inspection visit to their school, head-teachers not unnaturally want to demonstrate that the processes they have put in place match up to those judged excellent elsewhere. While in theory the real question concerns outcomes, in practice it is the processes which, being visible, tend to be copied. Over time, these same processes will infect the sector as a whole. Evidence from one context may, in this way, come to be used much more widely than originally intended or warranted.

The same effect can be seen where either economics or convenience dictates that individual organisations must borrow practices and processes from elsewhere. The widespread adoption of the Dewey Decimal Classification (DDC) system among British libraries could be cited as a case in point. Despite the dominance of the US world-view in DDC (at one time, homosexuality was classified under 'mental derangements' and even in 1989 entries could be found under 'social problems'!), and despite the existence of European alternatives like the Universal Decimal Classification (UDC), originally developed by the Belgian bibliographers Paul Otlet and Henri la Fontaine, DDC and the alternative US Library of Congress (LC) Classification are dominant throughout the world. Evidence of appropriateness in one cultural setting has led to adoption globally. Where a particular world-view is dominant, as with the United States' in the last half century, it is all too easy for its practices and evidences to become the norm.

It seems likely that EBP encourages this kind of development when it emphasises the published literature as its source of evidence. Not only are developed countries able to invest more in scientific investigations, but their researchers dominate the scholarly literature. Since published evidence is privileged, it is hardly surprising that the perspectives of the developed nations take precedence, leaving developing-world practitioners struggling to make their voices heard.

Performance Management

A focus in management across all disciplines on effectiveness, outcomes, impact and equity, alongside more traditional performance measures related to economy and efficiency, has not unnaturally led to a search for sources of reliable evidence. Indeed, one of the maxims of management is 'If you can't measure it, you can't manage it.' Typical advice based on this mantra would be:

> For example, we measure number of lines of code written by each programmer during a week. We measure (count) the number of bugs in that code. We establish 'bugs per thousand lines of code' as the metric. We compare each programmer's metric against the benchmark of 'fewer than 1 defect [bug] per thousand lines of code'. (http://management.about.com/od/metrics/a/Measure2Manage.htm)

In fact, of course, few managers would be naïve enough to follow that advice to the letter. Are all software bugs of the same level of seriousness? Do they all take the same effort to put right? Are programmers judged more competent because they produce more lines of code than their co-workers, with the same number of bugs?

Nevertheless, the belief that what is managed must be measured in some quantitative sense is widespread. It follows that those professions, of which again healthcare is perhaps the most obvious, where there is a large body of quantitative data readily available, are likely to adopt an EBP which privileges such information. This is not to criticise the use of quantitative methods, for they are a significant part of the whole picture. It is to note, however, that where managers and professionals cannot draw on this kind of research-informed quantitative data, there seems less likelihood of the EBP approach being adopted.

The Bandwagon Effect

Finally, it is clear that EBP is as subject to the bandwagon effect as any other new organisational process. It is always problematic when a new technique attracts official endorsement, when large numbers of practitioners adopt it and when it can lay claim to some spectacular results. The temptation is to join the rush to adopt it, to pioneer new ways to use it, to exclude alternatives and to promote it among one's peers as the answer to the problems that all professionals face.

It is important to recognise that bandwagon effects can be both positive and negative. On the one hand, a bandwagon can result in the development of critical mass. With EBP, this is epitomised by the increase in the numbers of RCTs which then contribute to the evidence base. Even if practitioners and researchers sign up to EBP because it's what everyone else is doing, their subsequent efforts may be beneficial.

On the other hand, there are negatives to consider. Clearly the fact that everyone else is doing something is not of itself sufficient reason to join in – there were fatal flaws in what was being said at the Nuremburg rallies but it took a world war to demolish their effects. It is always difficult to stand against the flow, especially when society as a whole endorses the direction. Yet, as has already been demonstrated, there are serious doubts about aspects of EBP as it has emerged, not only in its core arena of healthcare but even more so in its broadening into other professional arenas. At the very least, professionals need to be alert to the dangers of following the herd.

Conclusions

There can be little doubt that EBP has brought significant benefits. The emphasis on RCTs, and continuous efforts to improve methods, has led to authoritative sources of scientific information being made available to medical practitioners. In other disciplines, there have also been significant benefits from adapting the approach.

But there remain doubts and gaps. While many professionals push ahead with the EBP paradigm, there are signs that complementary approaches may be needed. It is all very well to publish papers in peer-reviewed journals, to employ statisticians and others to analyse results and prepare overviews of what the evidence is saying, but not everyone is taking notice. Most importantly, in medicine at least, the clients (that is, patients) are less than convinced. Why should this be the case?

One reason is that people act on their perceptions rather than on 'objective' reality, as Garvin (1984) pointed out in the context of management many years ago. When assessing the quality of a service or product:

> ... all customers make their judgements on incomplete information ... they ... come to a judgement ... based on their preconceptions as users and on the reputation of the [service] among their colleagues and acquaintances. (Brophy and Coulling 1996: 48)

A second limitation of EBP is that it requires the consumer of the evidence to (a) agree with written evidence as a suitable source of information, and (b) to have the skills and competencies to understand and apply it. Yet many groups, especially of non-experts, neither wish to obtain information on which to base a decision in this way nor are equipped to process it if delivered to them. For example, in a paper entitled 'Information preferences and practices among people living with HIV/AIDS', Hogan and Palmer wrote:

> ... more information is not the answer for improving information services for PLWHA (people living with HIV/AIDS). Availability of information was not reported as a problem by many respondents. The more pressing need might be understanding individuals and specific groups, getting the right information out to them, tailoring it so it is applicable, and improving it in terms of readability, provision of actions steps, and consistency. This requires not only creativity

on the part of information producers and distributors, but also attention to what Resnicow et al. (1999) term the surface and deep structure dimensions of cultural sensitivity. Whereas surface structure sensitivity involves matching health information to observable characteristics of a group, deep structure sensitivity involves understanding the cultural, social, historical, environmental, and psychological forces that influence the health-related behaviours of a group. (Hogan and Palmer 2005: 438)

We can also question the use of EBP by asking whether in fact universal application is either appropriate or useful. Clarke (1999) emphasises the need to consider 'evidence' alongside experience, to use skill and judgement both in framing questions and in deriving answers. She quotes White in observing how EBP subtly commandeers the high ground:

> In EBP there is what can be described as a hierarchy of evidence. At the top is a kind of experimental research … At the bottom lies clinical anecdote, which may be defined as the knowledge gained from the clinical experience of the practitioner. (White 1997: 175)

Tanenbaum adds that anecdotes 'are more emotionally interesting because they happened to one or someone one knows. The information is concrete and vivid and especially potent when derived from a face-to-face encounter' (2003: 291). Holmes and colleagues are searingly critical, 'we are currently witnessing the health sciences engaged in a strange process of eliminating some ways of knowing' (Holmes et al. 2006: 181).

There is no doubt that EBP has brought great value. The question is how to enhance that value still further by addressing some of its limitations, especially in the broader practice of professional judgement: 'Best evidence should be judged as that which helps the client/patient rather than claiming that the best is scientific and that non-scientific is a poor last' (Clarke 1999: 92).

The paradigm of EBP gives us a starting point, but it poses the question of how to build on its successes in order to encompass and indeed focus upon a more holistic and person-centred practice. One possibility is to return narrative to a central place. It has in fact been used widely in medical practice for very many years. In the Preface, we noted its use in ancient Babylon. In modern times, the patient's own telling of their narrative has often been the first stage in diagnosis – what happened, when, what are thought to be the contributory causes. The very process of telling one's own 'illness narrative' can be healing. However, there is considerable evidence that medical practitioners frequently block the patient's narrative, usually by a technocratic (and possibly EBP-influenced) approach. Mishler, after presenting a detailed analysis of transcripts, suggests that the medical interview can be seen as

> ... a situation of conflict between two ways of constructing meaning ... the physician's attempt to impose a technocratic consciousness, to dominate the voice of the lifeworld by the voice of medicine, seriously impairs and distorts essential requirements for mutual dialogue and human interaction. To the extent that clinical practice is realized through this type of discourse, the possibility of more humane treatment in medicine is severely limited. (Mishler 1985: 127)

He goes on to point out that

> ... the practice of medicine is not a theoretical, but an applied science ... its focus and stance are tied not to the 'disinterested' stance of the scientific investigator but to the practical concerns of patient care and treatment'. (ibid., 128)

Of course what he describes is not universal medical practice by any means, and many patients (I count myself among them) experience a professional listening ear which engages fully with the narrative. But the important point is that it is *only* when the narrative is allowed to speak that an holistic attempt at treatment can be essayed.

Galves (2004), a child psychotherapist, reinforces this claim from the perspective of one of the professions allied to medicine:

> The problem with EBP is that psychotherapy is not an experimental variable. It cannot be such because of its, contingent, unstandardized, idiosyncratic nature. One of the truths that most psychotherapists subscribe to is that the relationship between the therapist and the patient is crucial. This can't be standardized or manualized. How do you subject play therapy to the kind of study required to endorse it as EBP? Yet, my experience tells me that play therapy is very valuable as a therapeutic intervention with certain children and adolescents.

So it is that there is a growing challenge to the dominance of EBP, at least in its current form. Concern for context, and above all for a holistic approach which acknowledges individuality, feelings, emotion, culture and society is becoming more widespread. Moving beyond the scientific paradigm to find ways to support such concerns brings into focus one of the dominant ways in which human beings communicate with each other and describe the world they experience, namely narrative. It seems likely that a rebalancing of the evidence used in professional and organisational decision making to privilege narrative would help practitioners to move beyond the limitations of EBP. To explore this question further, we need first to examine the theoretical foundations on which professional practice and organisational management is based.

Chapter 2
Theoretical Background

kii mai koe ki ahau he aha te mea nui o te ao? maaku e kii atu ki a koe – he tangata he tangata he tangata [Ask me what is the greatest thing in the world and I will reply 'It is people, it is people, it is people']. (Maori proverb)

My life as a student of mind has taught me one incontrovertible lesson: mind is never free of precommitment. There is no innocent eye, nor is there one that penetrates aboriginal reality. (J.S. Bruner, *Life as Narrative*)[1]

Introduction

Social scientists have long accepted that there are a number of fundamentally different approaches to the understanding of human behaviour. The determinist approach offers one frame of reference, often signified as *erklärung*, suggesting that human behaviour can be explained by the operation of external causes, themselves capable of being observed and analysed. An alternative viewpoint focuses on the interpretation of behaviour through the action of a observer, encapsulated in the concept of *verstehen*. In anthropology, and in ethnography more broadly, *verstehen* refers to the systematic interpretation of the behaviour of an observed (and participated in) culture, an approach discussed further below.

Underlying these differences lie opposing beliefs about the nature of reality and about knowledge. Ontological beliefs – views about the nature of the world – are intertwined with epistemology – understanding of the nature of knowledge. Both of these profoundly influence the ways in which life individually, in organisations and in society, is understood. All professional practice is informed and shaped by the practitioners' ontological and epistemological beliefs, even when these are not articulated. It is therefore important to explore the key differences which, perhaps subconsciously, underpin approaches to professional practice.

In terms of ontologies, there is on the one hand belief in a knowable, objective reality, a world which exists and can be described and known quite apart from any human observer. On the other hand, there is the belief that all depictions of reality are socially constructed. Again, we will consider these perspectives and their implications later in this chapter.

Theories of knowledge – epistemology – present a similar division. One standpoint is positivist, focusing on scientific explanations constructed on the

---

1   <http://findarticles.com/p/articles/mi_m2267/is_3_71/ai_n6364150/pg_12>

basis of verified facts using logical deduction. Research is undertaken to test hypotheses, eventually accepting or rejecting them, then formulating new ones to test and thus advance knowledge. From a different viewpoint, relativists focus on the unknowability of, in particular, social phenomena independent of our interpretations of them. The two viewpoints tend to come into conflict when scientific methods are applied to social settings – which of course includes all professional environments.

Positivism

The positivist standpoint, in its pure form, holds that all that we can know of the world is what we can observe and measure. It posits a deterministic world of cause and effect which we can understand by the application of rigorous scientific method. Deductive reasoning is used to test hypotheses and theories, which then add to the sum of human knowledge about the universe and its workings. It rejects thoughts and feelings because they cannot be measured scientifically. B.F. Skinner is probably the epitome of this approach, with his experiments on rats designed to show how their behaviour responds to positive and negative reinforcers. At the heart of this view is a belief in empiricism, which emphasises the role of direct experience and of evidence – but evidence of a particular kind and especially that obtained through carefully designed and implemented experiments. Indeed, to some who comment from a positivist perspective, science and experimental method are virtually indistinguishable.

Within evidence-based practice (EBP), the emphasis placed on the RCT as a 'gold standard' reveals a view of evidence based on a 'scientific', positivist paradigm. In this view, scientific method, based on the testing of hypotheses (usually a 'null hypothesis' and an 'alternate hypothesis') by reference to experiments, dominates. The RCT is in a real sense the purest form of this approach, with its requirement for double-blind trials using properly constituted control groups. Commentators often speak of a hierarchy of evidence with the RCT at the top. Eldredge, for example, refers to a preference for '… more rigorous forms over less rigorous forms of evidence' and goes on to state that 'adherents to … Evidence-Based Medicine (EBM) … consider the RCT to be the highest level of evidence found in a single research study.' (Eldredge 2002: 72)

There has been some recognition that RCTs are not always the most appropriate methods. For example, Brice and colleagues suggest that 'randomised controlled trials, although offering the most reliable results for effectiveness questions, are not always the most appropriate study designs for other types of questions' (Brice et al. 2005: 8). However, there is little evidence that alternative approaches are given anything like equal prominence to quantitative ones in EBP. Eldredge simply suggests that they are useful to 'generate valuable exploratory hypotheses' which can 'subsequently [be] confirmed through larger, quantitative based research designs' (2002: 72).

The result of this approach is that the quantitative evidence collected becomes privileged to the extent that it is transmuted into what are in effect 'laws', believed to apply to any outwardly similar situation and as close as can be achieved to a 'correct' description of how the world operates. There is no other authentic knowledge.

Post-positivism

To an extent the above description of science at the beginning of the twenty-first century is something of a caricature, although the quotations immediately above indicate that it has its adherents. However, most discussion of scientific method and certainly debate on the philosophy of science has moved from a pure positivist viewpoint, aided by a recognition that the Skinner type of approach is hopelessly inadequate to describe animal, let alone human, behaviour. For example, Karl Popper argued that as it is never possible to include all possible observations, theories could never be proved – merely disproved (*'all theories are hypothesis*; all may be overthrown' (Popper 1963: 29, original emphasis)). For example, if we see one albino giraffe we can disprove the theory that all giraffes are brown, but there is no way of proving that all giraffes are either brown or white.

Another issue with the positivist approach is that it has an irreconcilable difficulty when applied to real-world social systems, namely, that it is literally impossible to control all the variables. A scientific experiment relies on the ability of the researcher to carry out the experiment within a closed system, or as close to that as is possible to achieve. Thus medical researchers go to enormous lengths to minimise any bias introduced by external factors – even in the laboratory this is a major issue, never mind in clinical practice. But while positivists view organisations as mechanistic systems which perform well if the right inputs are provided and the right processes put in place, post-positivists would want to take a more complex, and much richer, approach.

A further problem for positivism is that the only way in which we can communicate with each other about our observations, or anything else, is through language. The eminent twentieth-century philosopher, Ludwig Wittgenstein, focused his attention on this problem in his later philosophical writings. He used a simple example in his *Philosophical Investigations* to illustrate it.

> Let us imagine a language … The language is meant to serve for communication between a builder A and an assistant B. A is building with building-stones; there are blocks, pillars, slabs and beams. B has to pass the stones, and that in the order in which A needs them. For this purpose they use a language consisting of the words 'block', 'pillar', 'slab', 'beam'. A calls them out; – B brings the stone which he has learnt to bring at such-and-such a call. – Conceive of this as a complete primitive language. (Wittgenstein 1953: 2)

The question to which Wittgenstein is drawing attention is that in order to elicit meaningful dialogue – and I am using the term 'meaningful' deliberately – we have to assure ourselves that we share the meaning of the words we use. In other words, language is a social process. Externally defined meanings have limited value – real meaning exists in the sharing of concepts and ways of acting. Wittgenstein characterised the process by which we operate within a social setting as a 'language game' – 'meaning is embedded within a social context and so finds expression through the use made of particular terms' (ibid.). Just as a game must have rules – though not all of them may be written down – so any social context has its rules, both explicit and implicit. Without acquiring enough understanding of the rules to, as it were, play the game, we cannot participate in sharing and developing meaning.

But the rules of these language games are ever-changing, and unless we immerse ourselves in their social spaces we lose whatever familiarity we once had with their practitioners. What Eliot referred to as 'the intolerable wrestle with words and meanings' is the inevitable price of joining the game. Dewey put it like this:

> ... no sound, mark, product of art, is a word or part of language in isolation. Any word or phrase has the meaning which it has only as a member of a constellation of related meanings. Words as representative are part of an inclusive code. The code may be public or private. A public code is illustrated in any language that is current in a given cultural group. A private code is one agreed upon by members of special groups so as to be unintelligible to those who have not been initiated. Between these two come argots of special groups in a community, and the technical codes invented for a restricted special purpose, like the one used by ships at sea. But in every case, a particular word has its meaning only in relation to the code of which it is one constituent. (Dewey 1938: 55)

Lyotard extended the concept of the language game to include what he called *régime de phrase* and developed the idea of a 'genre of discourse':

> Phrases from heterogeneous regimens cannot be translated from one into the other. They can be linked one on to the other in accordance with an end fixed by a genre of discourse ... [which] supply rules for linking together heterogeneous phrases, rules that are proper for attaining certain goals: to know, to teach, to be just ... . (Lyotard 1988: xii)

Related to this, the concept of a 'linguistic code' is widely used in human communication theory and elsewhere to express the idea that the language which any one group of people uses demonstrates a different understanding of the world from that of other groups. It is simply not the case that each word in one language has an exact equivalent in another. Culler, for example, points out that

> ... speakers of English have 'pets' – a category to which nothing in French corresponds, although the French possess inordinate numbers of dogs and cats. English compels us to learn the sex of an infant so as to use the correct pronoun to talk about him or her (you can't call a baby 'it'); our language implies that the sex is crucial ... But the linguistic marking of sex is in no way inevitable; all languages don't make sex the crucial feature of newborns. (Culler 1997: 59)

Clearly, linguistic codes apply not just to the languages used by people in different nations but to the way in which any particular language – English, French or any other – is used by specialists. Furthermore, understanding of the linguistic code comes about through use just as much as by language learning. As von Glasersfeld (1999) has put it:

> ... children are not given a linguistic code in order to speak and understand language – they have to discover it on their own. They have to construct for themselves the meanings of a good many words before words can be used to expand the range of their linguistic communications. (von Glasersfeld 1999: 10)

It follows from all of this that the endeavour to find descriptions of the world and what happens in it can only be meaningful to the extent that we share understanding of the underlying concepts which we use in our descriptions. Within a scientific paradigm it is possible to approach a consensus of meaning – for example, through the use of a scientific formula with precisely defined variables. But once we move into social systems, when we move from one genre of discourse to another, this common understanding very rapidly breaks down. This again suggests that a 'post-positivist' approach is needed.

Unfortunately, 'post-positivism' is a term which is quite ill-defined – or rather is defined by different commentators in very different ways. (In a sense, of course this is inevitable since the concept carries within it a need to acknowledge different perspectives.) To some it draws heavily on the notion of constructivism (that is, the idea that we each 'construct' our understanding of the world – we will examine this in more detail in Chapter 4). To others its foundations lie in epistemology, an area we consider in Chapter 5. Yet others locate the term within critical theory. Perhaps the most common understanding is one which has come to be labelled 'critical realism', which believes that there is an objective reality but accepts that observations of it are prone to error and conclusions can only be tentative. One way to think of the difference is that positivists are goal-oriented while post-positivists are journey-oriented. The latter still keep the goal in view but accept that we can only strive towards it. As a result, post-positivism moves away from an identification of method with experiment towards multiple methods, each of which has its own fallibilities, and the need for triangulation so that observations using different methods are cross-checked for consistency.

Post-positivism recognises that anyone who carries out an experiment or other study comes to it with a particular world-view. However, it also argues that there are similarities between our understandings and that one way in which we can advance knowledge is by comparing and sharing the meanings we have individually, and as groups, extracted from the studies which we undertake. Processes such as the peer review of scientific papers exemplify this approach, for they enable shared meanings to emerge from formal discussion of findings from multiple sources.

It is important to recognise that some criticisms of positivism remain even within this very different kind of interpretation. In particular, where the objective is the study of human behaviour, the espousal of a series of viewpoints, each of which comes from within a scientific paradigm (and especially where quantitative data is privileged) runs the danger of returning to a simplistic 'observation of the observable'. Thus Laing writes:

> ... the error fundamentally is the failure to realize that there is an ontological discontinuity between human beings and it-beings ... Persons are distinguished from things in that persons experience the world, whereas things behave in the world. (Laing 1967: 53)

It is also worth emphasising that post-positivism is open to 'critical approaches', such as the feminist paradigm, which attempt to counter the prevailing assumptions which so easily slip into so-called objective research. This is surely a more appropriate stance within any professional discipline which claims to be focused on human beings and which relies on human judgement for so much of its operational delivery.

Relativism

The relativist, sometimes called interpretivist, paradigm argues that reality can *only* be described through the eyes and understanding of the observer. Each observer is culturally, historically and socially situated and thus brings preconceptions which inevitably colour his or her interpretations. To add to the complexity, all we have to describe the world and thus to share our understandings is language, which itself introduces ambiguity, bias and difference.

The relativist viewpoint has a long history, traceable at least as far back as Plato (369 BCE), who quoted Protagoras 'things are to you such as they appear to you, and to me such as they appear to me.' There is, of course, a logical inconsistency in the extreme forms of this approach, since if all views are equally valid to the individual who holds them, there is no room for consensus and agreement is meaningless – another person can come along with an entirely different viewpoint, which must be treated as equally valid. By this argument, it is just as valid to argue that the mountains of the moon are made of green cheese as to visit the place and carry out experiments which demonstrate that much of its surface is composed of anorthite, a type of feldspar. However, this is to take relativism to its extreme; its central tenet that, as Taylor put it, 'we have to think of man [*sic*] as a self-interpreting animal ... there is no such thing as the structure of meanings for him independently of his interpretation of them' (1987: 46), is critical to our understanding of the world. This shift in thinking from positivism has been called the 'interpretive turn' (Rabinow and Sullivan 1987a).

Relativism has a critical contribution to make to any study of social systems – which of course include organisations of all types. It warns us that we need a deep and holistic understanding of the entity being investigated. In social sciences and humanities, this has led to the development of a variety of relativist research methods, of which ethnography is perhaps the most important.

Ethnography

Ethnography is simply the study of people in their natural environments. It seeks to understand *what* it is that people believe and do from their own perspective – their own understanding of the world – rather than what they *say* they do or believe, still less what other people say of them. It is not necessarily interested in *why* things are done as they are, although this may be a subsidiary question. Ethnographic studies involve intensive fieldwork, sometimes over many years, and go to great lengths to avoid introducing any bias which could occur if the study itself affected the behaviour of the people being studied. Ethnographers seek to immerse themselves in the lives of the cultures they are studying – to 'go native' while retaining the role of observer. They are interested in a holistic description of the culture: 'social action is a part of the whole and derives a meaning through the place and purpose it has in the context of the (whole) system' (Sarantakos 1998: 196).

The initial work using ethnographic methods was undertaken in the early twentieth century by anthropologists like Bronisław Malinowski and Margaret Mead and published in a number of classic books including *Argonauts of the Western Pacific* (Malinowski 1922) and *Coming of Age in Samoa* (Mead 1928). They spent a considerable amount of time living among the people they were studying, participating in as much as possible of their daily life, observing what they did and making detailed notes on all aspects of their existence within their cultural setting. Early anthropologists were often particularly interested in the ways in which culture affected behaviour, and this has led to the development of cultural anthropology. Ethnography as a research methodology, using methods like participant observation, is now very widely used in the social sciences.

One of the key concepts of ethnography is that of seeing the world as 'anthropologically strange' – treating what the observer would naturally regard as 'normal' as unfamiliar, so as not to make assumptions. In this way, observers try to avoid suppositions based either on past knowledge or on their own cultural standpoint, although it must be recognised that this is an ideal which cannot in reality be achieved, since interpretation is always influenced by the cultural background of the observer. Margaret Mead's early work was criticised strongly on these grounds, a controversy which still continues (see Freeman 1983; 1999).

Such critiques and disputes reflect the controversies in anthropology concerning the extent to which ethnography can enable the 'reality' of the culture or society being studied to be revealed. Many contemporary descriptions of ethnographic research contain this same underlying tension. The claim is that basic reality can be described in analytic accounts of what has been observed, leading to what is in effect an attempt to grant 'scientific' status to the findings, using a pseudo-positivist standpoint. From this perspective, while succeeding researchers might refine the account being given, it nevertheless corresponds in a significant degree to objective reality.

More recently, there has been a shift towards the belief that people construct personal and societal explanations of the world, that their view of what is (and of what is significant) are built up of observations and experiences which together form coherent ways of seeing *for them* and thus of acting. Hammersley writes:

> ... central to the way in which ethnographers think about human social action is the idea that people *construct* the social world, both through their interpretations of it and through the actions based upon those interpretations. (Hammersley 1992: 44, original emphasis).

The *starting* assumption needs to be made that these viewpoints are as valid a representation of reality as any others – no particular view should be privileged – unless there is strong evidence to the contrary. This does not mean that we must accept a schizophrenic's account of the world as of equal value to any other, but that we need to weigh claims to representativeness carefully against the evidence. Fundamentally, 'there exist multiple realities which are, in the main, constructions existing in the minds of people' (Guba and Lincoln 1988: 81). We will see that there are strong connections between this view and constructivist approaches to pedagogy, which are described in Chapter 4.

In one sense, there is great advantage if the person carrying out a ethnographic study is an insider, if they know the environment, the working assumptions and the language – and are known to the people who are being studied. This is sometimes referred to as being 'inside the whale'. Hannabuss comments:

> This was, of course, the experience of Jonah, who was swallowed by a whale. Being inside the whale gave him unique insights which, as we know, were put to good use later. At the same time, it cannot have been an unmixed blessing: it would almost certainly have been dark, smelly, short of air, dangerous, strange and Jonah's ability to conduct objective research would surely have been thrown by his strange surroundings and the imminent sense he must have had of instant and unpleasant death. (Hannabuss 2000c: 103)

An interesting further stage of ethnography was characterised by Hannabuss as 'being inside Jonah inside the whale' (ibid.: 104). In other words, it is possible to treat oneself as one of the subjects of study. This is of course fraught with difficulties over subjectivity, but it is in fact how we construct our own stories. They *are* more difficult to validate than third-person observations, but that does not make them valueless. Indeed by exercising empathy with – being at one with – the group being studied greater insights can be obtained.

Ethnographic Methods

Ethnographic studies use a variety of methods – indeed no social scientific methods need be ruled out – but usually rely heavily on discussion, either observed or participated in, reflecting the reality of human societies where working together in groups is the norm. From an organisational and professional perspective, this focus on the study of discussion is important, because much of what happens in organisations is itself based on the way in which discussion takes place.

Effective discussion, although it is something we learn in childhood, has certain key characteristics. It involves:

- two or more people both talking *and* listening – that is, it is a *social* activity;
- the sharing of ideas, feelings, perceptions and experiences;
- the playing of roles such as leadership;
- the development of group membership and cohesion;
- the pursuit of individual and common goals, although effective discussion tends to centre around common problem-solving rather than the furthering of individual objectives, and
- stated or implicit rules. For example, many groups set out ground rules such as the right of every member to be heard uninterrupted and the limits of confidentiality.

Where individuals in a group act in competition or seek to dominate, discussion becomes debate or argument. While these may produce insights, and there is a large body of research on argumentation theory, it is generally accepted that genuine discussion is a more creative process. However, creativity in a group demands that members spend time gaining a deep understanding of each others' insights and experiences, weighing each contribution carefully. It is no accident that much of this communication involves the telling of personal stories, since members are attempting to convey not just facts but their own engagement in the issue, their own feelings and their own emotions.

Discussion is also often used as a research method, particularly in the form of *focus groups*, to gather information about groups, societies and the services they receive or require through a directed discussion. The researcher takes the role of *participant-observer*, 'a person who is a regular member of the group, engaging actively in its deliberations, but who at the same time is observing, evaluating, and adapting to its processes and procedures' (Brilhart 1978: 45). The key to running focus groups lies in achieving interaction:

> It is this interaction that gives focus groups their power. One person may make a comment and this sparks off a reaction in another. Soon a discussion or conversation is in progress. The skilled focus group facilitator steers this interaction with a light touch – enough to ensure that the participants keep to the broad points being explored but not enough so that their contributions are being led. In this way, the focus group technique enables the identification of attitudes, beliefs, and feelings as well as facts and gives an opportunity for participants to reflect on their own behaviour and experiences. (Brophy 2006: 200)

It is useful to note here that discussion as a teaching and learning method has come to prominence in education in recent years. More will be said about this in Chapter 4 but, as Pilkington and Walker comment, it is very noticeable that

> ... small-group collaborative learning in which students have opportunity for critical discussion with the tutor and other students is a key element of effective teaching and learning in Higher Education. Such opportunities to interact with the tutor and with each other are said to develop students' abilities to reason in a specialist subject. (Pilkington and Walker 2003: 41)

Equally, the ability of professionals to participate in positive and effective discussions is a key skill.

Other Qualitative Methodologies

Although the concentration in the discussion above has centred on ethnography, it is not the only qualitative methodology and it is important to recognise that there are other approaches and paradigms which can provide important contributions to a post-positivist exploration. Among the most important are:

- *Hermeneutics*, which is the art and science of interpretation. Although it started as a methodology for use in theology to try to demonstrate the meaning of the Bible in terms comprehensible to modern societies, it is now used much more widely to encompass any activity which involves the interpretation of statements or texts into contemporary language and norms. Robson points out that the importance of hermeneutics lies in its contribution to the ongoing activity of all people of making sense of the world in which they live: 'As all understanding takes place in time and a particular culture, a lesson from hermeneutics is that the pre-judgements we bring to this process are to some extent culturally pre-determined' (Robson 2002: 196).

- *Phenomenology*, which is based on the work of the twentieth-century mathematician and philosopher Edmund Husserl, who was influenced by Descartes, Hume and Kant among others. He insisted on a move away from the testing of scientific hypotheses by the collection of large amounts of data and the elucidation of underlying theories, to a process of examination of particular instances without preconceived theories in order to determine what is essential to those experiences. He was concerned with the study of consciousness and defined phenomenology as 'the study of consciousness as experienced from the first-person point of view ... a distinctive science (a rigorous, objective study) of the "subjective" structures of conscious experience. Since consciousness is nearly always consciousness of something, the central work of phenomenology is the analysis of various types on intentionality' (Smith 2002: 107). He coined the term 'intentionality' to show how we represent concepts and meaning through language and thought. Martin Heidegger developed Husserl's work and used phenomenology as a method in the study of being (ontology); in turn, this was built on by later philosophers such as Sartre, de Beauvoir and Derrida and was of great importance in the development of existentialism.

- *Interpretive biography*, which uses documents and reminiscences to tell the story of an individual, a group or an organisation. The use of narrative is explicit in this methodology, which uses the concept of time as the unifying thread of a biography. It owes much to Paul Ricoeur, who wrote that 'time becomes human to the extent that it is articulated through a narrative mode' (Ricoeur 1984: 52). The question of narrative analysis as a research method, which is clearly related to this theoretical approach, is considered in the next chapter.

- *Symbolic interactionism*, sometimes simply called *interactionism*, was developed initially by Max Weber and later by George H. Mead and focuses on the subjective aspects of social life. Human beings are pragmatic and continually adjust their behaviour in response to others. To do this, however, we must interpret other people's actions and represent both the actors and the actions symbolically. We also react to ourselves as symbolic actors by rehearsing in our minds what we have done. Furthermore, we play out possible courses of action, imaginatively rehearsing what we might do. So society consists of all of these interwoven patterns of actions, actors and real and would-be courses of action together with the strategies, such as negotiation, which underpin them. Research is undertaken by observing the roles people play and often uses participant observation; some symbolic interactionists deliberately use the analogy of the theatre to describe society – and thus, of course, take a narrative-based view.

- *Ethnomethodology* has been developed from symbolic interactionism and explores how people create social order even when they have different, perhaps opposing, views or when they do not fully understand each other, using their imaginations to fill in the gaps. Essential to this process is a constant adjustment or reorientation together with sustained trust: 'Trust must be assumed first, by all members of a practice, and then confirmed constantly through various displays of attention and competence' (Rawls 2008: 712). We will see in Chapter 5 that trust is fundamental to knowledge creation and thus knowledge management and it is pertinent that many ethnomethodological studies have been undertaken in the workplace. Researchers in this field tend to focus on conversations (a topic examined in Chapter 4), analysing how adjustments take place and trust develops.

Ethnography and Narrative

In all of the above methodologies, but especially in ethnography, narrative is very often used as a way of recording observations, as well as being the common form of oral accounts from the societies being studied. The term 'narrative enquiry' is used more broadly than in ethnography since the examination of oral histories, diaries, grey literature, letters, autobiographies, and so on, can be used within many different research methodologies, including those outlined above. However, because knowledge of a culture is so largely tacit, and because explicit accounts of culture can be so partial and thus misleading, much of the raw data of ethnography is found in the form of narrative. We will be examining what is meant by 'narrative' in the next chapter, but a few observations may be made here.

First, narrative is a form of discourse which seeks to picture the society or culture being studied in a holistic way, even where a specific point is being made. Secondly, its purpose is to convey meaning, not as undisputed fact but usually by encouraging the drawing of inferences by the listener. Third, narrative conveys a point of view, without ever claiming that it is the only point of view which is valid. Fourth, it includes emotions and moods, conveying what it felt like to be part of the scene being depicted. Fifth, it offers a timeline (in the case of personal narratives this may be a 'birth to present' account) but differs from a mere chronology. Sixth, narrative deliberately highlights what is unique or different – unlike scientific enquiry it eschews the attempt to find common ground or discover what events have in common. Even from this brief overview, it is easy to see why the collection, examination and interpretation of narrative has been so important to ethnography and, by extension, to any post-positivist enquiry.

The Question of Validity

Anyone involved in the use of qualitative methods to study social systems must be acutely aware that the question of the validity of any conclusions must be closely scrutinised. 'Validity' in this context means that the findings are trustworthy, credible and authentic (Miles and Huberman 1994). Guba and Lincoln prefer a framework of credibility, transferability, dependability and confirmability (Guba and Lincoln 1981; Lincoln and Guba 1985; Guba and Lincoln 1982) rather than speaking directly of validity, and many other commentators debate the appropriateness and meaning of the concept. For Scheurich (1993), validity marks the boundary between what is acceptable and unacceptable within qualitative research, though this again raises many questions, such as 'acceptable to whom?'. Wallace and Wray summarise the discussion with the question, 'Why should I believe this?' (2006: 28). Such a summary is immensely useful when the material under consideration is narrative in nature.

A number of strategies are used to test the validity (or equivalent) of qualitative research results and these are equally useful when considering the validity of narratives. They include:

- *Triangulation*, which involves the use of multiple sources of data ('data triangulation'), of multiple observers/narrators ('observer triangulation' or, in the context of narrative-based practice, 'narrator triangulation') and the use of different methodological frameworks and different methods ('methodological triangulation').
- *Negative case analysis*, which seeks out evidence which counters the findings being presented. Are there alternative narratives which appear to produce a different result? This is a particularly important device when different people in an organisation are contributing their narratives. At what points do they concur? Where are they at odds?
- *Peer group debriefing*, which involves exposing the narrative, or other evidence, to people with expertise to critique it. This is very similar to the process of 'peer review' which many academic journals use to distinguish submitted papers which are worth publishing from those which are not.
- *Participant checking*, in which people who have been studied are later asked to check the results being presented. Where narratives have been transcribed and collected, for example, it is very often helpful to read them back to the original narrators. Are they accurate? Have important nuances been understood? Has anything been omitted?
- *Cumulative validation*, which seeks to align findings with those of other studies to see if similar results are being found. Of course this must not be allowed to mask unexpected or novel findings, but will raise questions where these appear.
- *Identification and analysis of outliers and individual unexpected results*, which actively seeks for observations which are outside the general norm

which is leading to the conclusions being drawn. These 'maverick' cases can be extremely revealing – after all it was the observation by Alexander Fleming that the Staphylococcus bacterium growing on one of the culture dishes in his laboratory was being killed by a blue-green mould that was to lead to the discovery of the therapeutic properties of penicillin.

- *Audit trail*, which is important in any research or investigation, and means that if challenged the researcher is able to show exactly what data has been collected, how it has been processed and what methodological framework has been used to arrive at the results. This opens up the possibility of other people deriving different conclusions from the data.

It is also worth noting that there is an important distinction between validity and reliability, connected with the reproducibility of the results being claimed. Thus,

> Suppose that an entrance gate counter in the library is faulty and is recording only every second person to enter the library. The fault is permanent so that the results are consistently wrong – instead of recording 400 visits a day it is recording 200. That result is 'reliable' but it is not 'valid'. If there was an intermittent fault so that the number recorded was always wrong, sometimes 300, sometimes 200, sometimes 100 and so on, then the result would be neither reliable nor valid. (Brophy 2006: 14)

There are some qualitative approaches to which the above tests may not be relevant, for example, critical approaches (see above) where the observer's experience is part of the data being studied – as, for instance, in feminist research, an approach where, in Koro-Ljungberg's words:

> … feminist ethnographers question the naturalistic, ethnographic description of validity and instead produce representations … in which the reflections and detailed descriptions of true notions of reality are revised and replaced by fragmented, power-laden, uncertain, and momentary conceptualizations of a real. The emphasis in validity discussions is placed on a successful illustration of asymmetry rather than on a privileged removal from the object of study. (Koro-Ljungberg 2004: 610–11)

We return to the question of validity in Chapter 8 when considering the notion of 'warrant'. At that point, having examined concepts such as truth from a philosophical standpoint, we will return to the question of truth as a key component of professional practice, reflecting the need for a balance to be achieved in the use of different kinds of evidence.

Particular questions arise where the data consists of individual narratives. Generalisability from such cases needs to be handled meticulously because they can as easily be used to communicate unusual and atypical cases. This is of course part of their value – the individual's experience is privileged over the group norm;

in professional encounters, such as those in the consulting room, this is where so much of their value arises. Narratives which are used to highlight a particular case may gather their impact by their selectivity, by concentrating on the particular rather than reporting the overall picture. Strange uses the account of the human experience of slavery depicted in *Uncle Tom's Cabin* to discuss the ways in which narratives, by their particularity, reveal rather than conceal. He quotes Harriet Beecher Stowe's own commentary on the novel:

> The atrocious and sacrilegious system of breeding human beings for sale … fails to produce the impression on the mind that it ought to produce, because it is lost in generalities. It is like the account of a great battle, in which we learn, in round numbers, that ten thousand were killed and wounded, and throw the paper by without a thought (Stowe 1853: 151–2, in Strange 2002: 279)

Thus narrative validity is in part a question of their effect, of the reaction produced in the listener, as well as an assessment of accuracy of depiction. Wallace and Wray's question, 'Why should I believe this?' remains key.

Conclusions

The study of human behaviour and of the world in which we live has moved significantly away from a purely positivist standpoint towards a post-positivism which, while ill-defined, acknowledges the value of both positivist and relativist standpoints. Such a paradigm gives proper place to the limitations of human communication and language and seeks to acknowledge both individual and societal perspectives. Its methodologies, most notably those based on ethnography, support this attempt to acknowledge and give proper weight to the complexity of human and social perspectives. Emerging from these methodologies it is striking just how much the emphasis has shifted towards a central role for narrative and story.

It is timely now to turn to a more in-depth discussion of these ways of depicting reality.

Chapter 3
The Nature of Narrative

Australian Aborigines say that the big stories – the stories worth telling and retelling, the ones in which you may find the meaning of your life – are forever stalking the right teller, sniffing and tracking like predators hunting their prey in the bush. (Moss 1998: 144)

Storytelling is the common person's logic. (Hinchman and Hinchman 1997: xxi)

Narrative is the primary genre of oral discourse. (Green, Strange and Brock 2002: 229)

Introduction

We all grew up with stories, told to us at our mothers' knees, related by our schoolteachers, read in books, seen in pictures, watched on film. We may learn a great deal by studying facts, procedures and abstract theories, and such learning is of vital importance, but we empathise with one another and we develop a deeper understanding of our world when we listen to stories. For centuries, knowledge and wisdom has been passed from generation to generation in stories, helping societies to conserve and reuse knowledge based on experience. Stories possess subtle, half-hidden rhythms of what it is like to be human, to live in this crazy, frustrating, fascinating, exciting world. Over the last fifty years, the social sciences have been enlivened if not revolutionised by the understanding that our lives cannot be extracted from their context in socially constructed narrative and that even our abstract theories are themselves stories of the world: in Denzin's words 'everything we study is contained within a storied, or narrative, representation' (2000: xi).

Narratives and stories – the distinction between the two is explored below – are a way of organising the complexity of real experience and of passing it on to others, both in the present and in the future. The characteristic of a narrative is that it provides a temporal framework, which links a chain of events through cause and effect – chronology coupled with causality. It provides us with a starting point – traditionally every story began 'Once upon a time … '. It provides a middle, a telling of what happened, to whom, where and when. And it provides an end – what was the result – and by implication what is the lesson to be learned from what is told. It is 'one way of depicting reality and of revealing the meaning beneath the surface of events, of "telling it as it is"' (Brophy 2004: 188). As Polkinghorne put it:

> Narrative is a form of 'meaning making' ... Narrative recognizes the meaningfulness of individual experiences by noting how they function as parts of the whole. Its particular subject matter is human actions and events that affect human beings, which it configures into wholes according to the roles these actions and events play in bringing about a conclusion. The narrative scheme serves as a lens through which the apparently independent and disconnected elements of existence are seen as related parts of a whole. (Polkinghorne 1988: 36)

Narratives appear to be simple but are in fact hugely complex. They incorporate judgement – the storyteller must decide what to include and what to leave out, what is relevant and what is not. They involve interpretation, for nothing ever just 'happens'. And narratives do not lie idle: they invite, indeed demand, a response from their listeners.[1] Furthermore, because the world in which the narrative is heard is ever changing, the meaning of each nuance itself alters, develops, takes on new, perhaps greater, perhaps lesser, significance. For all these reasons, narrative is complex not only for the narrator but for the listener.

It is common for people to find themselves 'lost' in a narrative – something called 'narrative immersion' – which, as Escalas and Stern (2007) point out, is similar to vicarious participation. This is related also to the concept of 'flow', explored in Chapter 4, whereby the listener is 'carried along' with an activity. We examine this property of narratives and stories in more detail later in this chapter.

Narrative is also the way in which we naturally express ourselves as human beings, whether in our personal or our organisational lives:

> Human existence is temporal – we grow older – but if we are to get at the more personal aspect of human existence we must see this temporality as a *history* ... When asked by others who we are, more often than not we are forced to give some account of our past life, and this will be predominantly narrative in form. Loss of this ability to narrate one's past is tantamount to a form of amnesia, with a resultant diminishing of one's sense of self. (Kerry 1991: 7)

Narratives can also be challenging. They may defy logic, as in the surprise twist in the story or unexpected ending. They are so much not the product of reasoning as of experience. They are not easily categorised, and the same events are used to create different narratives by different observers. They are hard work! As Ricoeur wrote: 'the ability to follow a story represents a very sophisticated form of understanding' (1983: 178).

---

1   The term 'listener' is used in this book to encompass all kinds of audience – viewers, readers, participants, spectators and others.

Narrative and Story

While it is probably unnecessary to be too definitionally prescriptive at a time when interest in narrative is emerging in many fields, it is useful to explore distinctions between 'narrative' and 'story' and to acknowledge that narratives are a subset of what scholars across the humanities and social sciences would characterise as 'texts'. For the Oxford English Dictionary, a narrative is 'an account of a series of events, facts, etc., given in order and with the establishing of connections between them' (OED 2005). Some would argue that this is in fact too broad a definition, since it would appear to encompass documents such as company reports or plans, which would probably fall outside the intent of most commentators on narrative and certainly beyond the scope of what is discussed in this book. Branigan, in the context of media studies, offers a definition which incorporates the idea that narratives involve judgements, presumably on the part of the author or narrator, as well as that of the audience:

> Narrative is a way of organising spatial and temporal data into a cause and effect chain of events with a beginning, middle and end that embodies a judgement about the nature of events as well as demonstrates how it is possible to know, and hence to narrate, the events. (Branigan 1992: 3)

Genette distinguishes between story, narrating and the narrative itself in the following way:

> In a nonfictional (for example, historical) narrative, the actual order is obviously *story* (the completed events), *narrating* (the narrative act of the historian), *narrative* (the product of that act, potentially or virtually capable of surviving it in the form of a written text, a recording, or a human memory). (Genette 1988: 14, original emphasis)

Denzin argues that 'narrative is a telling, a performance event, the process of making or telling a story. A story is an account involving the narration of a series of events in a plotted sequence which unfolds in time' (2000: xi).

Barthes (1966) deconstructs narrative into story and discourse. The chronological account of the observations and experiences being communicated is the story while discourse is the selection of what is told and how it is told, including the selection of the medium to be used, genre and (narrative) style. In other words, *story* is what is told while *discourse* is how it is told, including the point of view taken (see below). One important issue which arises from this formulation is that discourse is selective in its use of information contained in story.

In attempting to make these distinctions between story and narrative, it is important to reiterate that the terms are often used loosely and interchangeably. Thus Gabriel suggests that stories are

> ... narratives with plots and characters, generating emotion in narrator and audience, through a poetic elaboration of symbolic material. This material may be a product of fantasy or experience, including an experience of earlier narratives. Story plots entail conflicts, predicaments, trials and crises, which call for choices, decisions, actions and interactions, whose actual outcomes are often at odds with the characters' intentions and purposes. (Gabriel 2000: 239)

We will examine the place of plot in narrative later in this chapter. For the purpose of this book, however, we take the view that 'narrative' and 'story' are synonyms, following Denning's lead:

> In common usage, *story* is a large tent, with many variations within the tent. Some variations are more useful for some purposes than others. There are probably many variations that haven't yet been identified. If we start out with a predetermined idea of what a 'real story' is, we may end up missing useful forms of narrative. (Denning 2007: 230)

Why are Stories Important?

As the move towards post-positivist paradigms has gained pace, it has perhaps been inevitable that narrative and story should start to recapture their rightful place. Gabriel has pointed out:

> [Although] modernity, with its massive narratives with forged concepts, ideas and theories, seemed to sweep away the delicate arts of storytelling and story listening ... in a curious twist, this is the tradition that has triumphantly re-emerged in our times, as people's thirst for meaning and identity seems to call upon narratives and stories to provide them with what science, in its majestic objectivity, appears singularly unable to do. (Gabriel 2004: 1–2)

Stories may address an individual situation, but still open up a new world of experience and understanding. As such, they provide insights which the bare 'facts' can never reveal:

> When the sirens first sounded on that very bright warm day, I was playing in Cook Street, and immediately all the people came out of the little houses and rushed to the shelters gathering all the children with them, as a result I was not allowed to go home but had to go into the shelter. Back home my mother was frantic, the German bombers were overhead, bombs were exploding all over the East End, and no Jimmy. As soon as the all clear sounded my three sisters were sent out searching for me, and for Mum there was a happy ending. (Tait, 2003)

We could read that people on the Home Front, being bombed nightly, had to run and hide in underground shelters. But the personal narrative brings home the experience at a totally different level. Well-told, the story enables us to enter, at some level, into the experience. It is not necessarily a perfect recitation of every known fact and it may contain minor errors or inaccuracies, a question we will return to in Chapter 5 when we examine the nature of knowledge. As Weick puts it:

> ... if accuracy is nice but not necessary in sensemaking, then what is necessary? The answer is, something that preserves plausibility and coherence, something that is reasonable and memorable, something that embodies past experience and expectations, something that resonates with other people, something that can be constructed retrospectively but also can be used prospectively, something that captures both feeling and thought, something that allows for embellishment to fit current oddities, something that is fun to construct. In short, what is necessary in sensemaking is a good story. (Weick 1995: 60–61)

Slater (2002: 157) illustrates this exact point when he invites us to consider the likely effectiveness of two very different approaches to AIDS awareness in Tanzania. One is a typical, well-intentioned campaign with posters, exhortations to use condoms, and so on. The other is a popular radio soap in which a man with typical male indifference to messages about safe sex loses first his daughter, then his wife and finally his own life to AIDS. Which, we are asked to consider, is likely to have most effect on its audience?

A number of people working in the field of health promotion have deliberately espoused the idea of using short stories to communicate the effects of ill health, accidents and other undesirable life incidents. Cole (1997) referred to these as 'narrative simulations' and found that there was significant evidence for their efficacy. More recently, the same technique has been used in virtual environments, sometimes providing interactive choices to enable different courses of action to be illustrated by different outcomes.

This use of stories to circumvent the subconscious defence mechanisms of their listeners is highlighted by Strange, who notes that 'well-crafted stories hold an intrinsic appeal that draws listeners' interest and attention to topics they would tend to avoid in other genres' (2002: 280). An arresting introduction, which relates the account to the interests of the listeners, together with an unexpected conclusion may be used as mechanisms both to catch the listeners' attention and to hook the story, and its point, into the memory – to make it stand out from the buzz of everyday conversation or the sleep-inducing factual presentation.

It is not the argument of this book that stories are, of themselves, sufficient as a basis for professional action. In management and professional practice, we need hard, and often quantitative, evidence on which to base decisions. But this kind of evidence, on its own, is insufficient to prompt action, as has been shown time and again. It is because enthusiasm for action is only engendered when we enter into the experience itself, armed with the evidence, that there is such a pressing need to join together the two often warring strands of discourse in professional practice. As we saw in Chapter 1, evidence-based practice (EBP) cannot succeed if it continues to insist that scientific experiments in the form of randomised controlled trials (RCTs) are the only 'gold standard'. The nature of the evidence required is changing and expanding as the value of qualitative approaches is recognised.

It is not only that we understand better when we use stories to reveal underlying beliefs and attitudes, nor is it solely that we communicate better when we find narratives which express the meaning of what we are trying to accomplish. Our colleagues and business contacts communicate with us all the time in stories. So, by learning how to listen to the narrative as well as the 'facts', we understand better what they are saying and what they are. Narrative is a two-way process, with storyteller and listener. Wise professionals can readily adapt to both roles – often simultaneously – which is where real conversation and real understanding begin.

Social psychologists have explored how people respond to stories in some depth. At a basic level, engagement in the story evokes 'as if' responses: in a drama, the audience's response to hearing a shot fired might be very similar to their reactions if they heard the same thing in real life – including the terrified screams! But being engaged by a story may evoke more complex reactions. Considerable emphasis is placed on the idea of *transportation* into the world of the narrative – 'a distinct mental process, an integrative melding of attention, imagery and feelings … where all mental systems and capacities become focused on events occurring in the narrative' (Green and Brock 2000: 701). In particular, two common reactions are the *problem-solving participatory response* and the *replotting participatory response* (Polichak and Gerrig 2002). The former refers to the way in which listeners gather information from the narrative to try and work out what is going to happen, often favouring such evidence as leads towards their own preferred outcomes. The latter is a kind of retrospective retelling, as the listener, perhaps fearing an outcome they do not wish to see, goes back over the narrative and engages in 'what if' or 'if only' scenarios. There is also evidence to suggest that there is also a third reaction, the *evaluative response*, which occurs when someone considers what happens in a story and evaluates either its values or its relevance.

It has also been shown that we react individually to our perceptions of events by turning them into stories. If the train we are travelling in comes to a sudden and unexpected halt, we immediately think of scenarios to explain what has happened which we then replay to ourselves as stories. We've hit a car on a level crossing; the driver has collapsed; there's been a terrorist attack just ahead. We then play these stories out in our minds as we seek for a rational explanation, creating quite complex cause-and-effect linkages between events that may have just that one, single trigger. This reaction to a simple trigger event is also the mechanism which helps us to relate to the stories we hear – for example, we subconsciously take on the role of the hero in a film and play out an ending to ourselves. Sitting in the train, we imagine ourselves playing a part in the subsequent rescue.

Researchers, especially in the social sciences, often treat narrative as a particular form of evidence which is characterised by 'retrospective meaning making'. In other words, the creation of narratives is a way in which people organise their understanding of what has happened in the recent or distant past. Narrative also, as already noted, is concerned with a temporal account – it is interested in cause and effect, in the consequences of actions and in explanations for what has been experienced or observed.

These characteristics are particularly noticeable when people are constructing narratives of their own lives, sometimes called self-narratives. Gergen and Gergen describe these autobiographical accounts in the following way:

> ... self-narratives refer to the individual's account of the relationships among self-relevant events across time. In developing a self-narrative the individual attempts to establish coherent connections among life events. Rather than seeing one's life as simply 'one damned thing after another' the individual attempts to understand life events as systematically related. They are rendered highly intelligible by locating them in a sequence or 'unfolded process'. One's present identity is thus not a sudden and mysterious event, but a sensible result of a life-story. (Gergen and Gergen 1986: 255)

The whole question of identity is contentious, with some arguing that rather than an integrated, singular, harmonious and clearly situated self, we are multifaceted, changeable, changing and indeed multiple. Our identity in one group may not be our identity in another. Hall (1996) suggests that we make sense of ourselves by investing in *narratives of the self* which delineate what we call our identity. These are closely related to *narratives of the group* or *collective narratives*, which help us to achieve cohesion in our identities.

Lyotard (1984) argues that a key distinguishing feature of narrative is its self-legitimising character. It is important to recognise that individual narratives exist within a broader meta-narrative (whatever postmodernists may claim) and that to be accepted within a community – whether an organisation or a village – the narrative must fit within this broader conceptualisation. Here lies a real danger, for it is all too easy for acknowledged or hidden elites to project their own meta-narratives, especially in organisations where there is a strong hierarchy such that the only legitimate narratives become those given the imprimatur of senior management. Each organisation develops what has been called its 'epic myth' (Mitroff and Kilmann 1975: 18) or 'organizational saga' which is 'intrinsically historical but embellished through retelling and rewriting' (Clark 1972: 178 – see also Chapter 7). Gabriel (1991) investigated a range of organisational myths and characterised them as 'collective fantasies'. These observations lead to the suggestion that there is a responsibility on all participants in any organisation or community to challenge narrative as well as use it – some have spoken of a need for 'narrative insurgency' which uses narrative to challenge narrative. If narrative is powerful then, like all expressions of power and authority, it can be subverted – as the invaders of Iraq in 2003 used the storyline of 'weapons of mass destruction' to impose their meta-narrative of a 'war on terror'. Challenging these meta-narratives as they arise in organisational settings is an important role for the professional, drawing on professional values and ethics, on notions of impartiality and responsibility. In this sense, the hallmark of the professional is not Shaw's 'conspiracy against the laity' but the ethical imperative to serve the interests of clients without bias or self-interest. Narrative is itself a vital weapon in this endeavour.

Narrative Types

Schank (1990) suggests that there are five different types of story. While others use different categories, his classification is a useful approach:

- *Official stories*, which are usually broadcast to a large audience, often with an exhortation and often originating with government, business, or voluntary organisations. They may be long and involved, as with a nation's narrative of its own history containing a widely accepted yet essentially idiosyncratic selection of key dates and heroes. They may be short and pithy, relying on imaginative reconstruction for their power to persuade. Examples would be the government's 'Don't Drink and Drive' or Christian Aid's 'We believe in life before death.' Often these are accompanied by images which fill in the storyline. People also tell their own official stories, a prime recent example being Hillary Clinton's claim to have landed in Bosnia amid a hail of bullets. The claims made about weapons of mass destruction in Iraq, referred to above, are another example of an official story created to get across a governmental message; typically, such messages ignore inconvenient facts.
- *Invented or adapted stories*, made up to describe experiences or to relay what we have imagined, often with embellishments and perhaps reordering events to make a more coherent tale. Virtually all the stories we invent are adaptations of others we have heard. Unlike official stories, this type is often created for entertainment rather than to persuade. Various forms of adaptation can be identified including the addition of details, accumulation of commentary and role-playing – this last describing the way in which someone might retell the story from a different perspective (Wyer et al. 1995: 72–3)
- *First-hand or experiential stories*, which are relatively straightforward accounts of personal experiences although we often alter them in order to appeal to particular listeners. We adapt the telling of the story to the circumstances – as Schank says, 'nobody wants to listen to what happened to you today unless you can make what happened appear interesting'(1990: 36). And, of course, this means interesting to the current listener, not to oneself! As a result, the first-hand story will not necessarily be identical at each retelling.
- *Second-hand stories* are those we relay, having heard them from someone else and remembered them. Evidence suggests that we frequently change

such stories as we relate them, mainly to achieve coherence by filling in what seem to us to be gaps or to correct what we perceive as inconsistencies.

- *Culturally common stories* are those which we have imbibed from our social and cultural environment and which we use both to make a point about our experiences and to demonstrate our membership of a particular group. Often the story is encapsulated in a short phrase – so the stereotypical image of a door-to-door salesman or a librarian can be used to convey a point about someone's assertiveness or lack of it, no matter how inaccurate that description might be. Schank refers to 'ossified stories' as those where the critical detail has become culturally embedded over time. Proverbs, such as 'blood is thicker than water', are ossified, culturally common stories where we supply the detail ourselves depending on the circumstances in which they are uttered.

This is not the only way to characterise types of narrative, of course, although it has resonance with organisational practices and helps illuminate some of the different purposes behind storytelling. Schank and his colleagues suggested that these kinds of stories are important in part because they assist memory, as was suggested above, the ability to retrieve relevant stories from memory being an important skill in many fields, including management and professional practice. Schank and Abelson assert that

> ... stories about one's experiences and the experiences of others are the fundamental constituents of human memory, knowledge and serial communication ... when it comes to interaction in language, all our knowledge is contained in stories and mechanisms to construct and retrieve them. (Schank and Abelson 1995: 1–2).

Narrative Impact

An intriguing question is: what makes for strong impact in a narrative? Schank and Berman (2002) suggest that the factors include:

- timing, so that the story is told when listeners want to hear what it has to say;
- relevance to listeners' personal frame of reference, so that they understand its significance in relation to their own lives;
- addressing topics about which listeners are curious; allowing the listeners to see themselves in the role of hero;
- rich detail, which may include the use of multimedia, including music to suit the mood or images to reinforce what is said, and
- information or images which enable us to file the story, and its relevance, in our memories.

There is some evidence that this last factor is linked to the human brain's way of storing information.

It is often the case that a narrative designed to be told is more compelling than one designed to be read – but this is not always the case (otherwise novelists would have been put out of business by the theatre) and much depends on the skill of the storyteller. Other factors include:

- a dramatic but believable setting, one which the listener can picture and imagine;
- a plot that keeps the interest flowing because new events keep occurring which catch the attention, often by being unexpected yet maintaining the temporal linkages throughout;
- characters we can empathise with – or hate – so that we relate our own lives to theirs;
- character development which assists in making the narrative believable because it reinforces the sense of time passing as well as confirming our knowledge that people change as they experience more;
- dramatic tension, which holds the attention of the listeners as they look for resolution of the dilemmas which the characters face;
- appropriate pace, which varies as the narrative progresses, allowing breathing spaces to intersperse fast action and tension; and
- the narrative invites retelling, partly through its own merits and partly because it can be used by listeners to communicate and explain their own quandaries and interests to others.

The Elements of Narrative

Literary theorists have provided extensive insights into the structure of narratives and stories, with narratology having emerged as a well-developed subdiscipline. Narratives are not just temporal accounts but have features which distinguish them from, say, a dispassionate (in so far as that is possible) log of events or a set of accounts – though even there narratives may make their appearance in the appended explanatory notes.

The study of narrative has not only taken place among literary theorists, but has encompassed disciplines such as linguistics, psychology and sociology and indeed has spread throughout the social sciences, alongside recognition that narrative is one of the primary ways in which human beings make sense of the world. In order to extract meaning from events, people use narrative, which provides a template for ordering experience, identifying the context and thus boundaries of what has occurred and establishing explanations by reference to cause and effect. In this sense, narratives are holistic rather than analytic and provide a means for individuals and societies to progress towards closure.

Semiotics, the study of signs and their meaning, has provided considerable influence on narratology. The classic work in this field is that of Saussure (1974), who argued that all signs are made up of two parts: the *signifier*, which is the term used to denote something, and the *signified*, the concept which is denoted by the sign. Within narratology, semiotics is often used as a methodology for analysis of narrative. Its importance was stressed through the work of Roland Barthes (see also above), who was concerned with elucidating the 'grammar' of narratives and wrote that semiology

> ... aims to take in any system of signs, whatever their substance and limits; images, gestures, musical sounds, objects, and the complex associations of all of these, which form the content of ritual, convention or public entertainment: these constitute, if not languages, at least systems of signification. (Barthes 1967: 9)

The work of the French philosopher Paul Ricoeur has been one of the most important influences on our understanding of narrative. He drew on Aristotle's *Poetics* as well as the work of Kant, Hegel and Heidegger, and suggested that stories are constructed by the use of *mimesis* and *emplotment*. Mimesis denotes the way in which, in constructing a story, we imitate events from life – Aristotle referred to narrative as 'the imitation of an action'. Emplotment is the way in which we link events and other elements together to create a holistic and coherent tale. Ricoeur defined three stages of interpretation:

- *Mimesis 1* refers to our basic competencies in the use of conceptual terms, our practical understanding of actions, goals, motives and agents. The storyteller and the listener have preconceptions which give meaning to the situation before any attempt is made to build and share the narrative.
- *Mimesis 2* relates to the field of action, the context which invests meaning, which Ricoeur referred to as 'the kingdom of the *as if*' (1984: 64). It is here that we use emplotment, giving the narrative structure.
- *Mimesis 3* is concerned with temporal structures, the 'now' and 'then' of lived time which are related to the narrative itself and thus provides the intersection where the time of the listener and the time of the narrative intersect. In this way, listeners are exposed to new understandings of their worlds, and thus to new possibilities for action.

In this sense, stories imitate – but clearly are not exact representations of – life. The events being narrated in story have a beginning, middle and end, termed 'concordance' by Ricoeur. However, there is always some lack of coherence in any plot – which is in part what gives it interest and grabs the attention of the listener – and this was termed 'discordance' by Ricoeur. Hence we have a paradox in any story, something he referred to as 'discordant concordance'. In this analysis, the plot is what enables concordance to overcome discordance and produce an effective and meaningful story (see Ricoeur 1983; 1984).

Work in cinematography and film led to the development of the concept of *diegesis*, a term used to denote the characters and events, times and places of the narrative. As Hannabuss remarks, characters 'can be aware only of some things which are happening but not all: so a film character will be aware (so far as we, the observers, can know!) that events are happening around them but they cannot be aware of the film music accompanying the sequence' (2000a: 224). In Monaco's words – drawing on the classic work of Metz (1974) – diegesis in this context means 'the narration itself, but also the fictional space and time dimensions implied in and by the narrative' (1984: 428).

Eight elements are key to understanding narrative structure.

Setting

Every narrative has a setting, a place – real or imagined – where the action happens. Settings are extremely important because the listener takes from them all sorts of assumptions and presuppositions. Where a narrative is set in an organisational context, for example, the organisation's epic myth (see above) may colour the listener's approach and understanding. Very often the narrator spends time at the beginning of the story elaborating the setting: hence the classic opening, 'it was a dark and stormy night and the rain came down in torrents …'.

Causality

Narratives capture and express cause and effect. One thing leads to another. One event happens only because something preceded it. As Kermode has put it 'first we look for story – events sequentially related (possessing, shall we say, an irreducible minimum of "connexity"). And sequence goes nowhere without his *doppelgänger* or shadow, causality' (1981: 80). Causality is at the heart of nearly all modern understandings of the world to the extent that it is usually taken for granted, creating a key role for narrative expressions to make cause and effect explicit. This centrality of causality in elucidating meaning derives from the work of the eighteenth-century philosopher David Hume, who characterised causal claims as empirical, that is, matters of fact rather than of analysis. Hume claimed that all empirical claims are based on sensory inputs. In narrative, these elements of the plot, coupled with actions of the characters, enable the listener to identify the starting point (cause) and what occurs, perhaps much later, as a result (effect):

> Storytellers, relying on sequence and causality, make sense out of nonsense; they impose order, economy, and moral consequence on the helter-skelter wash of experience. The notion that one event causes another, and that the entire chain is a unified whole, with a complex, may be ambivalent, but, in any case, coherent meaning, not only brings us to a point of resolution; it allows us to navigate through our lives. (Denby 2007: 1)

Plot

A narrative needs a plot 'because the past is formless, or at least it does not have rhetorical forms that alone make it meaningful in communication' (Jenkins 1999: 117). Plot is the container within which we find both events and causality. Although, classically, narratives were concerned with a temporal progression, from a beginning through a middle to an end (the 'episodic' tradition, described by Aristotle), they can relate the different elements of a story to one another in many different ways. Plot is at the heart of narrative, because it not only relates events to one another but crucially also the transformations that occur between them. The plot encourages the listener to ask, 'What happened next?' and 'Why did that happen?'. In other words, the plot enables the listener to establish the causality. E.M. Forster's formulation of the difference between story and plot is helpful. He wrote that while 'The king died and then the queen' is a story, 'The king died and then the queen died of grief' is a plot, since the second invites the listener to understand the sentence in terms of causality. Some have argued that 'then' in the first sentence serves the same purpose, merely inviting use of the imagination, but the point is made (1927: 86).

The plot is never explicit; rather it is inferred by the listener from the discourse. At the same time, different discourses may have the same plot, which is why it is possible to translate narratives successfully in a way that is difficult with, for example, non-narrative poetry. But because certain plots are frequently encountered, they achieve familiarity and enable the listener to explore meaning in the particular context of the story and the storyteller. In organisational settings, this can be an important way to achieve relevance.

Style

Narrative style refers to the way in which the narrative is presented. It includes *point of view* (considered further below), but also refers to the manner in which the story is told. For example, a newspaper report could be written in short, staccato phrases using contemporary jargon and references, or in longer, complex sentences perhaps with subclauses and explanations in parentheses using formal terminology. The latter would be perceived as a more 'academic' style and perhaps treated with more gravitas. The former would be more immediate, grabbing the attention. However, the two would not necessarily convey the same meaning, even to the same listener because style affects what is perceived.

The way in which concepts are connected is also critical in conveying meaning, as Winterowd illustrates in the following observation:

> Take the two propositions *The Lone Ranger rode a horse* and *The horse saved his life* and combine them thus: *The Long Ranger rode a horse that saved his life.* The result is that one preserves the meaning of each proposition and creates their new, relational meaning.. Nor is the creation of meaning through embedding a trivial

quality, but rather one of the great creative powers that the language confers upon its users: the power to express relationships through a finite series of recursive devices. (Winterowd 1975: 29)

Point of View

The point of view of a narrative refers to the standpoint or standpoints of the narrators, not to an opinion which they take – it sometimes referred to as the narratives 'focus' or 'angle':

> Like the camera in a film, the perspective of a narrative is always located somewhere, up above events, in amongst them, or behind the eyes of one or more of the characters involved. Like the film camera, the narrative voice can move around from one point of view to another, often shifting undetectably from outside to inside views. (Currie 1998: 18)

The point of view is usually revealed by the voice which is used. The first-person singular tells us that the point of view is that of a participant in the story (known as *autodiegesis* if a person is telling their own story or *homodiegesis* if telling someone else's). The third person, single or plural (*heterodiegesis*), tells us that we are hearing the story as observed by someone external to it, but a person who has knowledge of what has happened and often claims understanding of the thoughts and feelings of the protagonists. The third person can also be used to create what is called an 'objective' point of view, where no attempt is made to penetrate the thoughts and feelings of the actors, but the story is narrated simply as a series of events which happened.

Character

Character (sometimes called 'narrative personage') is a critical element of narrative, for the obvious reason that virtually all stories concern the interplay between human (or quasi-human) beings, each having their own traits. The listener's understanding is formed in relation to the characters who 'act' in the narrative. As Bredin puts it, 'with character, stories cease to be types, and become individuals' (1982: 298). Listeners relate to characters emotionally, which greatly affects what they hear and the meaning they ascribe to it.

Narrative Presence

The idea of narrative presence refers to the listener's relationship to the story, which in the extreme can involve feelings of being transported into the action, of being part of the narrative. (It may be noted that some commentators have used the term 'narrative presence' as a synonym for 'narrator', which can cause some confusion and is not the sense in which the term is used here.) Listeners have a sense of the reality of what is occurring as if it were part of ordinary (or extraordinary) events in which they are involved, becoming absorbed in them. Studies of presence go well beyond narratology and there has been considerable interest in the topic from researchers in the field of virtual environments (see Chapter 6). It is related to the concept of 'flow' (considered in Chapter 4) and centres round degrees of involvement and immersion.

Hermeneutic and Proairetic Codes

Roland Barthes introduced these terms to describe the two different ways in which suspense can be created in a narrative. The hermeneutic code refers to elements of the plot that raise unanswered questions, which create or add to our interest in the narrative by raising tension in our minds and so maintain our interest – we want to know how these will be resolved, so we keep our attention on the unfolding story until all these loose ends have been tied up satisfactorily (or left for us to ponder). Detective stories are based entirely on this idea – a murder is committed and the whole narrative is focused on answering the question, 'who did it?'. The proairetic code is simply the actions which occur and which will have consequences – we wait to find out what these will be so our attention is caught by anticipation of the outcome. For example, an aircraft's undercarriage fails to drop into position as it comes into land. What happens next?

While these are the elements of narrative, it is important to stress that many of them can be *implied* rather than made explicit. Take, for example, the well-worn joke that academics tell about working in a university: 'I hate Wednesday meetings; they eat into both weekends!' This is, effectively, a story. The hearer is invited to imagine a life with a uninterrupted, temporal progression from weekend to weekend. The setting is the university, or rather the privileged life of the academic who is employed by it. Causality is explicit – calling a meeting has disrupted this lifestyle. The plot is classically episodic. The style is pithy humour. The point of view is that of the professor, who is also the character, presenting his story in the first person. The narrative presence is an invitation to mock the supposed laxity of academic life. In one short sentence, when coupled with the listener's imagination, all the elements of narrative are present.

The implied make-up of a narrative is sometimes called the 'suggestion structure' and is made up of all those aspects which the listener brings to the experience, including shared knowledge, emotions and connections. This leads to 'realisation', which is the enactment and re-enactment of the story in the mind of the listener. As this occurs, connections are made with prior knowledge and beliefs leading to reconstruction of the mental world of the listener. This is a key concept in pedagogy and will be discussed further in the next chapter.

Narrative Analysis

Before concluding this chapter, it is important to make mention of the use of narrative analysis as a research methodology within the social sciences. There are in fact a number of different paradigms underlying such methodologies but they can be revealing of the nature of narrative, as well as its use in such diverse fields as linguistics, literary criticism and psychotherapy. The sociolinguists William Labov and Josuah Waletzky are key figures in the development of this field; they worked in Harlem in the 1960s and 1970s, analysing some of the stories told to them by interviewees. They, as did Paul Ricoeur, stressed the importance of narrative as representing a temporal account of events. One of their examples illustrates this through the responses of an interviewee asked, 'Were you ever in a situation where you were in serious danger of being killed?'. The response is 'I don't really like to talk about it ... Well, this person had a little too much to drink, and he attacked me, and a friend came in, and she stopped it', which they deconstruct into a temporal sequence as:

a. Well, this person had a little too much to drink
b. and he attacked me
c. and a friend came in
d. and she stopped it. (Labov and Waletzky 1997)

From the analysis of such stories, Labov developed a general theoretical structure of narrative which includes six elements:

- abstract,
- orientation,
- complicating action,
- evaluation,
- result (or resolution) and
- coda.

The abstract and coda are what we might think of as optional elements since they are at the boundary of the narrative – the abstract, self-evidently, providing a summary which helps the listener decide what the story is about, while the coda summarises in a different way and indicates that the story is complete. (Methodist preachers used to be taught that when delivering a sermon they should 'tell them what you're going to say, tell them, and tell them what you've told them'!)

The orientation tells the listener about the circumstances of the narrative – where it is set, when it takes place and the surrounding circumstances. Complicating action tells the main temporal events which are taking place. The order in which this part of the narrative is presented is critical to what is being told – changing the order changes the story. The evaluation is the point at which the narrator pauses to make clear the importance of the high point or denouement of the story. The result or resolution answers the listener's question, 'What happened in the end?'. So Labov and Waletzky demonstrate how the story is linked together within its timeframe to enable the identification of key events:

> A simple sequence of complication and result does not indicate to a listener the relative importance of these events or help him distinguish complication from resolution ... Therefore it is necessary for the narrator to delineate the structure of the narrative by emphasizing the point where the complication has reached its maximum: the break between the complication and the result. Most narratives contain an evaluation section which carries out this function. (Labov and Waletzky 1997)

However, Squire points out that it is unhelpful to be too prescriptive about narrative structure since narrators, as anyone undertaking narrative analysis soon realises, very often break the rules and the most compelling narratives can be found among those which lie outwith this kind of neat structure. She suggests that the different interests are linked by what she terms 'a kind of pragmatic politics' which has the function of 'broadcasting "voices" that are excluded from or neglected within dominant political structures and processes':

> Whether we link narrative analysis to the personal preoccupations of biography, to psychoanalytically-informed tracings of emotions, to structural concerns with language or to cultural patterns of representation and action, it can be argued that 'narrative' operates throughout as a kind of theorization of unrecognized or undervalued texts, and hence as a kind of politics for post-political times. (Squire 2005: 103)

Narrative and Truth

It is easy to get carried away with the power of narrative, to the extent that there is a failure to acknowledge that it can be as much a tool for falsehood as for truth. The twentieth century gave us plenty of examples of the 'grand narrative' that at heart denied fundamental human values, whether the anti-Semitism of Hitler which led to the Holocaust, the socialist utopia of Lenin and Stalin that paved the way to the gulags, or the rampant racialism of South Africa which opened the way to apartheid.

It is just as easy for narrative to be used to mislead on a much smaller scale. Indeed, one of its most common uses is to 'sell' an image of a product or service which is, in the common phrase, economical with the truth. A car is shown as part of the story of the free and easy lifestyle of a 'model' family. Ownership of it symbolises being 'cool'. It is a vehicle which cares for the environment. It always finds empty roads to drive on, never a traffic-jam in sight. Take the recent Citroen C4 advert:

> Last year, a seemingly innocuous car sprung from the slightly grim surrounds
> of an urban carpark, and started dancing just like the geeky guy out of the Lynx
> ad from whenever it was. How good was that?! Everyone loved it, everyone
> spoofed it, and subconsciously everyone started to think of Citroens as funky
> cars laden with technology ... As importantly, people started to like them. (http://
> motortorque.askaprice.com/articles/auto-0701/top-ten-tv-car-adverts.asp)

More will be said about truth in Chapter 5 and, in relation to brand identity in
Chapter 7, but it clearly lies at the heart of any attempt at a narrative-based practice.
A commitment to truth-telling will be one of the characteristics of that paradigm.

Conclusions

Narratives are hugely complex, yet they occupy a central position in human
communication. They enable us to share, discuss and debate all the multifaceted
aspects of complex human relationships, systems and organisations. They enable
us to represent cause and effect without oversimplification and allow listeners to
engage in a situation in a holistic way, recognising that thoughts, feelings and
emotions are at least as important as actions. They enable us to reveal ourselves to
others in a way which represents not just our explicit, observable acts but includes
our motivations, feelings, thoughts and beliefs. They also provide a means for
excluded and disadvantaged members of society or of organisations to make their
voices heard.

The place of narrative in organisational settings will be explored later (Chapter
7), but next we turn to examine how pedagogical theory and practice can help to
illuminate the use of narrative to achieve learning.

Chapter 4
Learning

It remains something of a mystery why narrative text is so easy to comprehend and remember. Perhaps it is because the content of narrative text has such a close correspondence with everyday experiences. Perhaps it is because the language of oral conversation has a closer similarity to narrative text than other discourse genres. Perhaps it is because there are more vivid mental images, or a more elegant composition of the conceptual structures. Narratives are more interesting, so perhaps they are more motivating to read. (Graesser, Olde and Klettke 2002: 240)

When a meeting of the minds isn't enough, try a meeting of the emotions: tell a story. (Bill Burchard[1])

Introduction

Professional practice involves continuous learning. Every decision is itself an occasion for learning, involving the marshalling of evidence, analysis of significance, the choice of a course of action and evaluation of the outcome. Each individual decision draws on prior experience. As the poet and philosopher George Santayana famously put it: 'Those who cannot remember the past are condemned to repeat it' – if we don't learn from what we have done, we will never progress. Learning is clearly more than memorising facts, although it does involve the acquisition of information and knowledge. Yet in an increasingly complex and interrelated world, learning is concerned far more with developing the ability to discern the significant from amongst a deluge of experiences, developing advanced literacies, skills and abilities, transferring the essence of one occurrence to novel situations, extracting meaning from intricately woven narratives.

In learning, as much as in any other field, there are underlying theoretical assumptions which draw, sometimes unconsciously, on well-embedded philosophical positions. As outlined in Chapter 2, positivist and relativist beliefs contend for attention and are often held in uneasy alliance. Pedagogical theories have drawn on these positions to provide underpinning for the ways in which teaching and learning are promoted, encouraged and managed.

In the past, there tended to be a concatenation of the terms 'teaching' and 'learning': teachers taught, learners learned. Behind this usage lay an understanding

---

1 http://alumni.media.mit.edu/~brooks/storybiz/storytelling-in-business.pdf.

of learning which saw the teacher as omniscient, with the learner simply absorbing whatever was taught. Typical of this approach was learning by rote or repetition, focusing on the '3Rs', nowadays familiar (at least in the West) only in Victorian schools rebuilt in theme parks:

> ... in the Victorian schoolroom at the Ironbridge Gorge Museum, Shropshire ... children and their teachers wear replica Victorian clothes and have a day's reading, 'riting and 'rithmetic lessons, giving them a taste of a school day in the late 1800s. (http://www.johnmalam.co.uk/creating10.htm)

Something not altogether different can be found to a rather alarming degree in much of higher education even today, where the lecture still retains something of a stranglehold on methods and too often consists of the lecturer or professor imparting 'knowledge' to quiescent students. (In fact, many of them spend their lecture time near the back of the auditorium constructing personal narratives through the medium of SMS text!) The irony is that at its best the lecture can be compelling – especially when it uses the narrative form to engage students. To achieve this, however, it needs to take participation seriously, valuing students' contributions and constructing a shared narrative – in the well-worn phrase, the teacher needs to move from being the 'sage on the stage' to the role of 'guide on the side'.

Learning in organisational settings, however, is very different from that in the classroom. It takes place in the course of everyday activity, dips into formal training courses, reflects on experiences of task completion (or non-completion) and finds its context in relationships with clients and colleagues. It tends to be far less formal than in educational institutions and far more context-dependent, since organisations are pursuing their particular missions and strategies and harness their staff's learning to better achieve these. Thus while formal and informal learning have much in common, and it can be argued are moving closer together, there are significant differences.

Theories of Learning

The pedagogical underpinning of learning comes from a number of different traditions, with behaviourism and cognitivism being prominent. The former is the theory that learning takes place through conditioning, the classic experiment being that of Pavlov's dogs, which were taught to salivate when presented with a stimulus other than food after they had repeatedly received the same stimulus followed by food. John Watson, one of the foremost behaviourists working in the first part of the twentieth century, famously declared:

> Give me a dozen healthy infants, well-formed, and my own specified world to bring them up in and I'll guarantee to take any one at random and train him to

become any type of specialist I might select – doctor, lawyer, artist, merchant-chief, and, yes, even beggarman and thief, regardless of his talents, penchants, tendencies, abilities, vocations, and race of his ancestors. (Watson 1930: 82)

To be fair, this was actually part of a critique of those who claimed that heredity was the key determinant of success in learning, the principle which had informed university entrance, at least in Europe, for centuries. It also has to be said that there is significant evidence that behaviourism can be effective in learning in some circumstances, as, for example, when a teacher lavishes praise on a pupil who does well. If good work is always rewarded and poor work criticised then one effect – though not the only one – will be to encourage pupils to seek rewards by submitting good work.

The cognitive approach, on the other hand, emphasises the importance of the mind and memory, giving prominence to thought, feelings, emotions and personality traits. A lot of attention in cognitivism is focused on problem solving, often based on the pioneering work of Newell and Simon (1972), who used computational techniques to analyse problems and possible solutions in laboratory settings. Interestingly, however, problem solving was one of the key learning skills identified by John Dewey nearly a hundred years ago. As Tanner writes:

... if we follow Dewey, critical thinking is motivated by a problem. It must be a genuine problem – the pupil's own problem. Neither a simulated problem nor a practice problem intended to help pupils perform well on reasoning . would qualify. (Tanner 1988: 471)

Since organisations and individual professionals are often operating in problem-solving mode it is not surprising that there is extensive treatment of cognitivism in the management literature.

Objectivism

Many of these conceptions of learning, and particularly the behaviourist approach, are related to objectivism, which itself is closely related to positivism, arguing that there is one objective reality which can be discovered through the senses and by the application of logic. Objectivism

... views the world as an ordered structure of entities which exists and has meaning quite apart from the observer or participant. Much of science and technology is taught on this basis: what needs to be achieved by learning is a closer and closer approach to complete (and thus 'correct') understanding. (Brophy 2001: 136)

As Duffy and Jonassen observe, in this understanding 'the goal of instruction is to help the learner acquire the entities and relations and the attributes of each – to build "the" correct propositional structure' (1993: 3).

While some, particularly those who espouse the purely relativist position described in Chapter 2, would reject this approach entirely, it would seem sensible to acknowledge that some learning does take place in this way. For example, if you want to learn how to use a new computer, it is quite helpful if someone points out to you how to switch it on – while some philosophers might argue as to the reality of the object in question (the on/off switch), it is of more use pragmatically simply to accept that it exists and that it is located in the indicated position!

To an extent, the amount of information which we are willing to accept in this way depends also on who is telling us about it. The role of expert is a contested one, but again there are pragmatic reasons for accepting some learning on the basis of a person's expertise. Over time, we find out who we can trust in this way and who to treat with scepticism, and of course this depends on the subject matter being dealt with. So a person is trusted within a particular field of expertise – we may believe what an engineer tells us about the load-bearing properties of a new bridge, but we wouldn't necessarily trust her to advise us on surgery for a replacement knee joint. Thus the extent to which we learn according to objectivist approaches depends both on the subject matter and on the relationship which we have with the 'teacher'. Since professionals are by definition experts, with some kind of qualification and accreditation, the question of trust is an important one.

Again, there is a considerable literature on trust, both as a philosophical concept and within professional and organisational settings. McAllister argues that it has both affective (emotional) and cognitive (reasoned) dimensions and defines trust in organisational settings as 'the extent to which a person is confident in, and willing to act on the basis of, the words, actions and decisions of another' (1995: 25). Brien argues that 'trust is the essential and central element in the development of a professional culture and trustworthiness is the first virtue of professional life' (1998: 396). Other approaches to trust will be examined in Chapter 5.

Constructivism

In contrast to objectivism, constructivist approaches stress that we come to conclusions about the world and our place in it by drawing both on our perceptions of it, including what we are told about it, and on our prior understanding, so that learning is in essence a matter of 'constructing' a new world-view. This approach is closely related to post-positivism, as described in Chapter 2. Bednar and colleagues put it this way:

> … learning is a constructive process in which the learner is building an internal representation of knowledge, a personal interpretation of experience. This representation is constantly open to change, its structure and linkages forming

the foundation to which other knowledge structures are appended. Learning is an active process in which meaning is developed on the basis of experience. This view of knowledge does not necessarily deny the existence of the real world . but contends that all we know of the world are human interpretations of our experience of the world ... learning must be situated in a rich context, reflective of real world contexts for this constructive process to occur. (Bednar et al. 1993: 21)

In recent years, constructivism has been dominant in education, at least in theory, and most discussion centres round how it can be encouraged in learners by taking steps to encourage students to take responsibility for their own learning – it is their own world-view which is being constructed. But since we are all individuals, with unique experiences and understandings of the world, it can be argued that constructivism is not so much a pedagogical approach as a description of the inevitable reality of being human. Everyone has a world-view – the question is how to enable its development.

Related to constructivism, metacognition is the process whereby learners are able to 'elaborate [their experiences] and construct explanations for themselves' (Greeno et al. 1996: 19). In essence, it involves the management of one's own learning experiences, including goal setting, ongoing motivation and self-evaluation:

Metacognition refers to one's knowledge concerning one's own cognitive processes or anything related to them, e.g., the learning-relevant properties of information or data. For example, I am engaging in metacognition if I notice that I am having more trouble learning A than B; if it strikes me that I should double check C before accepting it as fact. (Flavell 1976: 232)

Social Constructivism

The original theories of constructivism have been criticised as placing too much emphasis on each *individual's* attempt to make sense of the world they inhabit. In response to this analysis, efforts have been made to develop the notion of social constructivism. This argues that the construction of meaning, and thus learning, is a shared enterprise. Proponents of this view lean heavily on the theories of Lev Vygotsky, who argued that

... every function in the child's cultural development appears twice: first, on the social level, and later, on the individual level; first, between people (interpsychological) and then inside the child (intrapsychological). This applies equally to voluntary attention, to logical memory, and to the formation of concepts. All the higher functions originate as actual relationships between individuals. (Vygotsky 1978: 57)

Fundamental to this view is the idea that learning occurs through *interaction* between an individual's internal and external conditions. Since external conditions include other people, interaction with people is a very important part of learning. Simpson and Galbo define interaction as

> ... behavior in which individuals and groups act upon each other. The essential characteristic is reciprocity in actions and responses in an infinite variety of relationships: verbal and nonverbal, conscious and nonconscious, enduring and casual. Interaction is seen as a continually emerging process, as communication in its most inclusive sense. (Simpson and Galbo 1986: 38)

In parallel with work on social constructivism, 'activity theory' has been developed as a way of investigating human life as a complex system of constantly evolving relationships, concerned not only with people but also with the tools they use in their activities (Engestrom 1996). Activity systems include organisations, groups of individuals and professions, but they are constantly changing as a result of dynamic interactions between the people involved – and as others move in and out of the system. The object of the activity system remains unchanged – it could be something like the rules governing company takeovers – but the actors, actions and activities evolve. Leont'ev (1978) suggests that as human societies evolve so the complexity of activity increases, as does the number of activity systems.

An important concept within social constructivism is that of 'intersubjectivity'. This refers to the shared understanding between individuals in a social group on which they base their communication and from which they derive meaning and understanding. In part, this is derived from the group dynamic – those things which are shared and evolve in terms of their meaning – and in part from the group's history and culture. Acquiring familiarity with group intersubjectivity is an important part of learning.

Situated Learning

Arising from the observation that social interaction can only happen, by definition, within groups of people, the concept of situated learning has emerged, emphasising that learning takes place by participation in situated communities (that is, in a particular place, society and time) and the undertaking of developed social practices:

> ... a person's intentions to learn are engaged and the meaning of learning is configured through the process of becoming a full participant in a socio-cultural practice. This social process, includes, indeed it subsumes, the learning of knowledgeable skills. (Lave and Wenger 1991: 29)

So learning needs to be thought of in the context of the learner's social (using that term in its broadest sense) situation. Again, there are echoes of John Dewey in this understanding, for one of his emphases was on the importance of cooperative play if children were to learn. This was taken up by Piaget (1923; 1932) who argued that it is in dialogue with others that children learn to understand that there are different perspectives on problems and issues and that strategies are needed to cope with this in the real world. From this, there can be a development from egocentrism to empathy and understanding, leading to shared, that is, social action. As was noted above, narrative is a primary form of discourse within such dialogue. There are strong links between this work and Wittgenstein's notion of the language game, Lyotard's 'genre of discourse' and the concept of linguistic codes (see Chapter 2).

From all of these perspectives, it is possible to see that learning is intimately bound up with the situation and activity in which it is taking place:

> Situations might be said to co-produce knowledge through activity ... approaches such as *cognitive apprenticeship* ... that embed learning in activity and make deliberate use of the social and physical context are ... in line with the understanding of learning and cognition that is emerging from research. (Brown et al. 1996: 32).

Communities of Practice

One of the developments of this idea in the adult world can be found in Lave and Wenger's notion of 'communities of practice', an idea developed further by Wenger:

> Being alive as human beings means that we are constantly engaged in the pursuit of enterprises of all kinds, from ensuring our physical survival to seeking the most lofty pleasures. As we define these enterprises and engage in their pursuit together, we interact with each other and with the world and we tune our relations with each other and with the world accordingly. In other words we learn.
>
> Over time, this collective learning results in practices that reflect both the pursuit of our enterprises and the attendant social relations. These practices are thus the property of a kind of community created over time by the sustained pursuit of a *shared enterprise*. It makes sense, therefore to call these kinds of communities communities of practice. (Wenger 1998: 45, original emphasis)

A community of practice is much more than a network of colleagues or friends. First of all, it is focused on a particular domain – which could be anything from sculpture through nuclear engineering to psychiatry – and through that focus its members lay claim to a level of expertise. Secondly, the members are practitioners – they put into effect expertise within the domain; they don't just talk about it. Third, they engage with each other in sharing information, debate and discussion, so that learning forms a central focus for their activity.

An important criticism of the concept of communities of practice, however, lies in the observation that for many people – and especially those who are attempting to learn something new – the key issue is how to become involved in such a community. Lave and Wenger did draw attention to this in their work, although there was an assumption that the most relevant community of practice would be open and welcoming to newcomers, which may be far from the case.

One way to develop this notion in relation to organisations and professions, however, is to think in terms of them seeking to create internal communities of practice. This idea has a great deal in common with that of the 'learning organisation' in its more enlightened forms, although it must be said that many corporate implementations of the concept seem to have little acquaintance with modern learning theory. As Leitch and colleagues say:

> … the dominant paradigm in whatever guise has been described as being rational, positivist and empirical … as it is largely functional in nature with an over emphasis on cognitive learning and the development of theory and quantitative skills … a didactic approach to teaching and learning has been adopted. (Leitch et al. 1996: 31)

Here we find another point where professional and organisational practice, if not fully thought through, can lead towards a naïve positivism when all the evidence points to the need for post-positivist, constructivist approaches. Communities of practice provide an ideal location for a more thoughtful approach to organisational learning, provided that the potential contribution of all members is fully acknowledged and encouraged. A critical component is the sharing of personal narratives.

Conversation Theory

One way in which various of these theoretical standpoints can be brought together is through Conversation Theory, which was developed by Gordon Pask (1975) based on his work on learning styles and instructional design. As its name suggests, this theory proposes that learning occurs through 'conversations' about a subject between learner and another agent – which may be human or, possibly, a machine or piece of software. Through these 'conversations', the learner 'comes to know', or to construct an interpretation or shared understanding of the world based upon a 'conversational framework'. An important aspect of this process is the ability to externalise understanding and to express it conceptually, so as to engage with others. This presupposes the use of a language which supports shared meaning, as described in Chapter 2.

There has also been considerable interest in the way that discussion and argument enhances learning, with a variety of studies showing that the process of engaging in a group conversation helps individuals to reach a better and more balanced understanding of an issue. Kuhn, Shaw and Felton undertook an empirical study which showed that even where participants shared the same basic viewpoint, new lines of argument were explored when the group met together to discuss a theme. Furthermore, where people question each other as part of a discussion, individuals start to explore their own positions and understandings and to develop the depth of their thinking. For example:

> In one case study … a participant, Alice (all names are pseudonyms), voiced an initial argument resting on a global claim that CP [capital punishment] 'is justifiable' and 'justifies the crime committed.' During the dialogues, three different partners, one disagreeing and two agreeing with Alice's pro position, press her to articulate further her position ('What do you mean by "justifiable"?' asks one partner) and, in particular, to specify the conditions under which CP is justifiable ('What would you call "justifiable"?' asks another partner). As a result, Alice begins to identify criteria that constrain the justifiability of CP (e.g., seriousness of crime, responsibility for actions, intent), some of which appear as new elements in her posttest argument. (Kuhn, Shaw and Felton 1997: 311–12)

Diana Laurillard has put forward a 'conversational framework' with the following twelve elements as a way to develop learning in the context of the modern university:

1. The teacher contributes theoretical frameworks and ideas, which the student considers and
2. communicates back to the teacher in terms of his or her conceptions
3. The process is iterative so the teacher will consider what the student says in terms of his or her own conception, feeding this back into the conversation and
4. receiving the student's feedback in return.
5. In the light of what the student has communicated the teacher adapts the learning task which is set
6. and sets a goal for the student.
7. The student acts on this and feeds back results to the teacher, who
8. in turn provides feedback, enabling the student to modify his or her work and again
9. feed results to the teacher.
10. The student can now adapt his or her actions in the light of both the theory and the feedback on actions
11. and reflect on what has happened and its significance in the light of personal experience.
12. The teacher can reflect on the actions taken by the learner and modify the conceptions used in the first step for future occasions. (Laurillard 2002: 30, original numbering of stages in the process)

Laurillard comments: 'the interplay between theory and practice – that is, making the abstract concrete through a reflective practicum – is essential, as is the continually iterative dialogue between teacher and student' (ibid.). Both Pask's and Laurillard's work (and of course the related contributions of many other authors) is extensively cited in pedagogical debate, with widespread acceptance of the centrality of conversation and dialogue. This is also the experience of most professionals, who rely on conversations with clients and colleagues in arriving at decisions.

There is thus very strong evidence that individual learning is developed significantly through social interaction, both with a 'teacher' and with others, and that this applies to theoretical and abstract thinking as much as to the acquisition of practical skills. Furthermore, conversation and argumentation are skills which can be learned. Children have been shown to respond well to explicit tuition in collaborative reasoning (Reznitskaya et al., 2001), where they develop 'argument schema' which provide a structure within which relevant information is assembled, arguments are constructed, reviewed and amended, and flaws in reasoning are anticipated and detected. The evidence shows that this approach helps students to produce work which contains significantly better-developed arguments and counter-arguments.

A further aspect of conversation theory is that the conversation is also internal to the learner – part of cognition and learning consists of conversing with oneself, carrying on internal arguments (within reason!) and trying out different positions. It is easy to see how this fits with the concept of constructivism – we reconstruct our internal world-view in part by mentally sparring with ourselves. Within these conversations, much effort is expended in trying to find plausible explanations of cause and effect, a feature discussed in the context of narrative construction in the last chapter. Conversations are, in fact, very often a type of narrative.

Immersion and Flow

It is generally acknowledged that we learn more and more quickly when we are immersed in learning, rather than simply acting as an observer or approaching the topic as a purely intellectual activity. In other words, learning tends to be more effective when we are fully absorbed by the experience, particularly when that experience is positive, when we are enjoying ourselves as a by-product of it. The connection between this observation about learning and the concept of narrative presence (see Chapter 3) will be obvious.

One theoretical explanation for this phenomenon lies in the concept of 'flow', advanced by Csikszentmihalyi (1997). The basis for Csikszentmihalyi's work lay in his interest in creativity and especially in his observation that artists and musicians are apt to become so immersed in their creative work that they become 'lost' in it, that is, focused on what they are doing but cut off from the outside world. He discovered through his research that exactly the same phenomenon could be observed in much more mundane tasks, which can become intensely pleasurable as the individual becomes immersed in them. Furthermore, this does not have to be an individual experience – a group of people can equally become immersed in what they are doing, gaining great pleasure from it. These observations led Csikszentmihalyi to formulate his theory of 'flow', which he defined as 'the state in which people are so involved in an activity that nothing else seems to matter' (Csikszentmihalyi 1990: 4).

Flow has been studied in considerable detail in relation to computer games, where people do become heavily immersed in the experience, and in their application to learning. It has also been used to describe the experience of other computer-related activities, including the use (and sometimes excessive use) of Web-based services and systems. Pace gives the following example from an interview with a 35-year-old man:

> I just come home from work and I just want to relax and I'll sit in front of the computer. You know, I'm tired and I'll think, 'I'll just surf the Web for a half hour or something and go to bed'. And before you know it, it's like two or three hours have gone. Sometimes my wife will be going to bed and she may put a load of washing on and she'll say, 'Can you just hang that out when it finishes'. 'Yeah righto'. And then you totally forget all about it. You know she spoke to you, but you just push it to the back of your mind and carry on. When you're really concentrating on one thing, you just don't retain any information about another thing. (Pace 2004: 341)

Socially, this is clearly a negative experience (at least as far as his wife is concerned – there is even a Facebook group called Widows of Warcraft, tagged 'if you have lost a close beloved to this game, please join this group to mourn and celebrate the non-virtual life they once had …'!), but for the individual it can be intensely satisfying. It may also be socially positive in terms of virtual relationships – an issue considered in Chapter 6 in relation to Web 2.0. Csikszentmihalyi found that among the conditions for flow to occur was the balance between the skills of the individual and the challenge of the task. If skills greatly outweigh the challenge, then boredom is experienced. If the challenge is much greater than ability, then the person experiences anxiety. Thus matching the skills to the challenge – making it challenging enough but not too much so – is critical to achieving flow. Clearly, then, if learning events can be designed to match these criteria, then they are likely to be much more engaging and, almost certainly, much more successful. Activities which are most likely to produce flow have the following characteristics (Csikszentmihalyi 1993, xiv). They have concrete goals with manageable rules,

1. make it possible to adjust opportunities for action to our capabilities,
2. provide clear information on how we are doing, and
3. screen out distraction and make concentration possible.

The Reflective Practitioner

The idea of the reflective practitioner is one of the great contributions of Donald Schön, who argued strongly against the idea that professional knowledge and know-how is grounded in 'technical-rationality'. By this, he meant the positivist paradigm, one which, as we have seen, underpins the dominant thinking in evidence-based practice (EBP). Schön began by arguing that it was entirely appropriate for practitioners simply to apply 'appropriate' technical solutions which they have learned:

> Technical rationality holds that practitioners are instrumental problem solvers … Rigorous professional practitioners solve well-formed instrumental problems by applying theory and technique derived from systematic preferably scientific knowledge. (Schön 1987: 3-4)

However, he noted also that this view does not in fact reflect the reality of professional practice, being a kind of 'ideal' account which ignores what actually happens in professional disciplines. In the same volume, he writes:

> In the varied topography of professional practice, there is a high hard ground overlooking a swamp. On the high ground, manageable problems lend themselves to solution through the application of research-based theory and technique. In the swampy lowland, messy, confusing problems defy technical solution. (ibid.: 3)

He suggested, therefore, that it would be more helpful to examine professional practice from the practitioner's viewpoint – the point of view of those who actually face the problems – rather than as a simple problem-solving activity. In this way, the reality of practice – of complexity, of transitoriness, of differing values, of uncertainty – can be addressed because the practitioner is part of the problem and its solution. The practitioner's experience and engagement is critical to the situation: 'Let us search instead for an epistemology of practice implicit in the artistic, intuitive processes which some practitioners do bring to situations of uncertainty, instability, uniqueness, and value conflict' (ibid.: 49).

Drawing on the work of John Dewey, who had discussed the importance of reflection as part of learning fifty years earlier (Dewey 1933), Schön formulated the concept of the reflective practitioner. Dewey had suggested that a good teacher recognises when he or she is faced with a situation without an immediately obvious solution and steps back to reflect on the experience, contrasting routine action with reflective action. Schön built on this observation but rejected the notion that there are reflective and non-reflective teachers, focusing instead on what actually happens in the classroom. Laurillard's model (above) is clearly based on this understanding of pedagogy.

Schön suggested that there are actually three different types of reflection:

- Intuitive reflection, or 'knowing in action', which occurs during what Dewey had termed 'routine action', but which displays a high degree of skill without necessarily being explicit about the reflective process. Examples might include riding a bicycle or being able to interpret a balance sheet at a glance. It may be impossible to verbalise this type of reflection, but the skill is there none the less.
- Reflection-in-action, where the professional considers what is happening and is able to reflect on it and find solutions or new approaches without interrupting the flow of the event. Obviously, this is important in classroom situations where a teacher cannot just disengage in order to consider possible solutions. It is equally important in other professional contexts – for example, where a patient is consulting a doctor or a policeman is responding to an unforeseen incident.
- Reflection-on-action, which occurs after the event and consists of discussing (with others and with oneself) what has happened. By reflecting on what has happened, the practitioner is able to learn from experience and thus to become more skilled at finding solutions in the future. Unless there is reflection-on-action, the professional does not develop transferable expertise.

One common feature of reflection is the recognition of a problematic situation where different courses of action were possible. The way in which the situation is understood, and the assumptions which the professional makes about it, influence understanding of the possibilities it presents. For example, recognition of the power exercised by people at different levels in an organisation affects perception of the options which are available. In every situation, we make presuppositions: reflection on our own experiences helps us challenge and reform what we had previously taken for granted. In the context of teaching, Brookfield suggests that listening to the stories of fellow professionals helps to contextualise professional experience:

> … what we thought were idiosyncratic features of our own critically reflective efforts are paralleled in the experiences of many of our colleagues. We discover that what we thought was our own idiosyncratic difficulty is actually an example of a wider structural problem or cultural contradiction. (Brookfield 1995: 219).

Loughran offers the following example of a student teacher reflecting on the experience of taking a class:

> I assumed as a consequence of my own lack of enthusiasm that the students had a negative relationship with the subject. I sought to identify the factors contributing to their experience and experiment with alternative ways of teaching based on the feedback received … It was in their [students'] responses that I realized that my perceptions were not entirely accurate … I was surprised to find that the

students generally felt positive towards the subject, but identified key elements that took away from their learning experience ... This made me feel confident that choosing to pursue ways of responding to some of these 'highlighted issues' in my teaching practice could make the environment more stimulating for my students. (Loughran 2002: 36)

Loughran draws the important distinction between this kind of reflection and what can very easily become a process of rationalisation:

... reflection is effective when it leads the teacher to make meaning from the situation in ways that enhance understanding so that she or he comes to see and understand the practice setting from a variety of viewpoints. (ibid.)

This comment may be seen as a response to the finding in some studies that what is called 'reflective practice' can all too often become a mechanistic record of experience: so-called reflective activities can simply be 'far from reflection and indeed merely diary entries describing an event or activity' (Woodward 1998: 417).

Learning and Narrative

In essence, true reflective practice is a constructivist position which encourages a focus on building personal meaning from personal experience. However, if the full value is to be extracted from reflection, it needs to be more than deep analysis but also, as the social constructivist position would suggest, a shared experience. This is sometimes embodied in the concept of the 'critical friend', someone willing to provide an honest critique which aids personal development. In sharing experience, narrative has an important part to play. Both the act of writing a narrative of experience and that of subsequently reflecting on it are powerful ways of facilitating learning, leading to new understanding at both an intellectual and an emotional level. Chambers demonstrates by the use of a series of examples that 'a creative approach to the writing of narratives can promote learning from practice which is affective as well as cognitive' (2003: 412). He notes, in a comment which picks up on the discussion in Chapter 2, 'the profound significance of language in such an approach to narrative and reflective practice' (ibid.: 413).

Draper (2006) writes that 'stories use words to create imaginings in hearers. That could be a description of education.' As this perspective becomes more widely accepted, there are good reasons to believe that the use of narrative for learning and for reflection is expanding in formal education as well as in the continuing education of professionals, and that it offers a unique opportunity to engage learners in new ways. For professionals, Diekelmann has argued for a 'narrative pedagogy' which opens up new possibilities for reflective practice by 'explicating the narratives of students, teachers, and clinicians in a way that evokes thinking and converging conversations' (2001: 54). Ironside, in the context of nursing education, argues that narrative approaches are particularly helpful in facilitating analytical thinking especially when viewed as a shared enterprise:

> By focusing teachers' and students' attention on thinking and interpreting as communal experiences, Narrative Pedagogy engages teachers and students in pooling their wisdom, challenging their preconceptions and envisioning new possibilities. (Ironside 2006: 485)

An interesting example of this shift towards narrative-based pedagogies occurs in mathematics, sometimes called the 'Queen of the Sciences' and often regarded as the supreme example of a scientific, positivist domain – after all, 2 + 2 is always 4, isn't it? But a moment's thought tells us that mathematics is a socio-cultural construct, which develops to address particular problems in particular times and places. Apart from any other consideration, we could note that its practitioners are predominantly male and predominantly from developed societies, both factors almost certain to influence the problems it chooses to address. Baker, Clay and Fox argue persuasively that

> By engaging with the narrative, we place the mathematics in its context and personalize it, making it come alive to the conditions of the time. Context provides meaning and consequently learner motivation since it is exceedingly difficult to engage with context-less abstractions, as every teacher of mathematics knows! Contextualising the mathematics also means that the story is enriched in terms of the interconnection of disciplines ... By narrating we make use of our power to employ language to speculate about, enquire into, or interrogate. (Baker, Clay and Fox 1996: 33)

O'Neill (2004) cites empirical research which suggests that the level of oral storytelling skills among pre-school children is a good predictor of later mathematical achievement. She quotes Devlin (2000): 'reasoning about mathematical relationships between mathematical (abstract) objects is no different from reasoning about ... human relationships between people'.

The link between storytelling and literacy is of course much wider than in this one field and has been the subject of considerable research. Snow (1983) found that one of the critical issues in developing literacy is the ability to keep in mind the audience's viewpoint, that is, the perspective of the other. It is when children learn this skill that they start to relate the world to their own identities. Cameron and Wang (1999) speak of the need to learn to recontextualise a narrative so that it is meaningful to the listener, something for which storytelling ability is essential.

Conclusion

Learning is an extremely complex activity with a huge research literature and ever-evolving theories. However, an emphasis which is very evident at the present time, and for good reason, is on constructive learning as a social activity requiring participation in communities. As McDermott has written:

> Learning traditionally gets measured as on the assumption that it is a possession of individuals that can be found inside their heads ... [but] learning is in the relationships between people. Learning is in the conditions that bring people together and organize a point of contact that allows for particular pieces of information to take on a relevance; without the points of contact, without the system of relevancies, there is no learning, and there is little memory. Learning does not belong to individual persons, but to the various conversations of which they are a part. (in Murphy 1999: 17)

Learning encompasses the acquisition of reusable skills and competencies and the gaining of new knowledge but above all it requires the continuous development of new views and understandings of the world. There is increasing interest in the role of narrative in painting the wider picture and providing the context for the acquisition of skills and the development of the individual's knowledge. However, central as it is to learning, in the discussion in this chapter we have not considered in any detail how knowledge fits into the equation. It is to this subject, and to the concept of knowledge management, that we turn next.

Chapter 5

Knowledge and Knowledge Management

When a meeting of the minds isn't enough, try a meeting of the emotions: tell a story. (Burchard 2002: 1)

Introduction

It has been recognised for many years that knowledge is a critical asset for both public and private sector organisations. More than that, it is one of the major current determinants of the wealth of nations. The World Bank's 1998 World Development Report noted that

> For countries in the vanguard of the world economy, the balance between knowledge and resources has shifted so far towards the former that knowledge has become perhaps the most important factor determining the standard of living – more than land, than tools, than labor. Today's most technologically advanced economies are truly knowledge based. And as they generate new wealth from their innovations, they are creating millions of knowledge-related jobs in an array of disciplines which have emerged overnight: knowledge engineers, knowledge managers, knowledge coordinators. (World Bank 1999: 16)

It is now commonplace to refer to the emerging global economy as a knowledge economy. While definitions of what exactly that term means are often vague, in essence it refers to the belief that economic activity is increasingly concerned with the capture, storage, processing, sharing, selling and buying of knowledge. Yet knowledge is a peculiar resource which behaves rather differently from other assets such as land, buildings, personnel and finance. For one thing, giving knowledge to someone else does not deprive the giver of it, although it may affect its value. Much of an organisation's knowledge is locked in the heads of employees and closely linked to their know-how and skills. Protection of knowledge is difficult for those and other reasons, which is why complex intellectual property and other rights have been established.

The development of the knowledge economy has been closely tied to the deployment of advanced information and communications technologies (ICTs), which facilitate the capture, storage, processing and transmission of vast quantities of data. Although it is important to distinguish between data, information and knowledge (see below), the ability to store huge amounts of data and to transmit it globally, together with systems which allow sharing and collaborative information/knowledge creation, has been so critical to these developments that the terms 'information economy' and 'knowledge economy' have become almost interchangeable. It is also often taken as read that a knowledge economy will be highly dependent on ICTs and as a result, governments give high priority to ICT infrastructure and services.

Information and Knowledge

It is often taken for granted by contributors to the knowledge management literature that there is a hierarchical relationship between data, information and knowledge (DIK). For example, Feurer and Chaharbaghi write:

> Information is created by assigning meaning to individual pieces of data. However, information by itself only contains simple and discrete pieces of data. Knowledge is generated by integrating these individual pieces in a meaningful way. In contrast with information, which only contains individual pieces of data, knowledge can be regarded as a highly structured assemblage of data. (Feurer and Chaharbaghi 1995; 42)

Some would argue for the addition of wisdom as a higher level (DIKW) – this is discussed further below. The DIK model is variously defined, but it is useful to try and differentiate clearly between the three concepts, not least because the simple hierarchy masks critical differences between the three concepts. Thus:

- *Data* consists of symbolic representations of external events or objects, such as counts of items in a warehouse, an image of a distant galaxy, or a list of words encountered in a language. Data may be unstructured or structured – in the last example, the words may be held in an essentially random collection or they could be alphabetically ordered.
- *Information* is processed data. Buckland draws the important distinctions between information-as-process, information-as-thing and information-as-knowledge (1991: 351). The first is the act of informing someone or being informed, the second the use of the term to describe objects which contain data and are capable of 'being informative'. Hicks and colleagues suggest that it is useful to characterise information as *formal* or *informal*. Formal information is structured 'so that individuals exposed to it may infer the same knowledge from it, such as formal education, where the content and order is prescribed' (Hicks et al. 2002: 268–70); the informal variety is relatively unstructured and may be textual or visual, conversations, expressions (which could include such nuances as tone of voice to convey approval or disapproval) and individual memory. It may be noted that none of these definitions relate directly to the alternative, technical definition of 'information' formulated by Shannon (1948) and sometimes termed

'statistical communication theory', which forms the basis for modern developments in communications technology.

- *Knowledge* (information-as-knowledge in Buckland's analysis) is a cognitive construct and is what is communicated between people when they are being informed, that is, it is what passes between people in the first definition. As he says:

> A key characteristic of 'information-as-knowledge' is that it is intangible: one cannot touch it or measure it in any direct way. Knowledge, belief and opinion are personal, subjective, and conceptual. Therefore, to communicate them they have to be expressed, described, or represented in some physical way ... information-as-thing. (Buckland 1991: 351)

Davenport and colleagues suggest that 'knowledge is information combined with experience, context, interpretation, and reflection' (1998: 43). These definitions are not entirely compatible and illustrate the lack of terminological coherence in the field but are useful as illustrations of the ways in which distinctions are made between information and knowledge within the professional literature on the topic.

Knowledge, Understanding and Wisdom

As noted above, some commentators add understanding and/or wisdom to the DIK hierarchy. For example, Ackoff (1989) entitled his paper 'From data to wisdom' and suggested a five-tier hierarchy of data-information-knowledge-understanding-wisdom. Rowley comments:

> ... the hierarchy referred to variously as the 'Knowledge Hierarchy', the 'Information Hierarchy' and the 'Knowledge Pyramid' is one of the fundamental, widely recognized and 'taken-for-granted' models in the information and knowledge literatures. (Rowley 2007: 163).

The hierarchy is depicted in Figure 5.1 (see over).

Her analysis of the discussions of wisdom in the knowledge management literature led her to offer the following definition of wisdom: 'the capacity to put into action the most appropriate behaviour, taking into account what is known (knowledge) and what does the most good (ethical and social considerations)' (Rowley 2006: 257).

She went on to note, in a subsequent paper:

> ... wisdom is a neglected concept in the knowledge management and information systems literature. If the purpose of information systems and knowledge management initiatives is to provide a basis for appropriate individual and

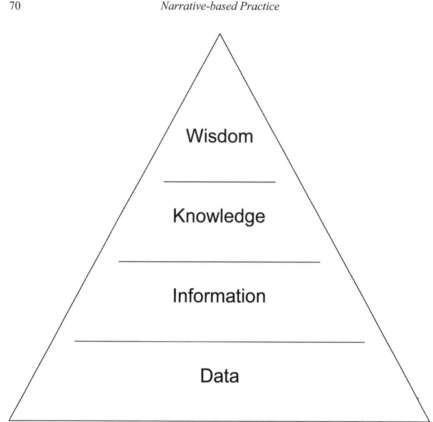

**Figure 5.1   The data-information-knowledge-wisdom hierarchy
(after Rowley 2007, 164)**

> organizational actions and behaviour more researchers and practitioners need
> to engage with the debate about the nature of individual and organizational
> wisdom. (Rowley 2007: 178)

These suggestions bring into focus a number of issues with the hierarchical
conception of DIKW. Before considering these, it is useful to outline a different
approach to the definition of knowledge, one derived from epistemology, the study
of the nature of knowledge from a philosophical viewpoint.

Epistemological Perspectives

The most common approach to knowledge from a philosophical and particularly
from an epistemological standpoint defines it as 'justified true belief', a formulation
which can be traced back to Plato. In other words, to know something a person

needs not only to believe it but also to have good reasons for that belief. So, I could stand at the roadside waiting for the bus to take me into town, but I could only be said to have knowledge about my intended journey if I had reasonable grounds to believe that a bus was likely to come along – perhaps from checking the bus timetable or from past experience. Another way of putting this would be to say that knowledge requires evidence, and that is what distinguishes it from belief, a stance called 'evidentialism', although this approach is not without its opponents in modern philosophy. (Issues arise because of the so-called 'Gettier problem', although discussion of that is beyond the scope of this book – for further information see, for example, Pojman (2003).) Knowledge also requires truth because belief in something which is false is not knowledge but delusion. Wittgenstein commented that one can say '"He believes it, but it isn't so" but not "He knows it, but it isn't so"' (1975: 42).

Thus, if we accept the broad thrust of this approach, belief, evidence and truth are all central to knowledge. Yet it is important to note that the epistemological approach says little about the relationship of knowledge to 'information'. It is simply accepted that information may form part of the evidence which is drawn upon to justify a belief. To take one example, it is interesting that Keith DeRose, who holds a Chair in Philosophy at Yale, never once uses the term 'information' in his extensive introduction, *What Is Epistemology?* (DeRose 2005). For philosophers, there is little sense of an hierarchical relationship between these concepts. Rather the situation is that depicted in Figure 5.2.

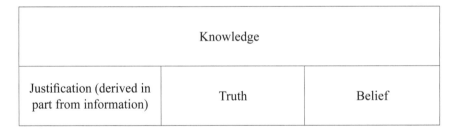

Figure 5.2   Knowledge as justified true belief

It is important to bear this in mind, because most of the knowledge management literature makes the assumption that the DIK hierarchy is an appropriate model, with the inevitable result that information management, including its ICT-enabled variations, and knowledge management become confused. The omission of belief, let alone truth, from the discussion marginalises the effects of human cognition, understanding, judgement and emotion. It strips knowledge of both human and social context and treats the language game which is needful for communication as a purely technical problem. Loosening the coupling between information and knowledge holds out the promise of a more holistic understanding of how knowledge is created and shared and one which better reflects the real world.

Knowledge is thus not simply a kind of rarefied information but is created in the human mind from a combination of belief – holding a proposition as true in your mind, evidence – which may in part be what we would term 'information' – to justify it, and truth. Because it requires belief, knowledge is a human attribute which, in Buckland's words, 'is intangible'. Note that it can be found even in the absence of what we would normally term 'information' – for example, a purely logical argument can provide the evidence needed for knowledge.

Truth

Truth forms one of the central concerns of philosophy and its huge literature cannot be summarised adequately in a short section. However, because truth is necessary for knowledge, it is important to examine the concept briefly in that context. There is a temptation to take a common-sense approach, but the danger is that this turns out to be simplistic. It is particularly important to be clear about the concept within the context of narrative knowledge because, as noted in Chapter 3, narrative is peculiarly susceptible to misuse, to the telling of falsehoods wrapped up in compelling stories. Yet narrative is also curiously resistant to bogus and sham accounts because of the human ability to discern what is being said beneath the surface of any presentation. We know, even as we watch it, that the car advert described in Chapter 3 is neither a literal nor a figurative account of the actual properties of the car in question.

Perhaps the most prominent school of philosophical thought treats truth as 'correspondence' with facts. Thus the statement 'the train is late' corresponds to the fact that, at the time that it was due, the train has not yet arrived in the station. In these circumstances, the statement is true. But note that if in fact I have arrived at the station late, and the train has already departed, the same sentence is false. It does not correspond to the latter facts. All of this presupposes, of course, that we accept a realist rather than a relativist standpoint, as described in Chapter 2.

An alternative way of thinking about truth, and one which is often embedded in narrative, is concerned with coherence. Thus Joachim states that 'Truth in its essential nature is that systematic coherence which is the character of a significant whole' (1906: 76). This approach sees the key issue as concern with an holistic view of the world: it will usually be concerned with truth in the singular rather than the truths of individual statements. Therefore, something is true if and only if it is in accord with a coherent system of belief, which may be expressed as a meta-narrative. This does, of course, present problems in a postmodern world where the very concept of a meta-narrative is contested. What it does suggest, however, is that truth is much broader than 'individual truths'.

This latter view also fits well with constructivist theories of pedagogy (see Chapter 4), where learning is seen as a continuing attempt to refine a coherent world-view. Coherence is also a key concept in discourse psychology (see Graesser et al. 1994). Graesser and colleagues suggest that, in the context of reading a textual narrative, coherence beyond the level of the individual statement may be achieved 'if the story is well written in the sense that there is harmony among the levels of representation, but not if the narrative is pointless, choppy and difficult to relate to general world knowledge' (Graesser et al. 2002: 246).

Glanzberg (2006) points out that the fundamental difference between these approaches to truth is that the correspondence theory posits truth as a 'content-to-world' relation, the statement's truth being dependent on its alignment to facts, while the coherence theory puts forward a content-to-content, or perhaps more accurately a belief-to-belief relationship.

A variety of other views are held by modern philosophers, many of which acknowledge the situatedness of judgements of truth. The pragmatic theory in particular implicitly accepts this by asserting that true propositions are those which it is most useful to believe. A further issue which is much debated is the relationship between theories of truth and theories of meaning. However, that takes us well beyond the scope of this volume.

Wisdom Revisited

Taking into account this epistemological perspective, then, it would also seem necessary to challenge the DIKW conception of an extended hierarchical relationship which links wisdom to data, information and knowledge. Rowley's suggestion, 'wisdom is only attained after much processing of data, information and knowledge, and the process starts with data' (2007: 175) needs to be contested.

From a knowledge management perspective, the discussion might be more fruitful if, instead of focusing on the individual levels of the proposed hierarchy, we turned instead to the question of how the transformations between the different concepts occur and under what conditions. What role does knowledge play in the achievement of wisdom? We have already seen that data is transformed into information by a process of organisation and structuring, which may include such things as making associations between different data elements. Information carries meaning in a way which data does not. We have seen how information contributes to the evidence needed for justification and thus for knowledge. How then does knowledge contribute to wisdom?

In classical philosophy, wisdom was thought of as the ability to discern good from bad. Alongside justice, moderation and courage, it formed one of the four principal virtues. Smith (1998) describes the Aristotelian approach thus:

> Theoretical wisdom (*sophia*) is *nous* (the ability to grasp first principles) plus *epistēmē* (scientific knowledge or understanding) ... which involves knowledge of the 'causes' – the 'why' of things. In so far as there can be different sciences with different first principles, there can be different examples of theoretical wisdom – one for each science. Practical wisdom (*phronêsis*), for Aristotle, is knowledge of means and ends.

Smith notes, however, that modern philosophy has paid relatively little attention to the concept of wisdom, although generally not challenging the notion that there is a connection between wisdom and the attainment of some outcome which is 'good'. Philosophers differ in their views on the place of knowledge in the equation. Thus some argue that wisdom can be equated to extensive factual knowledge, knowing a lot about the world, its history, human thought and how the universe is organised. However, the difficulty with this stance is that self-evidently some extremely knowledgeable people are not wise!

Another view is that wisdom is concerned with a wide variety of knowledge but only where this is coupled with understanding and judgement. Nozick puts it this way:

> Wisdom is not just one type of knowledge, but diverse. What a wise person needs to know and understand constitutes a varied list: the most important goals and values of life – the ultimate goal, if there is one; what means will reach these goals without too great a cost; what kinds of dangers threaten the achieving of these goals; how to recognize and avoid or minimize these dangers; what different types of human beings are like in their actions and motives (as this presents dangers or opportunities); what is not possible or feasible to achieve (or avoid); how to tell what is appropriate when; knowing when certain goals are sufficiently achieved; what limitations are unavoidable and how to accept them; how to improve oneself and one's relationships with others or society; knowing what the true and unapparent value of various things is; when to take a long-term view; knowing the variety and obduracy of facts, institutions, and human nature; understanding what one's real motives are; how to cope and deal with the major tragedies and dilemmas of life, and with the major good things too. (Nozick 1989: 269)

For Descartes, the question was about having a grasp of what is true:

> … it is really only God alone who has Perfect Wisdom, that is to say, who has a complete knowledge of the truth of all things; but it may be said that men have more wisdom or less according as they have more or less knowledge of the most important truths' (Descartes 1997: 262).

He continued:

> I should here have succinctly explained in what all the knowledge we now possess consists, and to what degrees of wisdom we have attained. The first of these contains only notions which are of themselves so clear that they may be acquired without any meditation. The second comprehends all that which the experience of the senses allows us. The third, what the conversation of other men teaches us. And for the fourth we may add to this the reading, not of all books, but especially of those which have been written by persons who are capable of

The well-known tale of the Traveller's Dilemma, used to explain the intricacies of decision-making where there are multiple variables and considerable uncertainty, provides a good example of why complex situations are best communicated through narrative. It goes like this:

Two friends, let's call them Simon and Angela, are on holiday in a remote part of Africa and each decides that they would like to buy a tribal mask. They explore the ethical dimensions and are assured that they are not stripping the country of its heritage – these are modern, but intricate, reproductions. They carefully wrap the objects in their luggage. But disaster strikes. On arrival back at Heathrow their suitcases have gone missing – along with the masks.

So they head off to report the loss at the airline desk, where they have to declare the value of the lost objects. Now the airline representative – let's call her Sandra – has come across this kind of thing before and she has a strategy to make sure that her company doesn't pay over the odds. She asks each of them separately to write down the value of the objects, without conferring. This is made easier by the fact that they've just had a row about whose idea it was to put the things in the checked baggage anyway!

The maximum the airline will pay per object is £100. If they both write down the same value she will assume they are being honest and authorise that payment to each of them. But if they write down different values she will assume the lower is the honest answer and pay that. But there are also bonuses and penalties. The person writing down the lower, and honest answer, will get a bonus of £10. The person writing down the higher amount will get the lower sum less £10.

So what do they do? Simon thinks about it and is about to write down £100 when he has second thoughts. What if Angela tries to trick him by putting £99? She would then get £109 and he'd get £89. So maybe he should clam £99 to forestall her? But what if she's being clever and predicting he'll do just that, in which case £98 might be the best bet?

It turns out that according to game theory, which is the logical analysis of this kind of behaviour, the best answer is £10. That is the 'rational' choice which either Simon or Angela would arrive at if they rigorously applied what is known as 'backward induction'. Logic tells us that it is the best choice regardless of what the other person does. But experiments in real life show that most people actually go for £100 or something close to it. This is because we do not behave according to strict logic. We weigh advantages, take risks. The inventor of the Traveller's Dilemma, Kaushik Basu, wrote that he devised it 'to contest the narrow view of rational behavior and cognitive processes taken by economists and many political scientists, to challenge the libertarian presumptions of traditional economics and to highlight a logical paradox of rationality' (Basu, 2007). He comments: 'If I were to play this game, I would say to myself: "Forget game-theoretic logic. I will play a large number (perhaps 95), and I know my opponent will play something similar and both of us will ignore the rational argument that the next smaller number would be better than whatever number we choose"'.

Figure 5.3   The Traveller's Dilemma: storytelling to illustrate game theory

> conveying good instruction to us. It seems to me that all the wisdom that we
> usually possess is acquired by these four means only. (ibid.: 263)

For others, wisdom involves action as well as knowledge and judgement, so that a critical issue is not just knowing 'how to live well' but putting that understanding into action, being a wise person in how one leads one's life: 'living well in general, which requires the wisdom to deal well with many particular situations. We do not live life in general, but rather, in a multiplicity of particular situations' (Grunebaum 2006: 120). Again, yet others would argue that a wise person is someone who, as well as other characteristics, holds very few unjustified beliefs, that is, does not claim knowledge where there is a lack of evidence.

Ryan (2007) summarises the discussion by suggesting that someone is wise if and only if they:

- have 'extensive factual and theoretical knowledge',
- 'know how to live well',
- are 'successful in living well', and
- have 'very few unjustified beliefs'.

Clearly wisdom is closely associated with decision making (in Rowley's words choosing 'the most appropriate behaviour'), involving selectivity between courses of action. We judge a decision as 'wise', usually with hindsight, by reference to its outcomes – Aristotle's 'practical wisdom', although clearly the notion of 'good' is highly contested. As Rowley suggests, wisdom has both ethical and social dimensions within which the notion of 'good' is resident. The Traveller's Dilemma (see Figure 5.3) is an interesting example both of the difficulty of representing wisdom in formal terms – which in effect is what game theory is attempting in its modelling of decision making – and of the way in which ethical and societal considerations affect what we would regard as 'wise', that is, that which is a 'good' outcome. What kinds of knowledge lead to a 'good' outcome? What else is required?

Drawing on Aristotle, Descartes and others, as well as Ryan's synthesis, we can therefore note that in addition to knowledge (as defined epistemologically), wisdom includes reasoning (whether by logic, intuition or revelation), judgement (and thus selectivity), action (since it is not enough just to select a course of action as a hypothetical case; rather it needs to be pursued), a concern for truth within an ethical framework, and a holistic perspective which acknowledges both complexity and social situatedness. Figure 5.4 represents this relationship.

All of this suggests that in order to manage knowledge for individual, corporate, or societal benefit, and to act wisely, we need to acknowledge and fully represent the interrelatedness of the wide range of cognitive, ethical, emotional, situational, societal and organisational issues which lead to wise action, which in turn enables individuals and societies to 'live well'.

Wisdom					
Knowledge	Reasoning	Judgement and Selectivity	Action	Ethics and Truth	Holistic Perspective

Figure 5.4   The components of wisdom

Tacit Knowledge

A very important distinction needs to be made between tacit and explicit knowledge. Tacit or intuitive knowledge is what we know without being able to describe logically what we know – it is a-logical but not illogical, and non-rational but not irrational. Explicit, sometimes termed 'analytic' or 'propositional', knowledge is derived from a logical process which can be explained and documented, although still requiring belief on the part of the individual if it is to be accepted as personal knowledge.

The concept of tacit knowledge has been explored in some depth, most notably by Michael Polanyi, who coined the term. An example which he used to illustrate the concept was the human ability to pick out a face in a crowd. We can all do this, but it is impossible for us to explain how it is that we achieve it. Research shows that the ability is much more than simply recognition of a series of individual features, each of which might be described. Instead, it relies on both the features and the way we perceive them as a whole (Polanyi 1966: 10).

Polanyi stressed three notions: first, that discovery, the uncovering of new knowledge, cannot be described by a set of rules or algorithms; secondly, that knowledge is both public and private, but that all knowledge contains emotions; and third, that tacit knowledge is more fundamental than explicit knowledge – all knowledge is either tacit or rooted in tacit knowledge. He stated that 'complete objectivity as usually attributed to the exact sciences is a delusion and is in fact a false ideal' (Polanyi 1958: 18). However, it would be inaccurate to interpret him as conceiving of two opposed kinds of knowledge: rather, he suggested that all knowledge can be placed on a continuum, from the 'ineffable', where it is impossible to verbalise or otherwise represent the knowledge to the almost entirely explicit, where what is known can be expressed in a form which would be intelligible to most people.

The acquisition of tacit knowledge cannot occur through the study of texts or by listening to an account of it. Polanyi (1958: 53) used the example of an apprentice who can acquire some knowledge by listening to the instructions his master gives him. So he can be told to hold the hammer by the handle and to move his thumb out of the way! But to gain the skills of the master, he must observe what is done and practice for himself. Many of the actions are subconscious, and they must be learned subconsciously, not by a process of analysis: 'practice makes perfect.' Polanyi inverts 'the hierarchy that privileged the propositional, analytic intelligence over the physical, subconsciously acquired and unconsciously employed skills of the craftsperson' (Adams 2006).

One group of medical students put it like this:

> What they wanted to learn …was a certain kind of knowledge that could not be learned from books. They studied their books dutifully, preparing for the quizzes that punctuated rounds and other such events, but believed that the most important knowledge they would acquire in school was not in those books. What was most worth learning was … 'clinical experience' – the sights, sounds, and smells of disease in a living person: what a heart murmur really sounded like when you had your stethoscope against a patient's chest as opposed to its sound on a recording, how patients whose hearts sounded that way looked and talked about how they felt, what a diabetic or a person who had just suffered a heart attack looked like. (Becker 1993: 33)

The organisation and management of such knowledge is quite obviously challenging. While it can be described in passages such as that above, it can only be experienced directly – the direct experience permits the student to move to a position of 'belief'.

Communication

The communication which happens between individuals – or groups for that matter – is not simply a matter of exchanging explicit and tacit knowledge, however, because we all have acquired sets of beliefs and presuppositions from the variety of experiences we have encountered and these influence how we express our knowledge. As we saw in Chapter 2, most of these beliefs are grounded in the communities of which we are a part, and the meaning we acquire is a result of shared understanding of language and of unspoken cultural heritage.

More than that, human communication draws on all the environments in which it occurs, including nonverbal signals, cultural assumptions and unwritten rules. Condon and Youssef relate a conversation with some Japanese students about the former US ambassador to Japan:

> One girl remarked, 'Yes, he was excellent, but … I think his wife was not such a good wife, if you know what I mean'. We didn't know. Was this some gossip from one of the notorious Japanese weekly magazines? No, the girl said, it was nothing like that. She simply had seen the ambassador interviewed on television a few times and 'noticed he had dandruff on his shoulders'. That was the end of the explanation … They patiently explained that in Japan a good wife is responsible for her husband's personal appearance. If he is not well groomed, it is obviously his wife's fault. But what did the girl remember hearing the ambassador *say*

when he was interviewed? She said she couldn't remember anything he said – just that dandruff. (Condon and Youssef 2002: 214)

Communication, as this experience shows, is a complex interaction between individuals and groups in which multiple messages are transmitted, received and decoded. Some of these messages are intentional, as with, say, the text of an email that is sent from one person to another, but many arise from the context and many are subconscious. This observation leads some to suggest that it is much more productive to think of interpersonal communication within an 'actor-audience' or 'co-production' framework than the more common 'sender-receiver' model. This alternative formulation is not intended to suggest that the 'sender' is consciously acting out a part, but to reflect the reality that all human communication involves people *presenting* themselves to others in order to make an impression. It is closely related to conversation theory, as outlined in Chapter 4.

'Impression management' is a well-established field in social psychology, based on seminal work by Goffman (1959) who showed that in everyday communication people take on roles as actors and audience and negotiate a 'definition of the situation', which then guides their behaviour. Schlenker defined impression management as 'the conscious or unconscious attempt to control images that are projected in real or imagined social interaction' (1980: 6), while Gardner and Martinko (1988) demonstrated that audience characteristics, such as personality traits and status, and situational cues like formality and familiarity, guide communication behaviour.

It is not possible to explore this literature in detail here, but its importance for the present discussion lies in the acknowledgement of complexity and role playing within the sharing of information and knowledge, which also characterise narrative approaches. Indeed, it is arguable that the 'actor-audience' understanding of human communication is simply a recognition of one common use of narrative in everyday life.

Towards the Management of Knowledge

In many ways, it is not surprising that much of the initial work on knowledge management stemmed from Japan, where there is a well-embedded culture of sharing tacit knowledge:

> Japanese managers spend many after-work hours together. Group dinners and visits to nightclubs are part of Japan's corporate culture. They function as an important knowledge-sharing mechanism as well as opportunities for establishing trust and ... opportunities for criticism. (Davenport and Prusak 1998: 92)

From this culture, the concepts of knowledge as a corporate resource and of the need to manage that knowledge emerged.

Nonaka and Takeuchi (1995) have provided the basis for most developments in knowledge management in the last twenty years. Their major achievement was to take the earlier work of Polanyi and develop it into a systematic account of organisational knowledge creation and use, creating in the process an ontology of knowledge levels, from individuals, through groups and organisations to inter-organisational knowledge. They believe that transformations between explicit and tacit knowledge do take place and can be managed, suggesting that there are four such transformations. Thus:

- Tacit to tacit communication takes place when people interact, for example, in meetings or social events, or in learning new skills. They termed this *socialisation.*
- Tacit to explicit communication happens when people articulate their tacit knowledge and engage in discussion – similar to the idea of social constructivism described in Chapter 4. This is *externalisation.*
- Explicit to explicit communication occurs when recorded knowledge is transmitted in some form from one person to others. They called this *combination.* It should be noted that confusion can arise here from the use of the term 'recorded knowledge'. Polanyi did not equate explicit knowledge with recorded knowledge but said that explicit knowledge was capable of being documented. Thus for combination to occur, one person's explicit knowledge must be recorded while another must use that record to arrive at 'justified true belief' – it is not a simple transmission model. Recorded knowledge in this sense equates to Buckland's 'information-as-thing'.
- Explicit to tacit communication arises from the process of encountering explicit knowledge, say in a report, and deducing new ideas, or new ways of looking at a situation, from it, again through justification, estimation of truth and belief. This is a process of *internalisation.*

They termed this four-stage process the 'SECI model', and it occurs widely in the literature of knowledge management. Socialisation can lead to externalisation, which leads to combination, then to internalisation, and so on round the circle – described as a 'spiral' on the basis that knowledge creation continues at a new level. In effect, tacit knowledge becomes externalised, shared and developed before being internalised again.

An associated theory of Nonaka and Takeuchi's is that of 'ba'. The word is notoriously difficult to translate into English but is concerned with the development and encouragement of a shared context for knowledge communication. Nonaka and Konno (1998: 53) described it as

> … a shared space for emerging relationships. This space can be physical …
> virtual … mental, or any combination of them. What differentiates *ba* from
> ordinary human interaction is the concept of knowledge creation. (Nonaka and
> Konno 1998: 53)

It should be noted that the context provided by 'ba' contributes to the individual's assessment of the justification for and truth of potential knowledge.

There is an extensive literature commenting on and developing Nonaka and Takeuchi's work and a wide variety of alternative formulations have been proposed. One useful distinction, proposed by Klamma and colleagues (2006), is that between *semantic* and *episodic* knowledge. The former relates to knowledge about organisational structures, procedures, and so on, while the latter is concerned with knowledge about experiences, usually in the form of incidents which are known, often personally, to the individual and which are usually recounted in the form of narrative. They comment:

> ... story-telling intertwines semantic knowledge ... by linking it with the narrative experiences gained from episodic knowledge ... telling, sharing and experiencing stories are a problem-oriented way to learn from the experiences of others. (Klamma et al. 2006: 177)

Theories of knowledge management often focus on the ways in which tacit knowledge can be transformed into explicit knowledge – Nonaka and Takeuchi's 'externalisation'. In some ways, this is an age-old yearning to systematise, analyse and re-express tacit understandings, often expressed in the oral tradition using storytelling, to create a permanent expression, usually in the form of a text. There has not been as much questioning in the knowledge management literature as one might expect on the feasibility, practicability and success of this endeavour, although something of a backlash can be detected in some spheres. Karen Armstrong, for example, comments on the work of Haym Soloveitchik, which 'argues that the shift from the oral tradition to written texts can lead to ... stridency, giving ... misplaced clarity and certainty about matters that are essentially elusive and ineffable' (2006: 164). The transformation from tacit to explicit inevitably both loses meaning and introduces nuances not present in the original. One role of narrative is to communicate what is tacit while minimising such distortions.

The Discipline of Knowledge Management

Knowledge management (KM) is now well established. Rowley offers the following definition:

> Knowledge management is concerned with the exploitation and development of the knowledge assets of an organisation with a view to furthering the organisation's objectives. The knowledge to be managed includes both explicit, documented knowledge, and tacit, subjective knowledge. Management entails all of those processes associated with the identification, sharing and creation of knowledge. This requires systems for the creation and maintenance of knowledge repositories, and to cultivate and facilitate the sharing of knowledge and

organisational learning. Organisations that succeed in knowledge management
are likely to view knowledge as an asset and to develop organisational norms
and values which support the creation, and sharing of knowledge. (Rowley
2000: 9)

While this is a useful definition, in practice, KM has been pursued from a wide
variety of different standpoints. Earl (2001) suggested a taxonomy based on the
identification of seven identifiable schools of KM, which can be characterised
by reference to three descriptors: the technocratic, the economic and the
behavioural. It may be noted that the term 'knowledge' is often used rather loosely
in these approaches, with a tendency to slip from definitions an epistemologist
would recognise into 'knowledge as information-as-thing'. As a result what is
termed 'knowledge management' can be no more than dressed-up information
management.

Technocratic approaches include the 'systems', 'cartographic' and 'engineering'
schools. The first focuses on technology, which is used to capture knowledge,
store it in databases and make it available to experts around the organisation. The
second is concerned with mapping knowledge throughout the enterprise, a kind
of electronic 'yellow pages' for anyone to use to track down who is most likely to
have knowledge about a given issue. The third of these schools, the engineering
approach, derives from business process re-engineering. For example, Hewlett
Packard developed systematic logs of past processes used in consultancies on its
intranet so that they could be used as input to new assignments.

Economic types of KM, characterised by the 'commercial' school, are
predominantly concerned with maximising the value of the organisation's own
knowledge resources – the exploitation of knowledge as an asset. Earl provides
the example of the Dow Chemical Company, which replaced an essentially
archives approach to maintaining its patents with a corporate 'Intellectual Asset
Management' group which actively analysed patents, identifying their potential
and value and thus encouraging the maximisation of asset value to the company
through commercialisation. Although this would at times involve sharing such
knowledge within the company, that was not the primary focus of this school.

Behavioural perspectives include the 'organisational', 'spatial' and 'strategic'
schools. The first of these concerns itself with the establishment of networks of
people, sometimes called 'knowledge communities', who are facilitated to share
or pool knowledge. Frequently, this sharing is relatively unstructured, person
to person or team to team, and has many of the features of a conversation, but
crucially includes the codification of knowledge, and of who knows what, so that
the right people can be brought together.

The spatial school of KM can be identified by its concern with the design of
work spaces to facilitate knowledge sharing. Descriptors such as the water cooler
as meeting place, the knowledge building and the knowledge café are typical of
this approach. The aim is to create environments in which people will mix socially
and share knowledge in a relatively unstructured way. An example is British

Airways Waterside development, described by the Commission for Architecture and the Built Environment (CABE) as follows:

> The icon of Waterside is the internal street. Everyone entering at ground level moves through this space, to use its facilities or to reach the office space. As the car park – situated below ground level – also exits onto this street, people leaving the car park are not able to by-pass the street by taking lifts straight to the upper floors. These flows through the street are key to Waterside's success in fulfilling the vision for the street as an active social hub ... The solution adopted gives the scope that British Airways sought for staff in different departments based at Waterside to meet casually – promoting the likelihood of chance encounters and of information being exchanged. (http://www.cabe.org.uk/default.aspx?content itemid=240&aspectid=7)

Some argue that this concept is becoming dominant in many of the buildings and other spaces which we encounter in everyday life. A recent report in *The Economist* discusses the views of William Mitchell, a professor of architecture at MIT:

> ... people are no longer tied to specific places for functions such as studying or learning ... [which] means that there is 'a huge drop in demand for traditional, private, enclosed spaces' such as offices or classrooms, and simultaneously 'a huge rise in demand for semi-public spaces that can be informally appropriated to ad-hoc workspaces'. This shift, [Mitchell] thinks, amounts to the biggest change in architecture in this century. In the 20th century architecture was about specialised structures – offices for working, cafeterias for eating, and so forth.

> The new architecture, says Mr Mitchell, will 'make spaces intentionally multifunctional'. This means that 21st-century aesthetics will probably be the exact opposite of the sci-fi chic that 20th-century futurists once imagined. Architects are instead thinking about light, air, trees and gardens, all in the service of human connections. (Anon. 2008)

This reflects an observation made some time ago by OCLC's Lorcan Dempsey:

> It seems to me that the role of the coffee house, and it must be said, Starbucks in particular given its reach, in the contemporary urban setting is becoming clearer. Starbucks provides time-place alignment in busy, moving lives: in other words it provides 'on-demand place'. It provides a place which is convenient at the time that it is required. This may be for downtime (a place to spend time relaxing), connect-time (a place to spend time connecting to the network), rendezvous time (a place to spend time with others), work-time (a place to spend time working). A colleague recently described Starbucks to me as his mobile office when he was on the road. It is not unusual to see job interviews take place there. (http://orweblog.oclc.org/archives/000799.html)

The strategic school of KM places the focus on knowledge as the key corporate asset, recognising that knowledge-based products and services are the key to future success. As Earl says, 'knowledge or intellectual capital are viewed as *the* key resource. The firm chooses to compete on knowledge' (2001: 228). This concept has led to knowledge-based theories of the firm (for example, Grant 2002), which encompass ideas like the knowledge marketplace – Web-based environments where knowledge-based products and services are bought and sold. Knowledge alliances become prominent and may replace other strategic alliances between organisations as they recognise the value of trading and sharing knowledge to mutual benefit.

Narrative in Knowledge Management

The word 'narrative' comes from the Latin *narrare* (to recount), which is itself derived from the Proto-Indo-European *gnō*, meaning 'to know'. Knowledge and narrative have in the past been recognised as closely related concepts, with the latter being a way to communicate the former without losing the context in which it is embedded. In more modern times, and especially during the second half of the twentieth century, there was a parting of the ways, with narrative and especially story divorced from the 'hard', 'factual' basis of knowledge. This is, of course, a false dichotomy. During the last ten or more years, various authors have explored the connections between narrative and knowledge management with experts in the latter field increasingly recognising that narrative is a key form of the knowledge they are seeking to capture and share. As Schreyögg and Koch (2005, 1) put it, 'narratives are viewed as a most promising feature in future knowledge management'. Some of these perspectives will be explored in more depth in Chapter 7.

Conclusions

An exploration of the concepts behind knowledge management reveals that there is a long distance to travel between the idea of knowledge as a resource and the reality of sharing and exploiting the knowledge which individuals in organisations possess. Knowledge can be an elusive concept, although the epistemological notion of 'justified true belief' is helpful. The application of knowledge, and its relationship to wisdom, is important but is an even more complex issue to investigate. As the modern knowledge management literature acknowledges, knowledge and wisdom are not simple resources to be shared and traded but open up major questions about the ways in which individuals, groups, organisations and societies operate and how they remain healthy and 'live well'. Narrative offers one way in which we may reach greater understanding of these issues.

Before turning to the use of narrative in organisations and professional practice, we will explore a rather different emergent trend which is of immense importance – the flowering of narrative forms in virtual environments.

Chapter 6
Narrative in Virtual Worlds

The current generation of young people will reinvent the workplace, and the society they live in. They will do it along the progressive lines that are built into the technology they use everyday – of networks, collaboration, co-production and participation. The change in behaviour has already happened. We have to get used to it, accept that the flow of knowledge moves both ways and do our best to make sure that no one is left behind. (Green and Hannon 2007: 17)

Introduction

Before turning to the use of narrative in organisations, it is useful to examine a broader arena in which storytelling has recently become prominent. In recent years, there has been an extraordinary blossoming of narrative using information and communications technologies (ICTs). The Web, especially in its Web 2.0 incarnation, offers a useful field of exploration into how people, both individually and organisationally, are employing narrative in the modern world. Other virtual environments, especially when they are immersive, such as many computer games, also raise intriguing questions about participation and collaboration using narrative forms.

Web 2.0, as is commonly observed, lacks any precise definition. It has, however, a number of distinctive characteristics – sometimes referred to as a 'gravitational core' (O'Reilly 2005: 1) – including:

- The idea that the web is a 'platform' – in other words, rather than use services or assemble content on our local computers, all this activity takes place in Webspace. Again, this is not a precise concept and can mean different things to different people. Programmers see it as the development of software in a virtual, shared space – a process lending itself to collaborative innovation and hospitable to open source approaches. For commercial organisations, the Web is a platform for doing business, whether direct service delivery (for example, bookselling or Internet banking) or forming corporate alliances. For journalists, the Web brings together global newsgathering with innovative media to provide an opportunity to use novel ways of communicating with audiences. Instead of carrying out tasks locally using local resources, we tap into the Web and use its resources wherever they may be.
- The facilitation of 'collective intelligence' through 'an architecture of collaboration' which provides almost unlimited opportunities to create links

between individuals' and groups' content and to post comments, revisions, opinions and so on, in open discussions which are limited neither by time nor place. Examples include Wikipedia, which has built an enormous online encyclopaedia through shared contributions and shared editing, del. icio.us which pioneered the art of folksonomy – user-generated descriptors or tags – and Cloudmark, which provides email filtering by dynamically gathering the judgement of millions of subscribers online to filter out spam. All of this is often referred to as 'the wisdom of crowds', though this phrase also draws attention to the downside – what happens when the crowd gets it wrong? Not so many centuries ago, Wikipedia would no doubt have contained detailed accounts of the forces which kept the sun in its orbit round the earth! However, while criticism is commonplace, the evidence suggests that such collaborative services are probably as reliable as many other published sources and simply require a degree of information literacy – and a modicum of common sense! – to provide useful information.

- New opportunities for place-independent interaction and the forming of deep, or at least long-lasting, relationships. Social networking services like Facebook and MySpace enable individuals to create a profile of their interests, to link to one another and to publish their own shared content. In this context, Web 2.0 can be characterised as a global network in which people are the primary content.

- Ownership of data, rather than of applications, provides the critical commercial advantage. This is why Facebook and other social networking sites fight so hard to dominate – it is not so much the services they offer as the acquisition of personal details of millions of subscribers which gives them competitive advantage. The data harvested by these sites includes user intentions (what was searched for), recommendations and user contributions, and is utilised through very large-scale analysis to identify such features as similarities with other users. At present that advantage is mainly seen in the ability to target customers with advertising but, as new services are launched, the ability to market selectively is seen as critical to success.

- Perpetual beta, the idea that software and services are released for use in what would previously have been regarded as their final draft or test phase, but are never finalised since they are overtaken by the next development. In effect, users are harnessed to undertake testing and bug-reporting; the next version released is an improvement as a result of this feedback, but contains new features to take advantage of new opportunities and so is itself also at the beta stage. In fact, it is arguable that software companies have always done this, since Microsoft, for example, relies on fault-reporting to identify shortcomings in its software. However, the change which is occurring with Web 2.0 comes from the idea of treating users as co-developers, often incorporating their own modifications into the product. A number of major software products, like OpenOffice – the alternative to

Microsoft Office – and Firefox – the competitor to Internet Explorer – rely on user involvement for development. Thus it is not only content which is always changing and increasingly collaborative, but the software and services which enable content to be manipulated too.

Various other features of Web 2.0 could be mentioned but those above are the key ones for the present discussion, particularly as they are the ones which lead to widespread adoption of narrative forms of communication.

What Kind of Data?

One of the most noticeable aspects of the Web is that it requires and exploits novel forms of organising data. Hyperdata actually preceded the Web by many years, HTML being a subset of Standard Generalised Markup Language (SGML), which was developed in the late 1960s for the description of documents held in data-processing systems. Since linking is the characteristic feature of the Web, it is not necessary for anything to be represented in multiple copies, pointers effectively providing the facility to include existing data in a 'text'. Thus any content which exploits linking is in effect built up over time from different fragments, themselves created at different times and often by different authors. Narrative structures provide a unifying framework for much of this content, especially where it contains biographical and autobiographical detail.

This focus on storytelling has been recognised as critical by the social networking services, which regard it as a key feature. Take, for example, this service announcement from Facebook, posted in May 2008:

> A few weeks ago, we told you about the new ability to import stories into your Mini-Feed from other sites. Since then, we've been working on increasing the number of sites that work with this feature. We're happy to report that now, you can import activity from YouTube, StumbleUpon, Hulu, Pandora, Last.fm, and Google Reader in addition to Flickr, Picasa, Digg, Yelp and del.icio.us. (Deng 2008)

Blogs, to give another example, often reveal narrative structures. They are temporal accounts but, unlike a diary, they appear in reverse chronological order. They also differ from diaries because they support linking to content anywhere within the blog, enabling chunks of text, images and so on, to be drawn into a new narrative. They no longer use the Web 1.0 concept of the page as the unit of organisation; instead the temporal account with embedded links is the organising concept, with data – in virtually any format and quantity – the linked target. Since some of the data which is linked into the blog may be dynamic, what results is a constantly updated multimedia expression.

Creating Innovative Content and Services

In the past, there was a very clear linear model of publication. The author wrote the text, the editor checked it and sometimes made suggestions for improvements, the publisher applied formatting, organised distribution and marketing, the printer produced the hard copy, the bookshops and news stands sold it, the libraries lent it, the end-user bought or borrowed it and then, some time later, read it. The Web radically alters all of this. Production and usage of content have become intertwined – Bruns coined the term 'produsage' to describe the phenomenon:

> ... the production of ideas takes place in a collaborative, participatory environment which breaks down the boundaries between producers and consumers and instead enables all participants to be users as well as producers of information and knowledge – frequently in an inherently and inextricably hybrid role where usage is necessarily also productive: participants are produsers. (Bruns 2007)

Some of the characteristics of this new style of production-consumption include:

*   continuous shifting of roles as people participate in different ways;
*   continuous revision with consequent difficulty in knowing which is the definitive version;
*   new approaches to intellectual property rights (IPR), with the emphasis on open usage with acknowledgement through Creative Commons licenses, and
*   exploitation of 'Long Tail' effects which make niche products viable by aggregating very small numbers of users on a global basis.

Herz has described these processes, in the context of computer games development, as 'harnessing the hive', bringing together ideas and content of value through the activities of literally millions of different contributors who gather information, contribute suggestions, discuss new methods of presentation and effectively donate all this for general use. Speaking of the hugely successful game *The Sims* produced by Maxis, Herz comments:

> ... more than 90 percent of The Sims' content is produced by the player population, which has achieved an overwhelming amount of collective expertise in all things Sim. The player population feeds on itself, in a completely bottom-up, distributed, self-organizing way; none of these people are on the Maxis payroll. (Herz 2002: 12)

Wilcox argues that it is this facility for sharing, for individuals to act in concert and gain from collaboration, which characterises online collaboration:

An idea is set in motion by being shared. The scope available to use for pooling, exchanging and developing ideas determines the extent of our innovation and creativity and so fundamentally our prosperity, well-being and hope for the future. Ideas grow by being articulated, tested, refined, borrowed, amended, adapted and extended, activities that can rarely take place entirely in the head of an individual; but which invariably involve many people sharing different insights and criticisms. The web allows shared creativity of this kind to involve more people, discussing more questions from more angles with more ideas in play. (Wilcox 2008)

What is created through these processes is very often a complex micro-web of different kinds of content brought together through a thematic thread. Text is interspersed with still images and video, both of which may be in the form of linked collections rather than individual items. Thus blogs link into Flickr photo collections, MySpace videos and Wikipedia descriptions which in turn link back into blogs and so on and on. Descriptions are provided with user-generated tags which are drawn together into folksonomies, collections of metadata selected by content creators and users, and displayed as tag clouds. Another user explores the cloud, contributing more content and thus affecting which tags are displayed and the prominence of any particular concept.

Collaborative Narration

From the individualistic perspective of twenty-first-century Western civilisation, we easily forget that the idea of individual, or even small team, authorship of narrative, enshrined in our legal system through the concept of intellectual property rights, is relatively recent. Few of the ancient classics arose in this way. We conveniently ascribe the name 'Homer' to the 'author' of *The Odyssey* and *The Iliad* when in fact we know virtually nothing of such a person and it is almost certain that both tales were recorded from oral tradition and thus multiple authorship some time before the eighth century BCE. The Old Testament similarly is not only composed of separate 'books' but most of those, and certainly the earlier examples, are the result of collaborative – and sometimes competitive – authorship, often spread over a considerable period of time. These narratives blend different individual and social perspectives, accrete asides and comments and are seen through the lenses of later generations' world-views.

There was a considerable number of experiments with the construction of collaborative narratives in the early days of the Internet, some resembling 'Chinese whispers' and others generating considerable controversy among their contributors. Simanowski reported on one example:

One of the pioneers of German collaborative writing projects is 'Beim Bäcker' (In the Bakery). Carola Heine started this project in 1996 when she wrote about a woman who encounters three preschool girls in a bakery. The girls want to buy lollipops, but are short a quarter. The woman is touched by these lovely girls, gives them the quarter, suddenly wishes for a baby, feels the need for a man and develops a sexual fantasy towards a worker having coffee in the background. Instead of talking to this man the woman buys herself a lollipop and leaves the bakery. And so the author leaves the text, leaving it to the next author to carry the story forward.

What we witness then is a fight for and with words. After the first author has introduced the female main character, another writer, a man, fills in some gaps. He turns the character in a direction the first author does not agree with at all. Now this author tries to rescue her figure and to retract the character the male author created. However, she can not just erase the former contribution: she has to take into account what has been said so far. This situation makes her both angry and inventive … It gets even more interesting when other readers turn into authors and jump in. Soon we can find all kinds of characters … . (Simanowski 2001)

There are now very many examples of collaborative, Web-based narratives. Among the best-known is *Mr Beller's Neighborhood*, which started in 2000 and contains well over a thousand contributions about life in New York. There is more than one way to navigate this collective creation, though the home page favours a geographical approach, featuring the relevant areas of Google Maps with pins for each of the contributed stories. The overall effect is of a complex, multidimensional narrative of life in New York, with all its ups and downs and highs and lows. For example:

It is rare, in New York, so I've noticed, that conversations pop up with strangers but I have experienced a few. I was in the bakery down the street from my apartment on the Upper West Side, the one with only two tables and a line out the door, and I was searching for the extra chair they have hidden behind the creamer station. A nice young man offered to help me with the search as he boasted that he was 'a regular' and 'a local' and knew right where the chair could be found. A conversation was born. (http://www.mrbellersneighborhood. com/story.php?storyid=2156)

This is a useful example of a number of Web 2.0 technologies coming together to help deliver, and provide a framework for, storytelling. For instance, the use of Google Maps shows a typical method of remixing data from multiple sources within a dynamic interface to create something new. Or stories might find new ways of distribution, perhaps from a blog by an RSS feed to an aggregator page like this one:

So you want to start your own business? Why? It's a lot more work than you might suspect. You'll have a jerk for a boss, and get to deal with everything, EVERYTHING, related to your business. You won't be able to call in sick, or take time off because the day is nice. And nobody, nobody, will sweep the floor as well as you will. Everyone else in your company will be an employee, and you know how much you care as an employee.

Yeah, I was told all this and more, but went ahead and did it anyway. In some ways, I was lucky in my choice of business (beer, who doesn't like beer?). So how did it all start?

Back in the middle ages, 1996 to be exact, I was down sized, right sized, laid off, use whatever term works for you, from the company I had worked for, for over 23 years. The company had been down sizing since 1987, and it became a rather depressing environment. I had been traveling to Canada on company business and had walked past a brew-on-premises operation one evening. It was intriguing to me as a home brewer, so I stopped in. Everyone was talking, smiling, having a beer or beers, good music in the background, and I fell in love. What a different environment from what I had been experiencing. So, a little bit of research, I found that there were some of these businesses operating in the U.S., and decided to check them out. I found one relatively close by, and spent a bit of time brewing there to get the feel for it. Same feeling to what I had experienced in Canada. It was a lot of fun..

But, that day in 1996 came, and it was time to find something new. So, with my wife's blessing, I embarked on the road to open my own business, a brew-on-premise. I contacted several of the BOPs operating in the U.S. and just started asking the questions I needed to ask, what equipment they were using, how they were doing, what they would do differently. I bought a software package to write a business plan, followed the directions, and Voila!, a business plan.

And so, shiny faced, full of enthusiasm and optimism, my newly printed business plan in hand, I gave a copy to a banker friend of the family, and anxiously awaited my funds. Well, the short story is he didn't approve my request or give me the funds. But he did give me some good advice ... (http://www.pc4media. net/Blog/Tag/storytelling)

Organisations are also using Web 2.0 services both to share internal narratives and to broadcast their brand stories to a wide community. Companies which are highly distributed are starting to find that sharing 'war stories' using blogs and wikis is an effective way of encouraging internal communication and collaboration where face-to-face meetings are infrequent:

You are involved in a business that is spread across different locations, cities or countries. Teams of people need to work together, but do not have many opportunities to physically meet. These blogs would allow people to create links through and around their work, without having to focus purely on tasks. Lots of our clients have people working for them who rarely make it into the corporate centre. Linking those people up through blogs like high-tech penpals, allows people to mentor and answer simple questions in a more efficient way. (http://blogs.hillandknowlton.com/blogs/davidferrabee/archive/2005/08/18/486.aspx)

Storytelling to promote a brand is, of course, nothing new but in the world of Web 2.0, where global *and* niche markets come together, it needs to be rethought. Just as companies like to get their logos on T-shirts so that consumers can become mobile billboards, so they are seeking to plant their stories in the conversations of the Web. A recent (April 2008) consumer trend briefing suggested:

As more brands [have to] go niche and therefore tell stories that aren't known to the masses, and as experiences and non-consumption-related expenditures take over from physical (and more visible) status symbols, consumers will increasingly have to tell each other stories to achieve a status dividend from their purchases. Expect a shift from brands telling a story, to brands helping consumers tell status-yielding stories to other consumers. (http://www.trendwatching.com/trends/statusstories.htm)

There is also considerable interest in using Web 2.0 technologies to share personal stories within professional groupings. The mobile phone company, T-Mobile, has experimented with setting up a Facebook group for new recruits to enable them to get to know each other and the company:

We set up a group on Facebook in May for the 2007 intake so that they could network informally with each other and the T-Mobile recruitment team before their September start date, enabling them to get to know each other and air concerns in a friendly, supportive environment. (Reported at http://www.personneltoday.com/articles/2008/01/08/43764/using-web-2.0-technologies-talking-about-my-second-generation.html)

In summary, as Green put it:

... mainstream companies look at the fast-growing social network scene as a place to market their products. But many are also adopting the same Web technology to create internal networks. It turns out to be an efficient way to mine for in-house expertise, discover new recruits, and share information within their own walls. (Green 2007)

It seems, then, that collaborative storytelling has found an outlet in Internet and intranet communication, using tools which encourage the telling of personal perspectives and experiences.

Narrative Generation

Recently, there has been a developing interest in the possibility of automatically generating narratives from Web 2.0 content, particularly by making use of the structures represented by user-generated tagging and folksonomies. Narrative generation has in fact been the object of considerable study since well before Web 2.0 services became available, although it has had limited success with a common criticism being the 'flatness' of automatically generated narratives. There are a number of different approaches being taken, including:

- author-centric systems which attempt to model the thought processes of the author and use formal logic to generate a chronological sequence of events;
- story-centric systems, based on the analysis of grammatical and linguistic features of a narrative, and
- character-centric systems, which start from the goals of particular characters and their *modus operandi*, including the ways in which different characters interact. An issue with this approach is that there is no obvious place for plot, although some suggest that this merely reflects the reality of emergent narrative arising from everyday human interaction or improvisation.

Riedl and Young argue that previous generations of narrative generation systems produced a

> … trade-off between plot coherence and character believability … systems that generate highly coherent narrative structures often neglect issues of believability and character. Likewise, systems that capitalise on the use of highly believable characters tend to promote poor narrative structure. (Riedl and Young 2003: 48)

The question, therefore, is whether the rich, user-tagged content created in the Web 2.0 environment can be used to overcome some of these shortcomings. The creators of computer games have been particularly concerned with this issue since believable narrative is at the heart of their products. It is worth looking briefly at some of the issues from that standpoint.

Computer Games and Narrative

The term 'narrative' is often used in connection with computer games, and rightly so, because critical features include plot, characterisation, chronology, and so on. However this genre pushes the boundaries of narrative as understood within literary theory or indeed everyday usage of the term, not least because each player in a multiplayer game contributes to the discourse and thus many different stories are being told at the same time. Such games are, in fact, a type of collective narration with varying degrees of contributor control. Again, the concept of narrator is redefined since, in some games at least, players take on the role of narrator, active participant and observer simultaneously. In a very real sense, there is an analogy with the contrast between the written text and multimedia hypertext, since each session of game playing provides novel and dynamic linkages which create a new story. The distinction is sometimes made between embedded narrative – that which the designer places in the game and which is revealed, at least in part, as the game progresses – and emergent narrative – which arises as the game is played from a combination of game logic and player actions. With multiplayer games, and especially with Massively Multi-Player Online Games (MMOGs), there is the added dimension of emergent narratives which are revealed, though not necessarily to every player, as the action progresses.

A further feature of MMOGs is that the narratives they embody are not dependent on the continuing active participation of any player but are ongoing, collaborative works-in-progress. So individuals may take a coffee break, go on holiday, go into hospital, or even die, yet the game continues. When they return – except in the last case! – the game has moved on but is still recognisable and still continues within its familiar logic and rules. It is in effect a social system in its own right – sometimes a very large one (*World of Warcraft* had over 10 million subscribing members as of January 2008). As games become established, they evolve forms of governance and a code of ethical behaviour. The narratives embody these values and participants may take punitive action when the social mores are challenged.

One of the critical issues for games designers is that of *interactivity*, defined by Crawford as 'a cyclic process in which two actors alternately listen, think and speak' (2002: 5); he refers to conversation as the most commonly experienced form of interaction. Crawford argues for a move away from the dominant action-oriented and often violent computer game towards a new concept of interactive storytelling in which 'plot and character command more design attention than cosmetic features' (ibid.: 339), with the broad concept or 'Big Idea' which the storyteller wants to convey represented by software. Different instances of stories based on the same concept would then be generated by interaction with an audience: 'the audience runs the computer programme, which interacts with the audience in such a way as to spawn a story expressing the "Big Idea" while matching the interests of the audience' (ibid.: 341). While initial attempts to achieve this kind of interaction have not been hugely successful, the idea – and particularly the separation of story generation from authorship, which becomes audience-controlled – points in one possible direction in which virtual storytelling could develop.

Interactivity in computer games leads to complex relationships between the game player and the narrative. Carr and colleagues commented:

> Players occupy different positions as regards the narrative: at times the player acts in the first person, generating events; at times in the second, being addressed as 'you' and being told of events by other characters or by an invisible narrator; and at times, the player's character is swept up in events … that evolve without any activity on their part, as if in the third person. (Carr et al. 2006: 182)

The use of computer games in professional and organisational training is not yet well established in most fields, but there have been many experimental studies of their potential and in some areas they are widely used – the most obvious being military training. A wide variety of computer games, including MMOGs, have been used in this field and there is experimental evidence for their effectiveness – Weil et al. (2005), for example, found evidence that MMOGs are well-suited for training in teamwork. Prensky comments:

> The military uses games to train soldiers, sailors, pilots and tank drivers to master their expensive and sensitive equipment. It uses games to train command teams to communicate effectively in battle. It uses games to teach mid-level officers (local Commanders-in-Chief or CINCs and their staffs) how to employ joint force military doctrine in battle and other situations. It uses games to teach senior officers the art of strategy. It uses games for teamwork and team training of squads, fire teams and other units; games for simulating responses to weapons of mass destruction, terrorist incidents and threats; games for mastering the complex process of military logistics; and it even uses games for teaching how not to fight when helping maintain peace. (Prensky 2001: 2)

Presence in Virtual Environments

In Chapter 3, we noted that one of the characteristics of narratives is the idea of *presence* – the way in which the audience becomes involved in a story and experiences it as 'real'. Chapter 4 explored the related phenomenon of flow. The same phenomenon can be found in virtual environments and has been studied in some depth. How do you achieve involvement and immersion such that the users lose themselves in the experience? Witmer and Singer suggest that four issues are involved: control factors, sensory factors, distraction factors, and realism factors. In brief these involve:

- Control: the ability to predict what is going to happen; involvement in the unfolding narrative; immediacy of feedback – as when the narrator responds to the audience.
- Sensory: issues to do with modality – for example, our visual ability is generally more developed and more sophisticated than our sense of taste – and multimodality – where more than one sense is involved. The richness of the environment being experienced is also a factor.
- Distraction: isolation of the participants from interruption and everyday stimuli and their willingness to engage in the virtual environment at the expense of other activities.
- Realism: consistency with the objective world of everyday experience and meaningfulness to the reader. A interesting additional angle to this occurs where the participants feel disoriented when the narrative is concluded and they return to the 'real' world, perhaps asking, 'but which is reality?'. (Witmer and Singer 1998: 228–30)

From the point of view of theories of perception, it is useful to remember that all experiences are mediated. A 'distal stimulus', which is the product of an object in the real world – let's say an ice-cream cone – provides information to the senses producing a 'proximal stimulus' – our internal image of an ice cream. We then attribute this latter stimulus to an external event, a process of 'distal attribution' which tells us to interpret the mental image as a real object. In virtual environments, the senses are stimulated by a different type of distal stimulus – maybe a particularly lifelike image of the ice cream cone. Of course, once we bring the sense of taste into the equation, the new distal stimulus corrects our proximal stimulus. Once virtual taste production is perfected, we will presumably have difficulty making the distinction! Loomis put it this way:

> The perceptual world created by our senses and the nervous system is so functional a representation of the physical world that most people live out their lives without ever suspecting that contact with the physical world is mediated; moreover, the functionality of perception impedes many reflective individuals from appreciating the insights about perception that drive from philosophical inquiry. Oddly enough, the newly developing technology of … virtual displays is having the unexpected effect of promoting such insight, for the impression of being in a remote or simulated environment experienced by the user of such systems can be so compelling as to force a user to question the assumptions that the physical and perceptual world are one and the same. (Loomis 1992: 113)

There is some evidence that three-dimensional environments like *Second Life* can be particularly successful at creating presence. Indeed, this is one of the reasons that these environments are being used in some organisations for training purposes – Stott (2007) reports on the use of *Second Life* in an MSc course on healthcare management at Coventry University and there are many other examples.

Social Networking

We have already seen that multiplayer computer games generate their own social structures but of course, the phenomenon is even more pervasive in the virtual worlds of social networking services like Facebook and MySpace. In order to participate in these sites, other than as an observer of public material, users must register and construct a profile or identity. This, because it is self-constructed, is a form of self-narrative and is, of course, partial or even deliberately misleading. Its purpose is to differentiate one person from another, to facilitate group memberships and to provide a 'post box'. It is a constructed representation of how the individual wishes to be perceived. However, it is also an expression of the individual's self-concept, of how someone sees themselves. Rafieli and colleagues ask:

> [I]s the ability to present an idealized self online similar to the ability to idealize one's physical appearance through the choice of clothing, haircut, makeup accessories and even plastic surgery? (Rafieli et al. 2005: 67).

It certainly enables individuals to place themselves within the perceived dynamics of those social groups deemed worthwhile and to which the individual aspires.

The concept of 'social identity' was developed by Henri Tajfel and John Turner (see Tajfel and Turner 1986) to describe people's self-concept in relation to the series of 'selves' which correspond to each of the social groups to which they belong (for example, family, work, neighbourhood, hobbies). It is what makes us 'us' as opposed to those outside, the others. The ways in which we describe this 'us-ness' are, of course, heavily reliant on narrative. Indeed, the term 'collective narrative' was used by Bruner (1990) to describe the collection of stories, memories, aspirations, explanations and beliefs which a group holds to define itself in relation to its surroundings and to other groups. The shared identity of the group thus established provides the individual also with a sense of identity. Again, there is a strong connection to language games and linguistic codes.

It is generally argued that the most important source for a collective narrative is the history of the group, and this would seem to be borne out by the popularity of social networking sites which enable links to be made with former schoolfriends or other acquaintances. However, just as Web 2.0 is highly dynamic and ever changing, there is also evidence to suggest that people in social networking groups are adept at creating a collective narrative with relatively little shared history.

Identity is particularly important in organisational and professional settings, both to enable the individual to create an acknowledged role (that is, one which is explicitly recognised by colleagues) and as a means of establishing a collective sense of purpose and mission. Whetten and Godfrey (1998) demonstrated the importance of organisational identity, arguing that it encapsulates what is deemed to be important about the organisation, those things which describe it uniquely and what is enduring about it. In addition, just as with individuals, organisational and professional identities serve to proclaim who is an insider and who is not.

The same authors also showed that personal and organisational identities are interrelated, so that there is an ongoing process whereby individuals shape the identity of the organisation, while it helps to shape theirs. It is important in this regard to remember that, as Cornellissen (2002) remarks, the term 'organisational identity' is a metaphor, a way of using language in order to make associations and bring out deeper meaning, in this case by pseudo-referencing which implies that the organisation is a cognitive organism. Thus it is that we find personal and organisational narratives intertwined.

Going back to the arena of social networking services, it is very noticeable that the predominant use is for sharing stories and narratives. Many of these are what we might call 'micro-stories', snippets of information about what a member is doing, but they are woven into the fabric of a shared narrative – what we might call 'interleaved narratives'. One of the curious features of this new framework is that the micro-stories contribute to a whole range of different interleaved narratives. Take the example of a micro-story written by one participant, let's call her Anne, using Facebook's 'What are you doing right now?' feature. Facebook displays this as:

> Anne is looking forward to seeing old friends for lunch in Gloucester today. Hope the train's on time!

Each of Anne's friends see this on the home page of their Facebook accounts, under 'status updates'. Brian is one of Anne's friends. He updates his status:

> Brian is on a tight schedule today. He didn't get that report on our new market strategy finished last night so it's got to be first priority today. He's got a meeting at 11.00 then lunch with friends.

Anyone who is a 'friend' of both Anne and Brian sees a story developing which tells of what is happening in Anne's and Brian's lives in the time leading up to lunch. But suppose Paul is a 'friend' of Brian but not of Anne. He writes:

> Paul isn't feeling too happy with life just at present. He has to go to the dentist this morning so it'll be liquid lunch today!

Brian's friends see this but Anne's do not. So we find that four different interleaved narratives have emerged from these short micro-stories by just three people (see Figure 6.1). And this is in addition to the stories seen by people who are only friends with one of these participants. Furthermore, this artificial example greatly under-represents the number of different interleaved narratives emerging, since most people on a social networking site will have considerably more than two 'friends'.

Quite apart from being a virtual meeting place for friends to share their social life, there is a plethora of professional groups active on Facebook as well as on other sites offering a similar service. A recent search (June 2008) revealed groups as disparate as Certified Public Accountants (1,471 members), Belgian

Friends of Anne, Brian and Paul see	Friends of Anne and Brian see	Friends of Anne and Paul see	Friends of Brian and Paul see
"Anne is looking forward to seeing old friends for lunch in Gloucester today. Hope the train's on time!"	"Anne is looking forward to seeing old friends for lunch in Gloucester today. Hope the train's on time!"	"Anne is looking forward to seeing old friends for lunch in Gloucester today. Hope the train's on time!"	"Brian is on a tight schedule today. He didn't get that report on our new market strategy finished last night so it's got to be first priority today. He's got a meeting at 11.00 then lunch with friends."
"Brian is on a tight schedule today. He didn't get that report on our new market strategy finished last night so it's got to be first priority today. He's got a meeting at 11.00 then lunch with friends."	"Brian is on a tight schedule today. He didn't get that report on our new market strategy finished last night so it's got to be first priority today. He's got a meeting at 11.00 then lunch with friends."	Paul isn't feeling too happy with life just at present. He has to go to the dentist this morning so it'll be liquid lunch today!	Paul isn't feeling too happy with life just at present. He has to go to the dentist this morning so it'll be liquid lunch today!
Paul isn't feeling too happy with life just at present. He has to go to the dentist this morning so it'll be liquid lunch today!			

Figure 6.1   Social networking interleaved narratives

lawyers (357), Theological Librarians (87), the American Society of Landscape Architects (1,489), the National Union of Journalists (1,649) and the Irish Society of Chartered Physiotherapists (1). While a proportion of the messages posted on these sites are job adverts, requests for advice and corporate propaganda, again it is noticeable that storytelling is a much-used approach. Indeed, the power of Web 2.0 technologies to enable the sharing of stories is itself a constant theme:

> Ok, I am a new media journalist. But I started out as a newspaper journalist. Print gave me a platform to express what I was required to express within a certain confine. The new media, however, enables me to express and share my experience with my audience any time anywhere. It even opened up new ways for me to narrate my story. (http://www.facebook.com/topic.php?uid=2310419 644&topic=3196)

It is interesting to note that the expansion of Facebook to corporate organisations has been carefully managed. The service began at Harvard University and rolled out to educational institutions by limiting membership to people with a .edu email address. It used viral marketing techniques to spread the word and rapidly became an application of choice for American undergraduates before going world-wide. At first hostile to non-educational membership, in 2006 it started to allow employees of selected commercial organisations, including Apple, Amazon, Microsoft and Intel, to join. Part of the motivation for this change lay in the desire to avoid the removal of members as they moved from education into professional posts, potentially resulting in the loss of people just as their spending power dramatically increased. For a service whose economic model relies heavily on advertising, this was hardly likely to be a winning strategy in the long term.

Conclusion

The widespread adoption of the Web as an everyday medium for creativity and communication, coupled with extensive use of other virtual environments such as multiplayer computer games, has introduced new forms of narrative. This is especially true where two or more, indeed often thousands, of people are making contributions and thus building up or participating in a shared narrative. Social networking services in particular have encouraged interactive and interleaved narrative composition in which autobiographical fragments are brought together in different ways to create multiple expressions. As the use of these services has moved out of academic institutions to encompass professional groups and organisations, it is becoming clear that they are facilitating uses of narrative expression as part of occupational as well as social dialogues. In these ways, the use of narrative is becoming an everyday experience for many people, even if they would not themselves characterise it in this way or claim to be authoring content.

We turn next to consider the wider issue of narrative use within and between organisations, bearing in mind the ways in which technology is becoming an enabling force in these environments and examining the different purposes behind narrative expression in organisations and professions.

Chapter 7
Narrative in Organisations

Scratch the surface in a typical boardroom and we're all just cavemen with briefcases, hungry for a wise person to tell us stories. (Attributed to Alan Kay, Vice-President, Walt Disney Corporation)

The tradition of an oral narrative history that records and hands down learning, insight or collective revelation still thrives in social communities and Shell has found it particularly effective in helping change our business mindset and improve our knowledge practice. (Shell International Exploration and Production 2001: 1)

Introduction

Every member of an organisation, and every client and customer, lives in a world of stories. At a high level, vision statements are developed to tell the story of what the organisation, or an influential part of it, wants to become. Stories use selective corporate memories to legitimise and glorify the past. They are used in training, and in spreading the organisation's ethos. What is it safe to poke fun at? What must be taken seriously? Who are the key players? What were the triumphs of the past? What is the vision of the future? What do our competitors think of us? What do we think of them? The organisational world is afloat in a sea of stories.

The same is true of the professions. We meet at conferences and seminars and exchange accounts of interactions with clients. We share ideas about the opportunities of the future. We bemoan the barriers put in place by lack of understanding by legislators and the near-sightedness of professional bodies. We commiserate over the stereotypical images that the public holds of our profession, whether it is accountants as bean counters ('There are three kinds of accountant in this world. Those who can count and those who can't!'), lawyers as ambulance chasers ('Why do so many lawyers have broken noses? From chasing parked ambulances!'), or librarians:

> I once had a 7th grade student library aide who was definitely not the sharpest knife in the drawer. I almost always had to undo the work that she had done, but she obviously loved 'helping' – so I used to save the easiest tasks for her to do. Open House night arrived, and her mother dropped in to talk to me. She gushed on and on about how much her daughter enjoyed being a library aide, and crowned it all by saying, 'You know, my daughter is not very bright, so

I figure when she grows up, maybe she can be a librarian'. I SWEAR this is
true – a word for word quote. I was speechless! (http://www.librarian-image.
net/2002/stories.html)

Narrative is not a replacement for problem specification, data collection, analysis
and synthesis. The post-positivist paradigm described in Chapter 2 does not reject
quantitative methods, either for investigation of a situation or for modelling
possible courses of action. Neither does narrative replace systematic processes
designed to assure and enhance quality of service. However, it is more than an
optional complement to those approaches. It deserves to be placed near the centre
of organisational thinking, not least because it opens up possibilities which a
purely analytical approach may neglect and better reflects the reality of complex
environments. It needs to be absolutely central in organisational communication,
because it helps employees to use their imaginations and their intuition to envisage
new situations and to understand what others in the organisation, and its customers,
have experienced. It provides starting points from which general lessons can be
learned, because although every situation is different, there are usually sufficient
similarities to enable knowledge and understanding to be transferred – otherwise
no one would be an expert in anything. As Hannabuss put it:

> One of the most frequent uses of narrative in organisations [is to generalise from
> them]. They are unique and idiosyncratic, but they are used as a key part of
> sensemaking because they tell us something important about the circumstances
> now, and they can also be used as pointers or lessons for the future (e.g.
> if the company were to do this, then similar or comparable outcomes would
> occur). They can also be generalised from and add to the store of exemplars of
> successful and unsuccessful management practice which becomes the folklore
> of management itself. (Hannabuss 2000b: 412)

This use of narrative fits in well with notions of critical reflection and reflective
practice. It helps us to 'enter' the experiences of other people in the organisation, to
compare our own understanding with that of others and to gain deeper insight into
which courses of action are likely to be appropriate in particular circumstances.

What Kinds of Stories do People in Organisations Tell?

Martin et al. (1983) attempted to categorise the stories which are commonly told
in organisations. They identified the following:

Rule-breaking stories

The majority of these accounts have the aim of revealing and sharing beliefs about
corporate culture, helping employees express and learn the acceptable attitude to

rules. A famous example concerning IBM relates how a very junior employee stopped Thomas Watson Jr, the all-powerful company chairman, from entering a restricted area because he was not wearing the correct badge. Watson accepted this and one of his aides was sent to get the correct identification. The story circulated around IBM and beyond as an indication that everyone in the company was expected to obey the rules. At the opposite end of the spectrum is the experience of a new employee joining NewWave, as recounted by Brown and Eisenhardt:

> Managers described their culture as 'rule breaking'. It was acceptable and even encouraged to minimize structure and violate rules. One manager related, 'It's part of the culture not to write things down'. Meetings existed, but they were free-form. As one project manager noted, 'One of the first things I noticed when I came here was the lack of organisation of meetings as a form of communication. Never any agenda, never knowing when the meeting is going to be.' (Brown and Eisenhardt 1997: 14)

Is the Big Boss Human?

Stories demonstrate that the chief executive or the prime minister is fundamentally the same as everyone else, often by demonstrating that they do not try to exert privilege. So there is no 'executive dining room', or everyone shares an open plan office. Images are used to reinforce the 'ordinariness' of those in power, just as politicians compete to be photographed kissing babies. Panda and Gupta tell the story of Air India's acquisition of its first Boeing 747:

> The person who broke the auspicious coconut on the (aeroplane) was neither JRD Tata, who was at the helm at that time, nor a minister, but a 57-year-old maintenance engineer Roland Fernandes, Air India's longest-serving employee. (Panda and Gupta 2001: 14)

Negative versions of this type of story depict the chairman (and it's nearly always a man) arriving at the factory gate in a chauffeur-driven limousine while workers are being made redundant: he lives in a different world.

Can the Little Person Rise to the Top?

Here, the question is about the openness of the organisation to promotion by merit. These stories focus on individuals at the bottom of the hierarchy and show how they moved up to the most senior role. Is ability rewarded? Issues about the 'glass ceiling' and the difficulties women face in securing senior positions fall within this category. Negative stories may refer to the 'double-bind' or 'lose-lose' problem, as Oakley remarks, 'typical double-bind for women in leadership positions is that they must be tough and authoritative (like men) to be taken seriously, but they will be perceived as "bitches" if they act too aggressively' (2000: 324).

Will I Get Fired?

In this type of story, the protagonists are employees and managers at relatively low levels in the hierarchy and the question often revolves around the issue of how decisions will be made if redundancies are in the air. Positive stories tell about managers' strategies for avoiding lay-offs, negative ones about randomness and unfairness. The underpinning logic is a narrative about the way the organisation treats its people.

Will the Organisation Help Me When I Have to Move?

Here, the issue is what happens when an organisation needs to redeploy its employees. In Britain, these stories are often found where government agencies are relocated and employees face the choice between moving and redundancy. The fictional *Yes Minister* discussion lampoons the issue but illustrates the point:

> … some servicemen could be stationed permanently in the north of England: other ranks perhaps, junior officers possibly. But he made it clear, very properly, that we really cannot ask senior officers to live permanently in the north. I asked for a list of reasons. He obliged: 1. Their wives wouldn't stand for it; 2. No schools; 3. Harrods is not in the north; 4. Nor is Wimbledon; 5. Ditto Ascot; 6. And the Henley Regatta; 7. Not to mention the Army and Navy Club … . (http://findarticles.com/p/articles/mi_m1316/is_n6_-_7_v20/ai_6495576/pg_1)

How Will the Boss React to Mistakes?

In these cases, the culture of the organisation is revealed by the way it reacts when someone makes an error, especially when it is a blunder of their own making. There are two scenarios. In the positive version, someone is at fault, goes along to their manager and confesses what has happened and is reassured that 'every mistake is a learning opportunity.' Recriminations are at a minimum and the person involved goes on to a successful career in the company. In the negative version, the mistake is discovered, they are bawled out in front of colleagues and their career is permanently blighted. Take this example:

> There comes a time in every job where you are taken to the boss's woodshed for a spanking. Or, in my case, an all-glass office with dreamy 32nd-floor views over the city, furnished with a quartet of green velvet-clad wing chairs traced by white leather piping and accented with toile throw pillows.
>
> I had always wanted to test those chairs and they are far more comfortable than I'd imagined, even when squirming in them.

'Quite frankly, I was disappointed,' was what was first uttered by my boss upon her closing the floor-to-ceiling glass door as we took seats in the green chairs. The moment I heard those opening words, I felt that same infusion of dread I remember from visits to the school principal. (http://www.boston.com/jobs/ news/articles/2007/01/21/at_my_age_admonishment_still_stings/)

How Will the Organisation Deal With Obstacles?

Martin et al. (1983) found this to be the most common type of story. Obstacles may be external, for example, a strike of post office delivery staff, or internal, perhaps when systems fail. There is also overlap with the previous category, since dealing with mistakes is an organisational as well as an individual issue. Stories may again be positive or negative. The former may tell how service was continued through the postal strike because employees took the initiative to find alternative methods of delivery, sometimes even using their own cars, and the whole episode enhanced the company's reputation. The latter relate the disasters that ensue when problems arise, for instance, when a key manager was taken ill and deadlines were missed.

It is interesting to consider why these stories are so common. Martin et al. suggest three possible explanations. A general finding is that stories tend to relate to points of conflict and tension in the organisation between its values and those of employees, the latter reflecting the mores of the external culture. They may offer a resolution to that conflict or they may suggest a way of living with it. For example, a major point of tension in all organisations can be found where one of the basic values of Western civilisation, equality, rubs up against the need for differentiation in staff roles and particularly for some to be in explicit positions of authority. Stories help to reduce the tension by positing answers, positive or negative, to this use of power. A second reason for storytelling among employees lies in the way that that power is exercised. Virtually all organisations retain the right to 'hire and fire'. Thus their underlying culture and ethic threatens the basic human need for security. So employees ask themselves and each other, 'What happens if the company runs into trouble?', 'What happens to me if I make a mistake?' The third explanation lies in the area of control. Becoming employees means giving up the right to control part of our lives, if only in such matters as when we have to be at the workplace and the need to allow others, in the name of the organisation, to exercise control over us. Again, this conflicts with the idea in modern society that individuals have the right to control their own destinies. The stories that people tell each other either offer a resolution to these questions or simply point up their everyday reality. In so doing they enable the pain to be shared.

A Typology of Storytelling Organisations

The questions of authority and control are critical ones in most organisations. Narratives and stories are powerful and as a result they are used by those in authority to exercise control, although, as the above analysis makes clear, this is often subverted by counter-cultural forms of narrative. However, for many organisations, the grand vision and the grand history are useful tools for attempting to promulgate a common purpose and ethos. Boje analysed the Disney Corporation as a storytelling organisation, commenting that 'The happy stories organisation members tell about themselves are as artfully constructed and as carefully edited as their legendary characters' (1995: 997), and characterising such organisational practice as the language game (see Chapter 2) of discipline: 'Walt's official story and singular worldview dominate, socialize, and marginalize others' experience' (ibid.: 1031)

Boje (2002: 43) suggested that there are five different 'ideal' types of storytelling organisation ('ideal' in the sense of pure types, which in reality are intermixed; not 'ideal' in the sense of perfection):

- bureaucratic – hierarchical, addicted to red tape and the 'right' way to do things, defined by functions and stuck in its traditions;
- quest – seeing itself on a journey, pursuing a call, open to reorganisation and change, adventurous, often granting heroic status to its leaders;
- chaotic – on the edge, thriving on complexity, used to adaptive systems which respond to the environment, recounting its stories without overall structure – almost an 'anti-narrative';
- postmodern – no single language game can be identified, multiple legitimacies, acknowledging aesthetics but with no real attempt to forge a collective narrative (see Chapter 6), and
- interstory – Boje's own suggestion for how organisations need to move forward: 'managers need to take advantage of the multiple, intertextual and polysemous (many meanings) strands of storytelling organisation processes' (ibid.: 48):

> For the manager … I feel that it is important for them to move between different types of narrative in a never-ending interpolation and entanglement of bureaucratic, quest, chaotic or postmodern – the creation of an interstory … while some organisational members may choose to reproduce the bureaucratic and quest stories presented in popular texts or as told by the CEO, such tales will be confronted by others, producing a much more contested landscape. (ibid.: 49–50)

One does not have to accept Boje's entire classification to appreciate the wisdom of this last model. Organisations which are dominated by one particular model of storytelling are unlikely to develop either self-understanding or appreciation of the potential contributions of all their members. In a fast-moving world where the environment forces rapid adjustment to continuous change, a focus on one type of narrative is bound to be damaging. Once the self-image becomes untenable, there remains little to fall back on. On the other hand, the organisation which opens itself to the multiple perspectives of all its members' stories is more likely to be able to find a way forward.

The remainder of this chapter is structured to examine the different ways in which narrative is being used in organisations and professional practice, focusing first on the ways in which narrative is used as an *input* – the opportunities for listening to narrative – and then the ways in which it is *created* in order to communicate both within the organisation and with its clients and customers.

Listening to Narrative

Organisations and the individuals within them spend a considerable amount of time listening to other people's narratives. Much of this is absorbed without a great deal of thought but it is arguable that much greater value can be obtained when deliberate efforts are made to listen to and understand the stories which form a kind of alternative description of organisational reality. A primary requirement for this to occur, of course, is the development of listening skills. Narratives are not just told and are not just heard as a kind of background noise, but engage those who are willing to become participants. A culture where listening is valued will therefore provide fertile soil for narrative:

> Firms that listen to what employees have to say rather than just telling them what to do are likely to perform better across the board. 'If a company wanted to make a difference in its workplace, the one single thing it could do is just start listening to people more', says Dr Pete Bradon ... All of the 10 companies which achieved the best scores for bosses who listen [in the 2005 *100 Best Companies to Work For* survey] ... are in the top 20 overall, and seven of those make up the top 10 itself. (Thomas 2005: 8)

Having said that, listening is a skill which needs to be learned. As Belker put it, 'there's a fine line between being a good listener and allowing people to get away from their work for two hours while they drink coffee and pour out all their problems to you' (1997: 56). But a good listener will allow both narrator and listener to gain value from the narration. As Linde put it, 'the hearer comes to participate in the construction of the story, and thus comes to have a stake in it' (2001: 163).

Understanding the Client

It has become a truism that services aim to be 'client-centred' ('the customer is king', 'the user at the heart of service delivery', and so on). The stories that customers tell can be invaluable in revealing their real attitudes to services and products and can reveal the reality behind such slogans. Furthermore, if the act of relating the experience as a story is encouraged, it helps the customer to put into words what may be a subconscious and subliminal feeling about the service.

A technique known as 'cultural probing' has been developed to assist organisations and researchers to collect customer stories. In essence, it is similar to diary studies, but the customers are also given a scrapbook to jot down notes and thoughts or paste examples, a camera to take photos of products or experiences, folders, maps and anything else that might help them to gather material together. The technique has been widely used in the design community, especially in relation to the design of home and other human environments, and is closely related to ethnographic research methods:

> ... cultural probes were successful for us in trying to familiarize ourselves with the sites in a way that would be appropriate for our approach ... They provided us with a rich and varied set of materials that both inspired our designs and let us ground them in the detailed textures of the local cultures. (Gaver, cited in Hemmings et al. 2002: 9)

With the widespread use of blogs, wikis and other electronic media, a new source of customer stories has been opened up. Brown and colleagues comment on a user's blog about encountering the new Volkswagen Beetle, noting that it 'is seeded with autobiographical detail and structured as a story. It has all the hallmarks of personal narrative':

> I inspected it in the driveway of our mom's home, where my brother and I were visiting, and then drove it around for half an hour on her neighborhood's streets, with light to no traffic, in a suburban area with no traffic signals, and in light rain and mist.. The overall impression of the exterior styling is 'extremely cute.' Almost huggable. The front of the car presents an almost literal face that appears to smile. The old running boards are just hinted at in the new design, which is nothing but round, sensual curves from stem to stern. The seats are VERY comfortable and firm, although they're equipped with perhaps the most bizarre set of adjustment controls I've ever used. The strange looking, wide stereo system is in the middle of the dash. Now comes one of the weirder parts of the styling— the huge, steeply sloped windshield must have been almost three feet from the steering wheel. It's the most unusual windshield placement I've ever experienced. The windshield is SO far away from your face as you sit in the seats, it's almost like you've turned around and are looking out the back window! This makes the top surface of the dash absolutely huge. The dashtop is so big and deep, in fact, you could probably set up an entire model train track on it. :) You could put a good sized dog on it. Or your entire collection of Star Wars action figures. You could plant a lawn on it. It's simply the strangest looking and feeling dashtop/windshield design I've ever seen in any car. Period. (Brown et al. 2003: 23)

What is fascinating about this account is that it incorporates so many of the different facets of narrative. It is personal and autobiographical ('the driveway of our mom's home, where my brother and I were visiting'), it uses compelling images ('you could probably set up an entire model train track on it'), it makes value judgements ('The seats are VERY comfortable and firm') and it is unashamedly emotional ('Almost huggable'). By putting all these different images and concerns together, what is conveyed is a rounded appreciation of how the potential customer reacts to a particular product. This clearly provides the manufacturer with much richer information about customers' preferences than would a tick list or simple observation – it gets inside their whole attitude to the products as presented.

An additional dimension of customer stories occurs where they pass them on by word of mouth; negative stories can spell the death knell for a product or even a company, recognition of which has led to a new discipline of 'reputation management', while positive stories are the gold dust of marketing. Solnet and Kandampully (2008) remark that

> ... positive stories passed between customers serve as a form of extended and enduring WOM (word of mouth) advertising. Stories often become connected with a brand or a company, such that the mere mention of that company or brand can evoke a folklore story that has an impact on the business fortunes of the company. (Solnet and Kandampully 2008)

Understanding the External Environment

Organisations and professionals also use narrative to explore 'otherness' – to reach understanding of worlds which are largely closed to them, which may include the everyday lives of customers and clients. This can be particularly important for professionals in service industries, such as doctors or nurses treating people with terminal disease, or social workers trying to engage with minority or disadvantaged groups. Washington and Moxley relate their use of narrative as a tool for understanding homelessness among a group of eight African-American women and report:

> The narratives proved very effective from three perspectives: first, they revealed the processes that pushed each woman into homelessness; second, they fostered catharsis of pent-up emotions among the women; and third, they indicated important advanced organizers of help and assistance (such as the substantive issues each woman faced). (Washington and Moxley 2008: 159)

They also noted that storytelling is well-suited to the use of mixed media, with the storyteller able to communicate her experience through non-verbal as well as verbal accounts:

> Collaborative production of a quilt over eight sessions with each woman
> contributing a panel that captured her way of thinking about the homeless
> experience strengthened the bonds among group members. Consequently, the
> women participated in their first public presentation on their homeless experience
> before an audience of 50 people. Their presentation of the encompassing themes
> of their narratives, supplemented by the performance of gospel songs and poetry,
> proved effective in arousing the audience emotionally. (Ibid., 159–60)

It is unusual in the literature of organisations and professional practice to find such
emphasis on emotional involvement, but as we have seen in earlier chapters – for
example, in relation to the concept of 'flow' in Chapter 4, 'ba' in Chapter 5 and
'presence' in Chapter 6 – it is this holistic approach which holds out the promise
of delivering improved and more human services.

Internal Communication

We have seen in preceding chapters how frequently people use stories to
communicate. One of the features of the stories that are told in organisations is that
while many of them relate the accepted norms of the workplace or the profession,
others focus on exceptions. They relate events and experiences which are outside
the norm – that, after all, is what often generates interest in listeners. Behn
suggests that these stories provide a useful source of information and opportunity,
especially for the manager adept at 'management by walking around', or, as Behn
puts it, 'management by listening':

> The stories that people tell managers are the ultimate in disaggregation; one
> such story can provide a single deviate datum that the summary statistics have
> completely masked but that, precisely because it was unexpected, prods further
> investigation that can produce some real learning (and thus, perhaps, some real
> improvement). (Behn 2003: 597)

An important aspect of storytelling for internal communication builds on Nonaka
and Takeuchi's concept of 'socialization' (see Chapter 5), the sharing of tacit
information. It follows that explicit actions to encourage informal interaction,
as well as encouragement to communicate through narrative, are essential for
effective knowledge sharing.

There is a wide range of ways of encouraging the use of storytelling for internal
communication. One which has proved successful is the use of the 'critical incident
technique' (CIT), which involves asking individuals to recall significant episodes
in their work. These could be instances of particular success or problems that they
faced, perhaps for the first time, where a difficult decision had to be made (see, for
example, Bitner et al. 1994). Although its more common use has been in examining
front-line interactions between staff and customers, CIT also helps staff to focus,
discuss and reflect on matters which are of importance to them. Importantly, it

enables a focus on perceptions. How did it feel to be in that situation? How do you think other people saw it? What was it that made that incident stand out?

Internal communication can also be enhanced by the use of digital storytelling techniques (see also Chapters 3 and 6). For example, Accenture used the following technique to gather a picture of the diversity of its employees (though note that this is the company's unverified official account):

> In the summer of 2004, ten Accenture UK employees were selected to participate in a week-long 'digital storytelling' workshop. The 10 short-listed candidates were drawn from across the organisation, from many different walks of life, from all over the UK. They were given access to a studio and asked to share a unique slice of life about themselves using their own photos and voice-over. The short films they created form a collection of intensely personal histories and experiences of family life, culture, religion, parenting, disability, values and identity, which can be viewed as a reflection of the extraordinary diversity of Accenture's people. (http://careers3.accenture.com/Careers/UK/AboutAccenture/Accenture+Digital+Stories)

This example is part of what has rapidly become an enormous new genre of digital storytelling, which has captured the imagination of many thousands of people around the world and given a new voice to those who would probably never have had an opportunity to tell their stories using traditional media such as the printed page.

Social Participation

One of the key issues for anyone working in an organisation is how to achieve and maintain social membership. In part, this concerns membership of the organisation itself; in part, it relates to the sub-groups which exist within it. In the former category are the stories about company culture, which may be related explicitly to new employees as part of their induction. Reissner tells of a study of an engineering company in north-east England where there was a very strong culture – interestingly including the explicit use of narrative for communication:

> The core group of ThyssenKrupp Automotive Tallent Chassis' workforce is highly loyal to the company and committed to give their best. The 'commitment narrative' is deeply embedded in the organisational culture with a remarkable 'can-do attitude'. Interviewees contended that there was actually a 'Tallent spirit in the air', which is hard to grasp or describe. The stories that capture this aspect of the company's culture play an important role in the induction and training of new employees, which are often perceived as a culture shock by new employees, as one interviewee pointed out: 'There's a certain Tallent way of thinking and you either sink or swim in that environment.' (Reissner 2005)

In large organisations, there will be overlapping and competing social groupings, which may be based on seniority, work divisions, professional affiliations, gender, or other factors. The narratives which gain currency in the organisation are one way in which this membership is achieved. Downing (2005) points out that the narrative integration achieved reflects shared ways of making incidents and experiences intelligible rather than necessarily representing shared meanings:

> Different storylines reflect competing evaluations of actions and identities; emplotment is based on a selective appropriation of actions and identities from storylines; and narrative structuring involves a selective working-up of a cause-effect logic. Different groups of stakeholders may enact competing social dramas by drawing on different aspects of storylines, selecting different plots, and elaborating different narrative structures. (Downing 2005: 195–6)

For individuals, it is important to find membership of the social group and this is achieved first, by selectively accepting particular stories, and secondly, by adding to them. So the discussion among the smokers outside the entrance bounces personal experiences around which confirm or challenge the accepted 'wisdom' among that group; cross-membership of different groups ensures that the differing versions are shared; and thus the story evolves. Hopkinson comments, 'meaning is never final or complete but is continuously constructed through the juxtaposition of competing views' (2003: 1944).

It is important to note that this kind of social bonding through narrative does not necessarily result in the story being closely related to the truth of what is happening (see the discussion on truth in Chapter 5). At the same time, the group bonding may give someone the courage to challenge company orthodoxy. As Snowden (2004, 203) points out:

> It only takes one person to say 'but that's not what really happened,' or 'but that's not the complete story,' and the whole process is undermined ... Several years of using anthropological techniques to capture water cooler stories after some official communication shows a near universal occurrence of anti-story: the cynical and naturally occurring counter-reaction to an official story of goodness that fails to reflect the reality of the audiences [*sic*] experiences. (Snowden 2004: 203)

Listening to one another's stories can be a healing experience – provided the listening is genuine. Gargiulo argues that stories in themselves promote healing:

> Like muscles that rip under the duress of heavy exercise, relationships are torn by the natural rhythms of people coexisting with one another. Without proper healing these tears cause long lasting damage that can be difficult and even impossible to heal. Stories open channels of communication and allow people to

meaningfully converse about the experiences and perceptions that can get in the way of trust and positive energy. (Gargiulo 2006)

That is, of course, one of the purposes of the 'water cooler' or smokers' meetings.

Conflict Resolution

One of the main tasks of managers is to resolve conflicts which arise between people within the organisation. This can be a particularly difficult task where the employees are professionals, since they will often have loyalties both to the organisation itself and to their own professional standards and ethos. One approach might seek simply to identify the immediate cause of the conflict and to propose a solution which is to be accepted by both parties, ignoring the question of why conflict arose and the underlying values which the two or more parties brought to the situation. A more sophisticated approach recognises that each professional is drawing on a personal and professional narrative which provides a sense of priorities and of what is important as well as differing understandings of and reactions to power structures (as explored in depth by Foucault (1980)) – this last being particularly pronounced where professionals are managed by non-professionals, as in hospitals or local government.

One way to approach such situations is to draw out the stories of the different players and to place these within the broader organisational narrative. Skjørshammer suggests this approach with an illustration, which he calls 'Story A', of a conflict between a nurse and hospital management. He writes:

> A conflict story is characterized foremost by differences in the version of the plot and not in the plot line with its beginning and end. In Story A, both the nurse and her leaders refer to the same eliciting events, even though they have different versions of the precursors and antecedent conditions. The most salient difference between the two stories is in the emplotment. Each party builds a moral order in the plot in which the other's behavior is a violation of an important value, principle, or rule and, accordingly, is labeled right or wrong, professionally or ethically. For the nurse, it is built around caring values related to herself and the foundation of the hospital; for her leaders, the values at stake are related to organisational rationality and their responsibility for securing sufficient administrative capacity in the hospital and avoiding creating precedents that could erode the management structure. (Skjørshammer 2002: 923)

What is vital in such situations, of course, is that both narratives are heard and that neither is dismissed. It is often valuable to have a third party involved, since it is well nigh impossible to stand aside from one's own story and dispassionately identify the points of difference. This is a particularly difficult task because the nature of the narratives spoken in these situations tend to be confrontational. Each party attempts, perhaps subconsciously, to put the other in the wrong – so the manager is portrayed as heartless, while the nurse is depicted as profligate with resources. They each see themselves as the victim of the other, or of 'the system' (which, of course, is the manager's fault). Each suggests, perhaps subtly, that the things which the other sees as wrong are in some sense their own fault. Exaggeration and hyperbole are used to paint a picture in absolutes – so accusations like 'you *always* let us down' fly around. To identify, and then gain agreement on, what are the real differences and why there are dissimilar views on them is a major challenge. Narrative, by encouraging the telling of the whole, complex story, provides a way in.

In this respect, managers can learn from the experience of mediation in personal conflict resolution, which uses narrative to allow the varying perspectives to be uncovered without allowing any one to dominate:

> There is no one 'truth' to discover, merely individual interpretations of what has transpired, is transpiring, or will transpire. One viewpoint should, therefore, not be privileged as being considered more 'true' than another. (Hansen 2003).

And, as Price (2007) argues, 'the centrality of story-telling ... involves the mediator in a process of assisting people to uncover their numerous understandings of the conflict.'

Price was commenting on the use of narrative in attempts to bring about reconciliation in post-apartheid South Africa. She remarks:

> The centrality of story-telling within narrative mediation resonates with wider conflict resolution and transformation initiatives in South Africa. There is abundant evidence of the powerful ways in which story-telling has effectively shifted individuals and communities. Story-telling offers a means to process painful memories and to help people to find the personal strength to confront their experiences, as well as the courage to confront each other's pain and discomfort. (Ibid.)

Performance Measurement

There is now much greater appreciation than in the recent past for the evidence that the performance of an organisation, or any other entity, cannot be measured only in quantitative terms. As the importance of the organisation's environment and its impact on the communities where it is based and whom it serves has grown, so too has the recognition of the role of narrative to portray the complexity and interrelatedness of its activities and their impact. Even in industries which traditionally have been very quantitative/results oriented, these broader perspectives have taken on renewed importance. Take this comment from Hodge, noting that measures of the economic contribution of mining need to be broadened if a full appreciation is to be gathered:

By embracing the concept of story there is much to be gained. Many aspects of contribution that the mining industry makes are simply beyond the realm of measured indicators. In many communities, the livelihood brought by mining is important not only because of jobs, wages, and cash contribution to the local charity but also, more importantly, because of the stability, respect, and confidence it brings to families and community during the life of the mine. There are many examples of where this sense of community leads to lasting relationships that far outweighs the significance of what can be short term mining income. This side of mining's contribution defies capture by measured indicators. (Hodge 2004: 9)

Salter, a mental health expert, commenting on a report recommending yet more reforms to Britain's National Health Service (NHS) with even more emphasis on quantitative performance measures, wrote that the author of the report

... is a surgeon, so he's accustomed to working with a branch of the medical profession where you can put your finger on outcomes: you can say this one survived or this one didn't. The two branches (of medicine) where it isn't that simple are general practice and psychiatry. At least 60% of patients who see a GP are there because of a psychological or social problem, and GPs look after 95% of psychiatry in the NHS. We go to them because we're feeling tired all the time, we feel sad, or we're having funny turns ... For psychiatrists, how on earth do you go about quantifying successful outcomes for people who by virtue of their illness are incapable of seeing themselves as ill? ... What we actually have to do is get away from measurements and statistics and calculations . and get back to what we know intuitively is the correct way to help people. That means doctors saying trust us, we're going to try to get you better using clinical skills, understanding and outcomes that simply can't be measured on paper. (Salter 2008: 6–7)

McLoughlin and Jordan argue for the use of logic models to structure the telling of performance stories. Such models bring together accounts, which will include some quantitative information, about the activities undertaken, resources used, customers reached, short, medium and long-term outcomes and external factors which are not under the control of those delivering the service or product. All of these aspects are then drawn together into a coherent story. They suggest that

Telling the story involves answering the questions: 'What are you trying to achieve and why is it important?' 'How will you measure effectiveness?' and 'How are you actually doing?' ... Because the story and the measurement plan have been developed with the program stakeholders, the story should be a shared vision with clear and shared expectation of success. (McLoughlin and Jordan 1999: 71)

Narrative is particularly suited to the assessment of longer-term outcomes, especially in public services where the client does not pay directly for the service and it is difficult to identify alternative measures. When the UK government funded the introduction of PCs and Internet connections in all the public libraries in England, one of the questions was whether this investment had made a difference to the lives of the people encouraged to use them, who very often came from disadvantaged groups. It was easy to come up with statistics about the numbers of PCs, the numbers of hours the libraries were open and the numbers of 'sessions' that users booked, but these did not answer the question. Instead, the experiences of users, narrated in their own words, told the story:

> Margaret, aged 70+, started with the Introductory Computer session because she wanted to find out what she was missing. She also wanted to be able to keep in touch with her granddaughter who was travelling. She took internet and email sessions and now uses the centre every week to check and send emails … Margaret wrote in one of her emails to a friend: 'This will come as a great surprise to you to get an email from me. I have started a course at the local library. The course is funded by the government and is free. What a great opportunity for people of all ages to get to grips with modern technology. I can now send and receive my own emails which is great fun.' (Brophy 2004: 8)

Appraisal of Individual Performance

There is considerable interest in the potential of narrative to unlock issues which may be hidden in the traditional employee performance appraisal interview. Rather than ask employees to analyse their successes and failures, the challenges they have faced and the achievements they wish to point to, it can be more productive to encourage them to place their year's activity in the form of a story. The natural temporal structure of a story fits well with the aim of reflecting on what is in effect a history of what has been experienced in a work situation. There will be a clear starting point, episodes which can be described by reference to the individual's perceptions of cause and effect, dramatic moments – which may be high or low points – and a conclusion focusing on what has changed as a result of individual, group and other decisions and actions. Exploring what has been emphasised in the narrative and why such points seem important to the appraisee provides ample opportunity for an appraiser, who will come to an interview with their own version of the corporate story, to gain real understanding of the situation as perceived by the appraisee.

Narrative is particularly important in performance appraisal because it allows the appraisee to express emotion in as non-threatening a manner as possible. This may be particularly important in professional roles, especially in the health and social services where everyday contact with people in need makes emotional responses critical to job satisfaction and feelings of either achievement or inadequacy. The spectrum of employees who feel emotional reactions to work incidents is, of course, much wider than this – call-centre staff must cope with rude, unpleasant, bullying and irritating callers as well as those who are pleasant or complimentary. However, there is significant evidence that it is emotional aspects of relationships with colleagues in the workplace which cause the most tension; Waldron claimed that 'the dynamics of organisational relationships are among the most frequently cited sources of intense emotion' (2000: 66), although this can also be a source of strength. Ray quoted a care worker who said:

> When I try to tell my husband or friends what it's like at work, to deal with 15 screaming, fighting attention-demanding kids for 8 hours straight, they don't really understand. The only people who really feel like I do are the people I work with. (Ray 1987: 174)

Miller and colleagues explored in depth the stories that employees tell, contrasting how negative and positive emotional experiences influence how they felt about their jobs. Take these two contrasting examples:

> It's just good people here. It's just like a big family. One gets sick, we all see to 'em. One's in trouble, we're all there.

> That's why I'm so tired while these young girls are going dancin' all night. They don't really put pride in their work. (Miller et al. 2007: 250)

These are not easy issues to deal with within a normal appraisal setting but encouragement to relate them as narratives provides much more scope to address the underlying concerns.

It is interesting to note that nearly fifty years ago Richards was also reporting that the storytelling approach proved valuable when he wanted to explore the attitudes of supervisors to performance appraisal:

> We have used two different methods to measure the attitudes of supervisors toward performance appraisal. One of these is the PEP Survey – a traditional type questionnaire which requires agree-disagree responses to thirty-seven specific items about the Personnel Evaluation Program. It was developed to measure the conscious attitudes toward personnel evaluation. The other, a projective device called the PEP Situation Survey, consists of four pictures related to personnel evaluation, with the respondent required to write a short story about each picture … The PEP Situation Survey pictures were designed to tap some of the attitudes and feelings at a deeper, unconscious level. The analysis of the stories brings out attitudes and feelings which differ considerably from those revealed by the traditional approach! (Richards 1959: 235)

The Creation of Narrative in Organisations

The above instances of the use of narrative in organisations have largely concentrated on the ways in which listening to stories is helpful in delivering services and products. However, organisations can also take the initiative in deliberately creating stories as a means of communicating both internally and externally. The following sections highlight some of the main ways in which this can be done.

Defining the Culture

Organisations are like any other social or economic grouping in developing and holding myths about themselves (see Chapter 3). The word 'myth' here has no connotation of truth or untruth, but is what is sometimes called a 'deep metaphor', which carries within it significant meaning. While it is sometimes argued that there is no place for myth in a postmodern world, many commentators have noted that what has happened is the replacement of religious and quasi-religious myth, for part of the world's population and most notably in the developed world, by alternatives. Organisational myth can play this role. Bowles writes that

> ... the work organisation, for many, has come to be seen as the creator of meaning
> in a confused world, where identification and commitment to the management
> and organisational ethos, can provide opportunities and rewards. (Bowles 1989:
> 411)

Kunde goes as far as to use the expression 'corporate religion', referring to 'the set of values that unites the organisation around a mission and vision' (2000, 111).

An important aspect of organisational myth lies in its relationship to power structures. By and large, organisations ascribe 'heroic' status to individuals who embody the deeply held values of the firm – sometimes through explicit reward structures, sometimes through simple recognition as a key character in the unfolding drama. At one level, this is what the gold stars awarded to model employees by MacDonald's exemplify – such people have absorbed the myth and now become actors within it. At the other end of the scale, multimillion-pound bonuses paid in the financial sector mark out what is seen in the corporate world as success – again they are recognised within the rather different myth. The flip side of these symbols of heroism is exclusion – those who do not conform to the myth are excluded from the stage.

Collins and Porras draw attention to the ways in which these organisational myths take on a life of their own and can go unquestioned by the organisation's insiders. They refer to 'the organisation's essential and enduring tenets – a small set of timeless guiding principles that require no external justification; they have intrinsic value and importance to those inside the organisation' (1998: 222). In fact, of course, organisational culture tends to be too fragmented (Knights and

McCabe 2000) to allow for this kind of monolithic organisational self-belief (or self-delusion!) to continue unchallenged for long.

Capturing the Vision

A related issue for organisations is to find ways in which to capture the vision of the future they wish to create. This is important not just to ensure that everyone is working towards the same goals but can also contribute to the process of actually starting to make the vision happen by galvanising people into appropriate action by providing motivation and encouragement. Levin suggests that to be effective the vision must be more than an amalgamation of mission, purposes, goals and strategies and that it should be 'a highly lucid story of an organisation's preferred future in action. A future that describes what life will be like for employees, customers, and other key stakeholders' (2000: 93). He argues that the most effective way to achieve this is through the use of narrative to create the 'vision story' and offers the following example of how a healthcare organisation could tell its vision story:

> The member, having just enrolled in the health plan completes a detailed personal health history questionnaire at a computer terminal in their home, office, or at one of the many kiosks located around our facilities. This highly interactive, point and click process is as easy for the new member to use as changing channels on their television set. The new health history is automatically entered into the system database. The new member is interviewed by a clinical team member to whom she tells of her and her husband's desire to become parents. The clinical team member brings up the 'physician database' on her computer terminal and reviews the biographies and experience of several family practitioners and obstetricians with the patient for her selection. After one is chosen, the clinical team member electronically contacts the physician's office and arranges an initial appointment for the new member. When the new member arrives for her initial appointment, the appointment clerk greets her warmly as if she were a family member. Her entire health history is brought up online at a small terminal in the examining room for the physician to review. Following her checkup, the nurse electronically schedules her with the health education center where she and her husband are enrolled in the 'Parents To Be' class. At the same time the nurse also schedules the patient's husband for a routine physical exam to coincide with the wife's next scheduled physician visit. During the prenatal period, if the patient fails to appear for a prenatal care appointment, the system computer automatically identifies this and electronically prompts the obstetrician's staff to determine if a follow-up phone call or notice is needed. (ibid.: 96)

While this may not be to everyone's taste, it does illustrate the value to both employees and customers of setting out what the future is expected to hold. The vision becomes accessible because it depicts the progressive client journey and even (though this is somewhat forced) includes emotional and affective aspects: the 'clerk greets her warmly'.

Exercising Leadership

It is very noticeable that business leaders often revel in the use of the quest style of narrative. Shamir and Eilam reported on an interview with a manager with an army background about his leadership style which evoked this story:

> We entered an ambush and were wiped out ... This is the kind of story that has to influence a person, to mould him ... I learned some of my behaviors from this story, my aggressiveness, my not giving in ... I am not yielding. I am seen as someone who is too stubborn. One who checks everything before he is ready to step aside ... And that is what I try to explain in this story, why I am so obstinate sometimes, why I am not ready to give up checking and re-checking everything ... If I believe I am right – no compromise! And that is how I educate everybody here. This is how I worked, how I work. I teach my son: check everything thoroughly. Even an order. Check every order, don't do anything blindly. (Shamir and Eilam 2005: 405)

Bennis and Thomas commented on a series of interviews they conducted:

> Whatever his or her generation, each of our leaders was the author, and critic, of his or her own life. In the course of our interviews, it became clear that each person has crafted a resonant story out of the important events and relationships in his or her life ... Their stories explained, amused, engaged, and often enrolled others in the narrator's vision. (Bennis and Thomas 2002: 160–61)

In taking this approach, leaders are following in what is now a long-established tradition, promulgated by Peters and Waterman (1982) among others, of using story to popularise the heroic decision making and sense of purpose of leaders. However, the reality of leadership is very different, frequently challenging and includes failures as well as successes. Leaders need to communicate clearly, even in adverse circumstances, as well as helping everyone in the organisation react to, learn from and overcome setbacks and obstacles. Stephen Denning, one of the foremost advocates for the use of storytelling in organisations, argues that the focus on 'heroic' leaders is damaging and unhelpful:

> ... change and leadership do not require exceptional people at all. Leadership and change are driven by ordinary people who act and speak in a different way. Once people grasp what is involved in acting and speaking in that way and take the trouble to master it, then they find that *anyone* can drive change, if they want to. (Denning 2007: 49, original emphasis)

He argues that the key to communication for leaders lies in the following sequence: 'first they get attention. Then they stimulate desire, and only then do they reinforce with reasons' (ibid.: 27). All of this, Denning argues, can best be achieved through narrative.

Formulating and Delivering Strategy

Strategy involves a focus on the long-term future of the organisation and is one of the key issues for organisational leadership. Traditionally, the process involves analysis of the current situation facing the organisation both internally and externally, which may include a SWOT (strengths, weaknesses, opportunities, threats) or similar analysis, focusing on a small subset of critical issues and formulating a set of possible paths to follow into the future. These will then be accompanied by implications for changes to the organisation's mission, goals, objectives and organisation. After due consideration, one particular strategy is chosen and this is then promulgated throughout the organisation and acted upon in a concerted manner, often with explicit performance measures built in to check on whether the goals are being achieved.

Scenario planning is often used in developing strategy, especially where the external environment is subject to changes which are essentially unpredictable. Used properly, scenarios can challenge conventional wisdom and encourage unconventional thinking, revealing new opportunities and possibilities. The term 'scenario', applied to management, derives from the American movie industry, where it is used to describe a detailed outline for a proposed new film – in effect, it is the 'story line'. Herman Kahn is credited with the broader use of the term, initially in planning for what might happen in the event of nuclear war. Subsequent use of the technique became widespread, although the distinction between scenario planning and forecasting, which relies on quantitative techniques, is not always made clearly. Wack wrote:

> Scenarios deal with two worlds: the world of facts and the world of perceptions. They explore the facts but they aim at perceptions inside the heads of decision makers. Their purpose is to gather and transform information of strategic significance into fresh perceptions. This transformation process is not trivial – more often than not it does not happen. When it works, it is a creative experience that generates a heartfelt 'Aha!' from you [decision makers] and leads to strategic insights beyond the mind's previous reach. (Wack 1985: 140)

Narrative has a number of other roles to play in strategy formulation, not least because it is important that strategy is memorable – it needs to be part of the underlying way of life of members of the organisation – and of course the compelling story of the future is an excellent way to achieve this.

Barry and Elmes argued that the use of narrative as a starting point for strategy development takes a fundamentally different approach from the standard methods of analysis and identification of options. They wrote:

> Traditional conceptualizations of strategy have tended toward notions of fit ('How might we fit into this or that environment?'), prediction ('What is ahead? Where will we be then?') and competition ('How might we "rule the roost," survive within the "pecking order," or gracefully "chicken out"?'). In contrast, a narrative view of strategy stresses how language is used to construct meaning; consequently, it explores ways in which organisational stakeholders create a discourse of direction (whether about becoming, being, or having been) to understand and influence one another's actions. Whereas authors of traditional strategy frameworks virtually ignore the role of language in strategic decision making, writers using a narrative approach assume that tellings of strategy fundamentally influence strategic choice and action, often in unconscious ways. (Barry and Elmes 1997: 432)

As they point out, no matter which approach is taken to strategy formulation, it can be regarded as a special form of fiction – it is not a report on something which has happened, but a projection, an imagining, of what might be. It is not surprising, therefore, to find that techniques honed in the development of writing fiction – such as plot and characterisation – have application in this sphere.

Sharing Knowledge and Communicating Complexity

The ability to share knowledge is critical to organisations and there is a wealth of evidence of the benefits of using narrative to achieve this, especially where the situation is complex and involves human behaviour. Annette Simons gives the example of how the dilemma of whether to launch a novel product into the marketplace ahead of any competitors, or whether to wait and see what problems could be identified by a market launch, can be captured. She illustrates the heart of the dilemma with a very short story: 'the early bird gets the worm, but something that is just as true – and people don't talk about as much – is that the second mouse gets the cheese!' (2006: 74) Promulgating this around the organisation gets people talking about which strategy is best and can help explain why in some circumstances it's better not to rush a product out ahead of the competition.

This perspective is confirmed by Denning who argues that successful stories tend to be those which enable an individual to describe a predicament with which others in the organisation can identify:

> The predicament of the explicit story was familiar to the particular audience, and indeed, it was the very predicament that the change proposal was meant to solve. The story had a degree of strangeness or incongruity for the listeners, so that it captured their attention and stimulated their imaginations. At the same time the

story was plausible, even eerily familiar, almost like a premonition of what the future was going to be like. (Denning 2001: xix)

Some approaches to knowledge management, as described in Chapter 5, explicitly set out to capture, analyse, store and share stories. In some organisations and professions, and especially where the importance of tacit knowledge is acknowledged, these have met with considerable success.

Product Design

The formal use of narrative in product design is well-established. In particular, *storyboarding* which breaks design, whether of processes or products, into an illustrative sequence has been adapted from its origins in the film industry into a sophisticated technique for analysing and sharing information in all kinds of organisations but especially in product design. In recent years, it has become a very common way to design interfaces for software; it sets out the basic design and shows how screens change as the user works through a task, illustrating images and text that might be used. It is an expression of the intended temporal experience of the user, from the initial engagement – say with a log-in screen – through to task completion. Storyboards are useful for discussing design with clients as well as for giving an overall 'feel' for what the end-product will look like. Software to support interactive storyboarding is now available and can be useful for engaging different individuals and groups in the process of design, providing a product or service 'walkthrough'.

John Seely Brown describes an activity based on storyboarding and comments that

> … we found this process based on narrative generated many valuable new ideas … the process becomes very powerful because it leads to the joint construction of the story endings, and it facilitates dialogue between people in distributed groups that are geographically dispersed. (Brown et al. 2005: 85–7)

Brand Identity

Organisations are very concerned to portray a clear identity for their brands, not only to customers but also to ensure that there is internal clarity about the market being addressed and the features and images that are deemed appropriate. This can sometimes form part of the organisational myth, and even becomes part of the 'corporate religion' in observations like that made by Randazzo: 'the brand's soul is its spiritual center, the core value(s) that defines the brand and permeates all other aspects of the brand' (1993: 17).

Within the process of design, there seems to be considerable evidence that the sharing of experiences and imaginative ideas in the form of stories can be extremely creative. Baek describes how sharing stories helped Mothercare to develop its brand:

> At one particular meeting, several designers were struggling to agree on a proposal for Mothercare's brand position; they spent a lot of time trying to find the right words to explain or to sum up what the brand was all about. One of them used the story of Mary Poppins – P.L. Travers's famous nanny, who uses magic, as well as dry humor, to get things done – as a metaphor to explain the concept. Other members agreed with the idea and added their own interpretations. This stirred up a group discussion and was eventually used as a basis for a preliminary design concept.
>
> At another early meeting, a male designer told stories about how completely different his post-baby life was. There was always something to be done, some disaster to avoid, or some breakthrough to enjoy. Nothing was what it had been, and you could never switch it off. All the other parents agreed, saying that life involved more work now – you didn't get enough sleep, you had to be more responsive. There wasn't much leisure, and your partner always seemed to think you weren't doing enough to help. One designer mentioned an acquaintance he had always considered shallow and brusque. Now that this acquaintance was a father, he seemed wiser, more generous, more sympathetic.
>
> This conversation created the inspiration for the work that came next. It was all about the reality of raising children, the ups and downs of parenting. After more long exchanges of parenting stories, the team came up with Mothercare's brand proposition and the radio advertisements that won accolades and a coveted prize. (Baek 2006: 37)

The development of brand identity is, however, a particular area where the professional needs to safeguard the truthfulness of what is being portrayed. Fineman and Gabriel have commented:

> Brochures and advertisements are designed by skilled public relations professionals to present a polished and selective image of the organisation, one that will attract the reader's attention. 'Truth' is adjusted to a particular purpose or goal – to get a recruit, to win a customer. Some people argue that this is unwarranted deception; others point out that few areas of life are free from selective distortions – but we must avoid downright lies. (Fineman and Gabriel 1996: 51)

More will be said about truth and professional responsibility in the next chapter. Here, we can simply note another instance of the power of storytelling.

Coordination

Because organisations are complex, involving many different people with different skills and different remits, achieving effective coordination of effort is a critical issue. It has become even more difficult, and more pressing, with the development of networked and highly dispersed organisations where people may not come into contact with each other regularly, if at all. The classic work in this field was carried out by Mintzberg (1979) who was concerned with organisational design. Prior to the publication of his work, the emphasis had been on the division of labour, splitting tasks down into their elements; Mintzberg countered by arguing that the really critical issue was coordination, putting things together rather than pulling them apart. He identified five key mechanisms used to achieve coordination: direct supervision, standardisation of work, standardisation of skills, standardisation of outputs and mutual adjustment. In the intervening years it has been recognised, however, that the modern organisation cannot succeed simply by standardising but needs to couple coordination with flexibility. As a result, the necessity is for shared understanding, which itself is dependent on shared meanings – which brings us back again to the issues discussed in Chapter 2 concerning language games, linguistic codes, and so on.

Brown argues that

> … coordination can be achieved, not through procedures, but rather through a deeper understanding of the goals. And you get a deeper understanding of the goals, not by creating mission statements, but creating stories. (Brown et al. 2005: 91)

Of course, common understanding of goals is not in itself enough. Jaatinen and Lavikka argue that there is a need to develop

- shared ways of thinking,
- shared ways of operating,
- shared knowledge,
- shared goals, and
- trust. (2008: 149)

This analysis, although not presented in the context of using stories, reflects many of the properties of knowledge and of narratives which have been discussed in earlier chapters.

Developing Meaningful Relationships

A final use of narrative in organisations is, quite simply, for creating positive relationships between team members, as well as encouraging the development of employees as people within a pleasant and effective working environment. In this sense, storytelling is both oil and glue, keeping the cogs of the organisation turning while helping to create a sense of belonging. Stories don't have to be deeply meaningful and may be little more than light-hearted anecdotes, though they will undoubtedly reflect aspects of the prevailing culture, not least because narratives are nearly always multidimensional. They may also go further than that. Ashmos and Duchon argue for a 'recognition that employees have an inner life which nourishes and is nourished by meaningful work taking place in the context of a community' (2000: 137), while Rego and Cunha suggest that there is a need for explicit recognition of a spirituality of the workplace:

> ... it does not necessarily involve a connection to any specific religious tradition, but rather can be based on personal values and philosophy. It is about employees who view themselves as spiritual beings whose souls need nourishment at work, who experience a sense of purpose and meaning in their work, and a sense of connectedness to one another and to their workplace community. (Rego and Cunha 2008: 55)

Spirituality is a very personal issue but one which requires a social setting in which experiences can be shared. If the work environment denies this aspect of individuals' sense of self and personal value, then it will discourage full engagement.

Since spirituality and religion have always relied heavily on narrative, it is not surprising to see a emphasis on this approach among writers who address this topic. Part of the reason for this is also that discussion of spirituality has been largely hidden, with many people expressing reservations about the appropriateness of the topic for discussion. Lewis and Geroy commented that 'many workers desire opportunities for spiritual expression in the workplace but are hesitant because of fears of offending peers and management' (2000: 683).

The following personal narrative, taken from an interview carried out in New Zealand by Lips-Wiersma, is illustrative of the issue for many people:

> I was taught by the old people. I know who I am, where I come from and what I believe in. So in taking this job I knew what I wanted to achieve, I knew my duty was to marry our old Maori ways and European ways of doing and being for the benefit of both people. I earn less here than I did in my previous job as supervisor in a commercial organisation, but I want to be here as it gives me a place to stand. (Lips-Wiersma 2002: 390)

Conclusion

Organisational use of narrative is multifaceted and complex. It reflects the culture, customs, conventions, beliefs, interests, concerns, politics and ethics of its leaders and its workers. The stories that they tell reveal nuances which are hidden from view when all that is available is formal reports and quantitative analyses. On many occasions, stories offer insights into an holistic view of the organisation, its people and its environment, demonstrating novel outlooks and revealing new perspectives, perhaps empowering those who do not have a voice.

However, corporate and professional storytelling is also dangerous, because it is very easy to misuse the power of narrative to convey falsehoods, to promote products and service with messages which exaggerate and embellish the real properties of what is on offer. For that reason if no other, we need a professional approach to narrative which takes its responsibilities seriously and which is as condemnatory of misleading stories as it would be of the organisation or individual who concocted spurious statistical data to support their cause. That is why we turn in the final chapter to consider what a narrative-based practice must embrace.

Chapter 8
Narrative-based Practice

Leadership is about change, about taking an organization or a group of people from where they are now to where they need to be. The best way to get humans to venture into unknown terrain is to make that terrain familiar and desirable by taking them there first in their imaginations. (Tichy and Cohen 1997: 174).

A man who has no story is a man with no truth to offer. (Keillor 1989: xviii)

Introduction

Chapter 1 began with an overview of evidence-based practice (EBP) and the possible reasons for its remarkable rise in popularity and endorsement, especially in the health services. Within this discussion, some questions were raised about the appropriateness of the paradigm both in that sector and in the disciplines to which it has more recently been applied. A number of philosophical and methodological positions were then examined to begin to throw light on these issues and, in the following chapter, the nature of narrative and storytelling was discussed. There followed an analysis of pedagogical theories and insights and then an analysis of the nature of knowledge in the context of theories of knowledge management. It was perhaps something of a diversion to examine how narrative is being used in virtual environments, but this revealed some of the most widespread and accessible types of storytelling in modern times. Narrative in organisational contexts was examined in the last chapter. Following on from all of the earlier discussions, the purpose of this chapter is to try to draw these different influences together in order to delineate a narrative-based practice (NBP).

The concern is with NBP as a way of working within organisations as well as an approach to professional and indeed personal endeavour. NBP values narrative, in its many forms, as one of the richest means of developing understanding, of informing decision making, of creating and sharing knowledge and of acting wisely. It is suggested that NBP can be distinguished by:

- a post-positivist approach which requires the use of a *broad evidence base*, acknowledging the importance of both quantitative and qualitative data but rejecting the notion of a 'gold standard' of quantitative methods;
- acknowledgement of *the complexity of decision making* in the real world, with the implication that holistic approaches are essential;
- recognition that all actions are *socially situated* and that civilised societies

can only function when there is due understanding and recognition of different points of view;

- awareness of the need to *learn continuously, actively and reflectively* including competence in storytelling as a key professional skill, and
- a commitment to *ethical conduct*, including dedication to truthfulness in the use of narrative.

These characteristics are considered in more detail in this chapter. In setting out the scope of NBP, it is claimed that narrative provides the appropriate means both to achieve understanding and to pursue purposive action. By centring narrative within professional and organisational practice, it is possible to overcome the limitations of evidence-based practice, as that approach is generally understood and applied, and achieve a more holistic and ultimately a more satisfactory and more satisfying way of working and living.

A Broad Evidence Base

We saw in Chapters 1 and 2 that the positivist approach, with its emphasis on quantitative evidence and the so-called gold standard of the Randomised Controlled Trial (RCT), has severe limitations. It is not that this kind of evidence is not valuable, but when it comes to be applied to real-life situations, it is so often found that the whole situation has not been reflected in the 'scientific' evidence. It is one thing to demonstrate that a particular treatment has no known scientific basis and can be replicated using placebos, but if patients report beneficial effects it is quite another to conclude that the treatment should never be offered. The narrow focus of scientific, experimental trials cannot replicate the feelings, emotions, understanding and beliefs of the patient who is suffering. As Watson put it, 'evidence-based medicine helps us understand populations, while narrative helps us understand individuals' (2007: 1285). Only a much more holistic approach can hope to address the complexity of the problem and offer truly appropriate solutions.

The value of qualitative evidence lies in its ability to reflect the huge range of issues which need to be brought to bear on any real-life decision. Of course it is not a panacea. Of course it is difficult to generalise from specific cases. Of course the quantitative evidence must be considered and given due weight. But we need a balance which truly values the whole range of information and knowledge which is available and which is fully relevant to the individual case. One of the leading proponents of narrative-based medicine, Trisha Greenhalgh, has written:

> How, then, can we square the circle of upholding individual narrative in a world where valid and generalisable truths come from population derived evidence? My own view is that there is no paradox. In particle physics the scientific truths (laws) derived from empirical observation about the behaviour of gases fail to hold when applied to single molecules. Similarly (but for different reasons), the

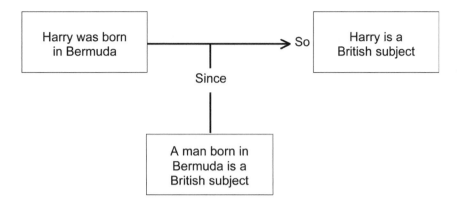

Figure 8.1   The concept of a 'warrant' for a claim to knowledge: example

'truths' established by the empirical observation of populations in randomised trials and cohort studies cannot be mechanistically applied to individual patients (whose behaviour is irremediably contextual and idiosyncratic) or episodes of illness. (Greenhalgh 1999: 323)

The question therefore arises as to the weight that should be given to all the various evidence available which bears on any particular problem. When knowledge is claimed in any organisational or professional setting, how do we assess its truth for that situation? Toulmin (1958) introduced the concept of a 'warrant' as the grounds for believing that data being adduced supported a particular claim. His example, now out of date though still instructive, is shown in Figure 8.1 above.

Incidentally, this example usefully emphasises that the warrant for any claim is often a social and cultural construct subject to change. Toulmin writes:

… the warrant is, in a sense, incidental and explanatory; its task being simply to register explicitly the legitimacy of the step involved … Unless, in any particular field of argument, we are prepared to work with warrants of *some* kind it will become impossible in that field to subject arguments to rational assessment. (Toulmin 1958: 92–3)

He also went on to argue that when appealing to a warrant, we need to discuss the extent to which it applies in a particular case, a statement which he termed the 'qualifier'. He further suggested that an argument may contain 'backing', additional information which supports the claim, and a 'rebuttal', which sets out the counter-argument. These six elements – claim, data, warrant, qualifier, backing and rebuttal – form the constituent parts of a persuasive argument.

The concept of 'warrant' has been taken up in many fields, not least in the health-related professions. Forbes and colleagues suggest that if we are to take post-positivist and critical theory perspectives seriously in weighing the evidence we use, then we need to acknowledge at least three types of warrant (see also the discussion on validity in Chapter 2):

- *Expert judgement*: 'careful scrutiny of findings and of methodological strategies is common practice in scientific communities. Those expert in the substantive area and in the particular methodology should judge the evidence' (Forbes et al. 1999: 376). They quote Schultz and Meleis to the effect that scientific knowledge is warranted dependent on 'the degree to which the researcher has followed procedures accepted by the community of researchers and on the logical derivation of conclusions from the evidence' (1988: 220). Note that the term 'scientific' in this context needs to be interpreted as encompassing any widely recognised research paradigm.
- *Corroboration*: evidence can be corroborated from other sources. It is important that such corroboration should include public scrutiny as well as triangulation of research findings. From a relativist perspective, it should also include 'intersubjective' warrant, that is, it should be 'recognized by others that the descriptions of the experienced phenomenon by the scientist captures their own experience' (Gortner and Schultz 1988: 23). Cronbach wrote that 'acceptance or rejection of a practice or theory comes about because a community is persuaded. Even research specialists do not judge a conclusion as it stands alone; they judge its compatibility with a network of prevailing beliefs' (1988: 6).
- *Scope*: the scope of the evidence is critical to ensure that the issue is being addressed in a holistic manner which enables the generation and challenge of different viewpoints. Critical theory would demand 'emancipatory understanding and contextual explanation' (Forbes et al. 1999: 376).

It is important to remember that our main concern when using narrative is to reach understanding of how individuals and social groups interpret experiences and events. We may also wish to compare their assessments with our own interpretive reality, but we do so in the knowledge that the customer, client, or colleague's standpoint is equally valid. Thus the information we select, and the warrants we call upon, will reflect a broad approach which refuses to privilege any one kind of data.

This leads to the question of *how* to include narrative in the evidence base; how to gather together the stories needed to provide the full picture. In part, of course, this means listening out for stories, especially those told by clients, and being willing to reuse them when appropriate. In part, it means creating a culture in which telling and listening to stories is acceptable and encouraged. It also means taking deliberate steps to collect narratives which can be used in decision making and in other professional situations. Figure 8.2 illustrates one way that the use of narrative has been encouraged within a particular profession – a vignette which used to be acted out by those training as librarians.

CAN I HELP YOU?

(The user looks at the librarian with a worried frown on his face) *Have you any books on houses?*

I THINK SO, WHAT SORT OF HOUSES ARE YOU INTERESTED IN?

Semi-detached.

(Short pause while the librarian digests this) AH, BOOKS ON ARCHITECTURE PERHAPS?

No, not really, it's just semi-detached

OH, IS IT A PARTICULAR HOUSE YOU WANT A BOOK ON? WHEREABOUTS IS IT?

I live in it

SO IT'S A BOOK ON LOCAL HOUSES?

Not especially

(another long pause. Tries a long shot) DO YOU THINK PERHAPS SOMEONE FAMOUS LIVED IN YOUR HOUSE?

(User looks startled at this) *I don't think so. No, is there anyone famous from round here?*

(Librarian swallows hard) NOT SO FAR AS I KNOW. WHAT IS IT ABOUT YOUR HOUSE?

It was last week

(an even more determined swallow) TELL ME WHAT HAPPENED

We had just gone to bed and my wife turned to me and said, 'Can you hear that?' and I said 'What?' and she said 'That. There, you must have heard it' and I said 'It's someone outside in the road' and she said 'No it isn't, it's closer than that. It's in the roof' and I said 'What's in the roof' and she said 'It's either bats or rats. You go and have a look' So I got out of bed and got a torch and pulled down the loft ladder and had a look and I think it's bats because I could see one of them hanging from the rafter at the far end and I don't know what you're supposed to do about them so have you got a book?'

YES, OF COURSE. I'LL SHOW YOU. YOU HAVE TO BE CAREFUL BECAUSE SOME OF THEM ARE PROTECTED SPECIES BUT IT TELLS YOU ALL ABOUT IT HERE.

Figure 8.2   A training exercise in encouraging customers to tell their stories

Some of the more formal methods include:

- *narrative interviews*, which aim to allow respondents to tell their own stories. The interview technique involves little questioning or even conversation, consisting largely of short prompts which encourage self-expression. Spontaneity is valuable in such situations as the interviewees relate personal experiences and perceptions in their own language and terminology, finding their own meaning in recounting a chronology.

- *inter- and intra-organisational case studies*, which are frequently found as temporal accounts of a sequence of events with key characters' roles depicted and cause-and-effect relationships explicitly described. Often they are simply used to document what has happened, but it is possible to construct them as narratives so as to bring out particular meanings.
- *the development of 'learning histories'* (Kleiner and Roth 1997; Thier and Erlach 2005) which bring together the different perspectives and memories of people in an organisation about a particular event and create a shared narrative as a 'jointly told tale' (van Maanen 1988).
- *collective sense making*, a process whereby the members of an organisation share and draw on story fragments to create their sense of the organisation's purpose and character – see above and Chapter 3 *re* organisations' epic myths. It requires a sense of membership and ownership – else it becomes an external critique – and shared experiences.
- *naturalistic or informal story-gathering*, which draws heavily on ethnography and gathers together the fragments of conversation and other story elements which members of the organisation exchange in the course of the day. Customer-oriented organisations will also gather the stories of users as they interact with the service. Where the work is undertaken by members of the organisation, it is sometimes termed 'auto-ethnography'.

The question of how professionals can become skilled in creating their own narrative expressions is discussed later in this chapter, while practical suggestions will be found in the appendices.

The Complexity of Decision Making in the Real World

We all know that the world is complex, that there are a huge number of dependent and independent variables brought to bear on any real situation with which we are faced. Decision making can all too easily become an exercise in sub-optimisation, an oversimplification whose import only becomes apparent later, when unconsidered factors have come into play. Narrative, both as a source of information and as a means of conveying strategic and tactical direction, offers a way to address that complexity.

There is a large number of different approaches to professional decision making represented in the literature. One way to categorise them – after Charles et al. (1997), writing in the context of medical treatments – is to distinguish between the paternalistic, the informed, the professional-as-agent and the shared models. The first is essentially the imposition of the decision by an authority figure, with little discussion or consultation. 'Informed' decision making arises when the client is given information about the options and enabled to make a selection – this has become more prominent in the UK National Health Service with the introduction of 'patient choice', meaning that before going for treatment, the patient is able to select from a range of hospitals to attend. In theory, this decision is supported by publicly available evidence for such matters as recovery rates, yet the reality is that the interpretation of such information often requires more knowledge and perhaps skill than the average patient possesses. Although in theory, this approach consists of the professional transferring information to the client or patient, who is then equally well informed, the reality is that the further transformation of information into knowledge is, as we saw in Chapter 5, far from simple.

The idea of the professional-as-agent approaches the issue from the other side by seeking the clients' authority to act on their behalf. Again from a medical standpoint, Evans characterises this in the following way:

> ... the professional-as-agent assumes responsibility for directing the health care utilization of the patient ... as an agent trying to choose what the patient would have chosen, had she been as well-informed as the professional. (Evans 1984: 75, cited in Charles et al. 1997: 684)

There are many situations where this can be an appropriate model, especially where the client is unable, for whatever reason, to participate fully in decision making.

The final model is that of shared decision making. In these cases, both the professional and the client are actively involved in the process. What is critical is that both parties seek to come to a full understanding of the other and that both acknowledge that neither of them has complete information nor absolute wisdom. The professional does not try to behave like a god and the client does not undervalue the professional's experience and knowledge. In other words, the decision-making act is a true partnership.

It is fairly obvious that for this kind of partnership to work information must be shared at a deep level. The client – especially when a patient – needs to be able to express emotion, feelings, doubts and uncertainties. Professionals need to be able to acknowledge the limitations of their own knowledge and to be open to other perspectives, culminating in a process of entering the story of the clients, seeing things from their perspective.

Barry and Elmes remark that 'narrativity emphasizes the simultaneous presence of multiple, interlinked realities, and is thus well positioned for capturing the diversity and complexity present in strategic discourse' (1997: 430). They continue:

> From a practitioner's viewpoint, the narrativist stance can encourage people to explore strategic issues in more meaningful ways ... narrativity encompasses both the telling and the told; it can be applied both to strategizing and to strategies. Extant, formalized (and perhaps realized) strategies can be examined as artifacts: their rhetoric, tropes, metaphors, and sequencing can be identified, compared, and evaluated in various ways. Strategy can also be examined as a narrative process, one in which stories about directionality are variously appropriated, discounted, championed, and defended. This view asks, 'How do people make sense of and narrate their notions about directionality?' 'When does

a strategic story stay the same and when does it change?' 'How does it survive "register" changes alternating between the printed and the auditory, the formal and informal, or between intrafirm and industry levels?' (ibid.: 431–2)

This quotation brings to the fore the question of how people create narratives as explanations, whether these are autobiographical with the intention of explaining their own lives or derive from a second- or third-party perspective to elucidate events that are essentially external to the self. There are many contexts outside the professional, and certainly outside medicine, where the creation of narratives is a common means of sense making, preparatory to making decisions. Jurors, for example, were shown by Pennington and Hastie to use narrative methods to organise and make sense of the evidence presented to them in criminal trials (1986: 1988).

Clearly, there is no point in simply extending the use of narrative within organisational or professional contexts just for the sake of it. Rather, its use needs to be purposeful. To achieve this, it is helpful to bear in mind the basic characteristics of narrative outlined in Chapter 3, especially that it is used to describe perceptions of causality within a temporal framework. Thus, a primary use will be to provide a logical, though multifaceted, account of events which have happened, or courses of action which could be pursued, but one which takes into account the human elements of feelings and emotions both for explanation and to gain empathetic involvement. As Charon says in the context of medicine:

> Sick people need physicians who can understand their diseases, treat their medical problems, and accompany them through their illnesses. Despite medicine's recent dazzling technological progress in diagnosing and treating illnesses, physicians sometimes lack the capacities to recognize the plights of their patients, to extend empathy toward those who suffer, and to join honestly and courageously with patients in their illnesses ... A scientifically competent medicine alone cannot help a patient grapple with the loss of health or find meaning in suffering. Along with scientific ability, physicians need the ability to listen to the narratives of the patient, grasp and honor their meanings, and be moved to act on the patient's behalf. This is narrative competence, that is, the competence that human beings use to absorb, interpret, and respond to stories. (Charon 2001: 1897)

What is noticeable in this account is that the patient is to be treated as a person, not as a pathological instance – the narrative can become a 'projection of the professional imagination' (May and Fleming 1997: 1098).

Socially Situated Action

The recognition that all actions are socially situated is central to the adoption of a post-positivist perspective. In Chapter 4, we examined the concepts of social constructivism, situated learning and the link to communities of practice. These concepts are all important to a narrative-based practice. What was emphasised there, and can be emphasised again here, is that all of these concepts can only be realised when there is a commitment to listening as well as to telling. This applies as much to professional-customer relationships as it does to those between professionals.

An example of how the narrative approach can inform understanding of the organisation as a social setting is provided in a remarkably frank and revealing paper, published in 2005, documenting the restructuring process at Oxford University's Bodleian Library. The saga of change management in a venerable institution was told from the perspectives of key players, including that of the new director, Reginald Carr. Long overdue reorganisation of the Library met with considerable resistance, both within the library and from academic staff. The story became one of confrontation and considerable ill-will:

> One librarian from a Bodleian dependent commented, 'We do have tensions. There is a lot of "us" vs. "them". Departmental and faculty libraries have too much say, and low seniority outsiders have more say than high seniority insiders.' (Moran 2005: 278)

> Some complained that Carr was too much a businessman. He was accused of 'management speak.' He introduced a new vocabulary to the Bodleian. 'We used to have "readers," now we have "users",' I was told. 'We used to have "staff" now we have "human resources".' He was viewed as someone who was 'trying to fit into an institution that values its medieval traditions and who is trying to drag that institution faster than it wishes into the future.' (ibid.)

> As an experienced manager, Carr realized that he was not meeting the expectations of the Bodleian librarians ... Although he said he had consulted with numerous groups and used their advice to make changes, he recognized that 'individuals are always complaining that they have not been consulted.' (ibid.: 279)

So the difficulties progressed, and the story reveals both major and petty disagreements. Reflecting on the tales that participants had told her when interviewed, Moran is able to draw conclusions about the change process and about the underlying issues which these stories reveal:

> In many respects, it appeared that the more Carr tried to communicate, the more criticism he engendered. It appeared that the problem was not lack of communication but something else. When issues are complex and threatening, it is often easier for an individual to criticize communication than to recognize one's inability to grasp the complexity or to face the changes that are to come. A large part of the communication difficulty could be traced to distrust and fear. Carr could most likely never solve the problem because the staff actually desired more than detailed communication. They wanted to know that the integration

was going to result in an organization that would preserve the importance and the meaning of their own positions and their own part of the larger reorganized structure. This was an assurance that was impossible to provide. (ibid.: 281)

But in the end the reorganisation proceeded and became recognised as a success:

Carr and the librarians have been able to do the necessary 'sorting,' and despite the difficulties encountered in the process, the new restructured library is overall a success ... 'Both users and librarians agree that overall services have been improved, and thus the integration appears to have succeeded in its ultimate objective.' (ibid.)

This is a good example of what is called 'situated action theory' which in essence argues that the focus for professional and organisational activity needs to be upon the everyday activities of people acting in their particular settings, so that the spotlight is on the interaction between the individuals or groups and their current environment. The same perspective argues that understanding is not just an individual achievement but occurs within the social grouping. This draws on Vygotsky's and Leont'ev's work (see Chapter 4) and emphasises that the storied description is what reveals the inner feelings and motivations of those being observed and observing each other.

In an interesting discussion in the context of librarianship, though unrelated to the account summarised above, Birdsall has suggested that

... it is crucial ... for those promoting evidence based practice to consider its methodology in the larger context of the transformation of librarianship; that is, a shift back to heterogeneous library practice arising out of the recognition there are multiple communities of knowing. (Birdsall 2008: 66).

This reflects some of the discussion in Chapter 6, particularly the observation that ICTs have encouraged and enabled local groups and specialised interests to take control of their own narratives, encouraged by services such as social networking sites and the phenomenon of the 'Long Tail'. The 'societies' in which action is situated are now tending to be organised on a more human scale – the small group, the local community, the virtual neighbourhood, the network of 'friends'. While government and large corporations continue to act on a global stage, for many professionals, it is the particular concerns of the locality and of the interest group which provide a focus.

Continuous Learning

The close relationship between storytelling and learning emerges in almost every account of the use of narrative in organisations or in professional contexts. This is hardly surprising, because anything which engages our attention and helps us to listen deeply is bound to reveal something new, and thus to add to our knowledge and understanding. Furthermore, because narrative is essentially a shared experience, it encourages social interaction – even when this is simply the reader responding to the written word – which itself creates a sense of community and an experience of learning. When we ourselves craft stories, the process carries with it learning, not least because it requires reflection on the situations we are addressing.

Becoming a Storyteller

While it is certainly true that some people are natural storytellers, it is perfectly possible to learn how to use narrative in professional settings. Indeed, we are all already storytellers in our normal lives, something we learned as children and practice unceasingly when we encounter other people. As earlier chapters have illustrated, narratives feature structure, characterisation and other attributes (Chapter 3) and describe particular environments which are recognisable to their listeners. They combine familiarity and surprise. Different types of story are known to be effective in different circumstances. All these aspects of storytelling can be learned and our natural, innate abilities as storytellers can be discovered, honed and improved. Katalina Groh, one of the leading exponents of storytelling in organisations, emphasises from her own experience that anyone can learn to express themselves in this way:

> If you'd met me fifteen years ago, you would have said that I was the quietest, shyest person. I didn't even speak English until I went to school, because we only spoke Hungarian at home … It was hard for me to communicate at school with my heavy Hungarian accent, and so I was very quiet. I lived through years of feeling I had something to say, but I never said it. And what helped me was when I had some teachers who pulled it out of me and got me to start. They thought, 'She must have something to say.' And now, I'm helping other people tell their stories. (Brown et al. 2005: 148)

Marc Davis and Michael Travers of the MIT Media Lab introduced the concept of 'narrative intelligence' in the field of artificial intelligence (Davis and Travers 2003), where the aim was to reproduce the human ability to tell meaningful stories. While this approach has not been overwhelmingly successful, it was not long before the term became more widely used, especially in connection with organisational management, to denote the human ability to create and tell effective stories. Stephen Denning uses the term in his books on the use of storytelling in organisations:

> … narrative intelligence is about knowing the different patterns of story, knowing which pattern works in which context, intuiting which stories one's listeners are

living, and having the capacity to judge how well they respond to new stories. (Denning 2007: 213)

The appendices contain some suggestions about practical storytelling in organisational and professional contexts, providing starting points for those who would wish to pursue the practice of narrative.

Using Narratives as a Learning Tool

As has been remarked already, stories and narratives seem to be a natural way in which we learn about the world. For example, the prevalence of storytelling as a way of communicating with small children is commonplace in every society. Indeed, some pedagogical experts (for example, Lauritzen and Jaeger 1997) have suggested that there is a need for a 'narrative curriculum' in schools which would embrace not just the narrative form but the development of storytelling skills. Such a commitment can be seen as a critical way in which children can learn within their social setting, encouraging empathetic reactions to what could be mere factual accounts. Cotazzi and Jin offer this example, an autobiographical account from the experiences of the Vietnamese 'boat people' by a child who had been in the UK for only eighteen months, to show how teaching narrative skills can produce accounts which are profound learning experiences for listeners:

> My name's Hoa, my name means flower. I lived in a big house in Vietnam with my mother and my father and Binh and Quan. In Vietnam it was sunny I can play out all day if I like. But one day I can not stay there because the was lot of bombs. So one day my mummy and Daddy packed all the thing that we want we well some clothes for some money when it was dark we when on a cart and a horse pull it we went on the cart and a horse pull it we went on the cart for just one night then we have to walk. When it was morning we saw a river and we went on a little boat. We told the man were we wanted to go and the man row the boat to a beach. We stay on the beach for four weeks and waited for the big boat. We went in the house with five peoples it was not our house. Then we went on the boat. It was very crowded there was 200 peoples. There was one toilet. It was very frightened when I looked down the hole in the toilet because I can see the sea. It was very dirty and wet and it was smelly we have a little bit to eat every day and my Mummy had a little bottle for us to drink. We stay on the boat for two months. (Cotazzi and Jin 2007: 658)

Within professional and organisational settings, the achievement of the same kind of contextual and situational understanding can also be achieved through learning narrative skills and listening to other practitioners' stories.

Ethical Conduct

One of the distinguishing features of a profession is that its practitioners have knowledge and skills which are not held by society at large. A critical perspective would add to this that professions exercise power and in some cases domination over aspects of social life. Becker (1970: 88) argued that in addition to these characteristics it is important to consider the way in which professional knowledge and expertise is enacted, what is sometimes termed 'professional spirit', which thus focuses on professional conduct and activity. This leads to understandings of professional knowledge as socially constructed (Abbott 1988). From here, it is natural to question the ways in which this knowledge is applied in social situations, in other words, to focus on questions of professional conduct. Hodgson (2002) argues that this leads us naturally to a Foucardian analysis, quoting Fournier: 'being a professional is not merely about absorbing a body of scientific knowledge but is also about conducting and constituting oneself in an appropriate manner' (1999: 287).

Codes of professional conduct are commonplace as a response to this issue but they have had a very mixed success in ensuring that the interests of clients are prioritised, as any individual who has tried to pursue a complaint can probably testify. Abbott (1983), having surveyed the field in depth, argued that such codes contain five common characteristics:

- *universal distribution*, in that all professional groupings (in which category Abbott included groups as disparate as certified accountants, Rotary Clubs and peanut growers!) have a form of ethical code;
- *correlation with intraprofessional status*, that is 'the status of an individual professional or professional subgroup in the eyes of other members of the same profession' (ibid.: 858);
- *enforcement dependent on visibility*; evidence that the most vigorous enforcement of ethical standards occurs when offences are visible to the public;
- *individualism*. They apply to the individual practitioner rather than to the aggregate performance of a professional group. Abbott gives the example of the medical profession where individual breaches of ethical standards are pursued vigorously while collective breaches – such as regional differences in recovery rates from the same procedure – are treated as managerial issues. It is worth noting that this is in itself an issue for evidence-based practice. And
- *an emphasis on collegial obligations*. Many codes of professional conduct concern themselves with behaviour between professionals – such as not poaching clients – rather than the rights and expectations of clients.

This analysis suggests that existing codes of professional conduct are probably insufficient for the purpose when it comes to establishing a firm basis for narrative-based practice. What is needed is a clear commitment to three principles:

- integrity in expressing our own stories in a way that reflects our honest perceptions of our own reality,
- acknowledgement of the validity of other people's stories, avoiding any temptation to dominate the dialogue with our own, and
- truth and integrity in using narrative to communicate corporate or professional values and issues, including descriptions of services and products, whether to colleagues, to clients or to the marketplace.

Underpinning such an approach would lie a form of 'process ethic' which concerned itself with how decisions are reached and not just with the decisions themselves. Gendlin gives the following example to illustrate what is meant by 'process' in this context:

> Suppose your good friend has decided to marry someone, and you like the person. Marrying that intended spouse seems (in general) a good thing. Is that enough for you to call the decision right? Would you not need to know more about how your friend decided? What if the decision was made on a drunken afternoon to get married that very day? Suppose your friend badly wants money and the intended spouse has some? Suppose the wedding was announced and your friend wants to back out but is scared of disappointing the relatives? What if your friend talks mostly of not wanting to live alone?

> We commonly call these 'wrong reasons.' Why? They indicate something about the process of arriving at the decision. The trouble is not exactly these reasons themselves. After all, one rarely marries for the 'reasons' one gives oneself. Many people spend the rest of their lives trying to discover why they married as they did. In my examples, these clearly wrong reasons indicate something more: the lack of the kind of decision-making process we respect.

> It is difficult to delineate 'the right kind of process' even though it is well known. Therefore, people describe it indirectly. For example, they describe the process in terms of time. You might ask how long your friend has thought about it. Or, it can be described in terms of a spatial analogy called 'depth': how far down inside has your friend examined his decision? Or, we describe the process in factual terms: how much is known about the person, the family, where will you live, and so on. (Gendlin 1986: 265–6)

Although Gendlin does not say so, the way in which we talk about process is commonly through narrative, and this can be seen in his example. We would rarely simply ask how long these people have known each other; rather we would

Once upon a time there was a small village. And in this village there lived men and women, boys and girls, dogs and cattle, pigs and hens – and a wise old man, who went by the name of Bertrand. When any of the people had a problem that they couldn't solve for themselves, they would seek out Bertrand and ask for his advice and he would do his best to help them.

One day a young man went to his house and knocked on the door. 'Come in' came the greeting and quickly he let himself into the single room where Bertrand lived and slept. 'How can I help you?' asked Bertrand. 'Well, it's like this', said the young man, 'I can't decide whether I should stay here in the village and continue helping my mother and father with the farm or should I go to the town and find work. What is your advice?'

Before Bertrand could respond, the young man continued, 'But if I stay I'll never make anything of myself. There's nothing wrong with being a farmer of course and it's not a bad living, but I can't help wondering … .' There was a long pause.

After a little while, Bertrand opened his mouth to speak, but before he could say anything, the young man went on, 'If I moved to town I might get a good job and if I worked hard and if I was lucky then maybe I'd make my fortune. But of course I might not be fortunate and I could just as easily fall on hard times. And I don't know anyone there so I would be on my own.' He paused again: 'It's quite a dilemma.'

'Well …', Bertrand started but was again interrupted. 'And then there's Maria, who thinks we should be getting married though I've never committed myself.' A shorter pause and then he continued again, 'I ought to talk it through with her … That's what I'll do. Thank you so much.' And with that, the young man left the house.

Figure 8.3   Allowing others to find their own answers

describe the relationship in terms of how they met, what they have done together and so on, selecting episodes and events that fit with the way we perceive their story. As the issue is discussed the story changes, both with new insights and through reworking of what is included and what is excluded. Thus when we apply this approach, we are looking at a holistic view of the decision process and one which includes our judgements – and therefore our ethical stance.

The Validity of Other Points of View

Stories can be used to dominate, especially in large organisations, although the brief characterisation of organisational storytelling in Chapter 7, where subgenres such as 'is the boss human?' were identified, should serve as a warning to any who are tempted to think that a compulsory corporate axiom is likely to be successful in the long term. Any serious commitment to the use of narrative needs to be a commitment to listening and valuing others' stories as well, bearing in mind that it is very easy for professionals and managers to dominate discourse. As a result, they often fail to hear other people. What is more, they often fail to provide the space in which others can use narrative to help clarify their own problems and identify their own solutions. The story in Figure 8.3 makes the point.

Being Honest: Telling Our Own Stories As They Really Are

Careful listening to others and creating spaces for them to tell their own stories is one side of the coin. But it is all too easy to script unrealistic and insincere versions of our own stories, which attempt to hide more than they reveal. It is even worse when others try to persuade us as to how we should perform our own narratives. Such stories are rarely either compelling or even interesting and very often they are counterproductive. Take this commentary by Stuart Jeffries on the UK government's ill-fated attempt to tell parents how to converse with their children:

> It will be a cold day in hell before I tell my daughter: 'You're my shining star.' Or indeed: 'You've got a friend.' Not to mention my personal favourite: 'You belong.' All of these, though, are among 100 suggestions for expressions of praise in the government's new guide for fathers.

> But, even though she is a Virgo and therefore, astrologists believe, will need a lot of positive reinforcement (which makes her sound like a tent peg), my daughter will not hear such suggested praise from me. This isn't because I don't love her. Rather it is because I think using many of these expressions would be counter-productive, not least because I expect that my nine-month-old will develop a yuck-o-meter at least as finely calibrated as mine. In a few years, if I say to her: 'You brighten my day' (also in the guide), the exchange would continue as follows. 'And you brighten my day, too, Dad.' 'Do I really?' 'No.' 'But you just said I did.' 'I was,' she would reply as her bedroom door closed slowly in my face, 'BEING IRONIC.' (http://www.guardian.co.uk/commentisfree/story/0,1799084,00.html)

It is not particularly unusual for organisations and professions to take the same line, albeit in a rather less cringe-making fashion. Pressure to conform to the corporate myth can be exerted in a way that denies the validity of employees' own personalities. This reaches the limits of absurdity for more junior staff in call centres, supermarkets and bank branches where every customer must be greeted in the same way by someone pretending to be something they are not, often all too obviously. So we have call-centre staff in India instructed to adopt Western names and schooled in regional British or American accents, with the obligatory 'Have a nice day!' to end every conversation. Hewlin (2003) characterised the approach that people take in these circumstances as 'facades of conformity' (FOC).

For professionals, the pressure to provide a uniform front is more subtle. Stormer and Devine applied Hewlin's concept to academics in Canadian universities and found that they too feel under pressure to conform to the perceptions of acceptable organisational norms. A typical example was as follows:

> I refrain from talking about pedagogy to my colleagues because when I do so, they remind me that teaching is something to which I should give little of my time and attention if I am to be a good scholar. I believe that teaching is as important as research, but I don't believe that I can openly articulate this sentiment to anyone in my profession. I work teaching at a major university. That university espouses teaching as a primary goal – the reality is that teaching really matters little in my annual review process. As a result, I 'talk the talk' about respecting students, having concerns about pedagogy, and doing course development. The reality? I spend as little time as possible on teaching as it has little payback to me during tenure and review. (Stormer and Devine 2008: 119)

Of course, NBP is no panacea to this situation but it does suggest one way forward, namely to attempt and share holistic descriptions of the reality of professional life through depictions which go beyond the institution's epic myth. Stormer and Devine again:

> Putting aside the costs of lack of transparency to the psychological health of the individual and the organization, how does the use of FOC affect society when professionals entrusted with upholding the public good are faced with situations that are blatantly problematic, either ethically or legally? As Oscar Wilde suggested, 'A brazen face is a capital thing to show the world, but now and then when you are alone, and have no audience, you have, I suppose, to take the mask off for mere breathing purposes. Else indeed, you would be stifled.' (ibid.: 129)

Truthfulness and Integrity

In Chapter 3, it was noted that compelling narratives can be written to promote falsehood. In Chapter 4, knowledge was equated with 'justified true belief' and the concept of truth was discussed from a philosophical viewpoint. In this section, truth has been discussed briefly as an aspect of ethical conduct. It is highlighted here, at the end of this book, not as an afterthought but to emphasise that without dedication to truthfulness, narrative is both useless and dangerous.

In his recent book *The Secret Language of Leadership*, Denning argues that truth is critical to success:

> Since transformational leadership is in essence a collaborative activity … truthfulness and integrity are essential. Lack of forthrightness or deliberate shading of the truth is devastating to trust and credibility: it undermines the

possibility of enduring enthusiasm. Even an apparent lack of openness ... can be disastrous. (Denning 2007: 119)

As he suggests, there are many subtle aspects to this whole area; integrity can be compromised by only partially revealing the truth or by emphasising aspects which are known to be of interest to the listeners or by building only on their expectations. A concern for *fairness* also suggests that the professional's deeper knowledge of an issue should not be used to create undue advantage over individuals who may be handicapped by lack of information, education, social status, or wealth.

While there is nothing peculiar to NBP which alone demands adherence to ethical standards, it is an important emphasis because of the ease with which storytelling can mislead. The discussion of branding in Chapter 7 provides examples from one particular field, but the issue is much more widespread. It is fundamental to professional identity:

> Each of us, regardless of who we are or what we do, is expected to be scrupulous and honest, but for some professions truthfulness is so fundamental that when it goes missing, that profession becomes completely worthless, and even dangerous. If judges, detectives, researchers, and reporters were to stretch the truth and, without any reason, say, decide, or write down anything whatsoever, then our society would be disrupted. (Pattyn 2006)

And surely the same is true in large measure for anyone who would claim to be a professional.

Conclusion

NBP offers an opportunity to make professional practice relevant to the reality of decision making and action in the complex, intricate, multifaceted actuality of real-world situations where human interactions involve far more than mechanistic actions. By listening to the stories that others tell and by crafting our own narratives we can gain and share knowledge which is hidden, or simply ignored, in purely quantitative studies carried out by excluding the very variables which add richness to our understanding. Bringing together all the evidence, deliberately seeking out the insights which narrative and other qualitative methods can provide, offers opportunities to enhance professional practice to the benefit of practitioners and clients alike.

Appendix 1
Telling the Story

Introduction

This and the other appendices in this book are intended to provide some practical suggestions which will help readers to make use of narratives in organisational or professional settings. There are thousands of resources available on the Web and elsewhere, many targeted at particular groups and others providing general introductions to techniques. Various consultants and trainers can also be used to help develop the skill and habit of organisational and professional storytelling.

The template provided in this appendix is intended to help anyone who is fairly new to storytelling within a professional or organisational context to make a start on their own stories. The outline presented here is an amalgam created from considerable personal experience, including consultancy with a variety of professional groups. However, what works for one person doesn't necessarily work for another, so it is a good idea to try different methods.

Storytelling is a *social* activity, so it is essential to become involved with a supportive group – who may also be the audience for some of the tales that are told. Why not set up a group to learn and critique each others' stories, either within the organisation or within a profession or elsewhere? However, whatever approach is taken, there is no substitute for practice!

A Template

The following guide is intended as a simple template to help in the process of storytelling. It is *one* way to create a story – not the *right* way, nor the *only* way, nor the *recommended* way, just one way!

ACTION	HINTS
Decide on the principal *character* who will be portrayed in the story	The first thing is to decide *who* NOT *what* is going to be portrayed. So the story is not 'about' a product or a service; it's about a person. This could be a customer or a member of staff.
Decide on the *ending*	It may seem the wrong way round to start at the end, but this helps to keep focus on where you want the story to go. What happened to your character in the end?
Think about the *plot* and decide the main events	Remember that most stories are temporal accounts so place the events in order – you might vary this later on when you come to tell the story but you need to be clear in your own mind.
Decide which other *characters* will appear in the story	Who does your main character encounter during the story? For example, a customer might encounter a sales assistant. You might also introduce characters as a way of telling your story. In the example in Appendix 3, the guard at the gate isn't really a key player but his attitude adds to the tension of the story.
Think of an arresting opening	This isn't essential and can be overdone but something which catches the attention is helpful. Sometimes this can play on the familiar ('They had a real set-to in accounts last week, according to Pat …'), perhaps with a twist ('Marvin fell out of the top floor window yesterday – you know, Pat's stuffed toy bear …'). You might also use the ending as an opening, which the story then explains ('one of the customers was so angry he threw the hat stand at Pat …').
Decide which *voice* to use	Is this something that happened to you or to someone else? (See Chapter 3 for a discussion of voice)
Think about how the people in your story *feel*	Emotions and feelings are at the heart of good stories. Were they angry, sad, pleased, overjoyed … ?
Write a first *draft* of the story	Try to put all the above elements together without worrying too much about getting every element exactly right
Read the story to yourself	Read out loud, putting the emphases where they sound natural. Make corrections on the script as you do this. Make sure that what you have written sounds natural.
Revise the story	Make the corrections you've identified. Consider whether the events are narrated in the right order.
Tell the story	Preferably in a small group of colleagues who can give helpful and positive feedback
Practice! Practice! Practice!	

The *History of the Future*: Storytelling in Team Building and Forward Planning

Introduction

One very successful technique for using storytelling in forward planning goes under the name of the *History of the Future*. It is particularly useful when a project team is being set up, perhaps drawing people from different organisations, or different departments in the same organisation. The author has used it frequently as part of the 'kick-off' meeting at the start of a project, where it provides a means of achieving cohesion and appreciation of different viewpoints among participants. It can also be used as part of an overall evaluation strategy, where it forms what has been called 'premative evaluation' – activity which starts the evaluation process before the project itself has even begun.

The purpose of the *History of the Future* exercise is to articulate the often unspoken assumptions of individuals regarding how the project will be undertaken, what it will achieve and what its outcomes or impact will be. It is usually the case that when a group of people are drawn together for a particular purpose they have different ideas about these issues, without always realising it. So a computing expert will see the project in terms of successful software development, someone from marketing will see it in terms of global brand reach, a finance director will view its fit with investment policy, and so on. It is important to surface all these assumptions at the outset so as to reach explicit agreement on coherent aims and objectives.

It is just as important to articulate who needs to do what for the project to succeed. For example, many projects involved in developing digitised materials state that the aim is 'to improve access', maybe for schoolchildren to find materials for their homework. Unfortunately, unless both teachers and parents are involved – or at the very minimum know about the project – it is unlikely that it will succeed, no matter how brilliant the programmers!

On day one of the project, therefore – or even beforehand – everyone involved independently drafts a story in the form of a press release which will be published some time after the project is completed. It explains what has been achieved, who the key players were, what the effects have been and why it is important. As far as possible, the individual documents follow a narrative structure. Experience shows that comparison of the press releases always seems to reveal different perspectives!

Further details of the background to the technique can be found in Markland et al. (2007).

Method

The following method can be adapted to fit any particular requirement and context.

1. A briefing is held to acquaint participants with the purpose of the task and the procedure. It may include the provision of a role that each participant should take (for example, they could each be asked to imagine themselves as a user of the new service), or they may simply undertake the exercise from their own perspective. The briefing should include some basic ideas about storytelling (see Appendix 1) but needs to emphasise that:

- the requirement is for them to imagine that the project has succeeded in its objectives;
- success should be illustrated by writing about its effects on someone outside the project team – generally a customer – preferably with a quotation from that person's perspective along the lines of 'it's changed my life, because now I ...';
- it should refer to what people in the team, or others they have involved, have done to make the achievement possible;
- it can refer to obstacles that have been overcome, although this aspect should not dominate, and
- the style must be highly readable. It is useful to pretend that the press release is for use in a popular national newspaper. The suggestion can be made that the paper is in the habit of using press releases verbatim so it needs to be written as if it were a finished news item of general interest, avoiding specialist jargon at all costs. It is worth emphasising that most easily accessible newspaper accounts are presented in the form of stories with an arresting introduction – which might be in the form of a headline – with characters, progression and a conclusion. However, participants should be able to use whatever form they wish.

2. Participants then spend about twenty minutes working individually on their press releases. While the facilitator can answer questions about the process, it is important not to guide participants in the content or style of what they are writing and to avoid the temptation to share with others. A relaxed atmosphere is needed and sometimes participants need to be reassured that there is no 'right' answer.

3. At the end of the twenty minutes, participants should be invited to share their press releases. This is an important part of the process, since it enables them to

appreciate that there are differing perspectives. However, it is not a competition and it is best to avoid any value judgments. Once again, every perspective is valid.

4. The facilitator should collect all the press releases and analyse them by noting:

- who the 'customer' is,
- what benefits that customer is reporting,
- who has been identified as a key player in the process of reaching a project conclusion,
- what steps were taken in reaching that stage, and
- any other notable features of the account.

5. The facilitator then feeds this summary back to the team, with time for discussion and agreement on what needs to be done to ensure that a common perspective on aims, objectives, methods and desirable outcomes is achieved. This is also a good opportunity to agree on what actions the team needs to take to ensure that external parties are on board – in the example above, should there be early contact with parents and teachers so that they can be persuaded to play a part from an early stage and can plan their involvement and take-up?

Example (*Note: this is a fictional case based on an amalgamation of real examples*)

At the beginning of a major international project concerned with the development of a repository of online lessons, intended to facilitate learning by schoolchildren, the History of the Future exercise was carried out with a mixed group of developers and teachers. The task they were set was as follows:

Time has moved on three years. The project was completed six months ago and the repository was launched to groups of teachers in a variety of schools.

Tomorrow at a press conference you will present its accomplishments to local journalists. Write a press release for distribution at this meeting, explaining succinctly:

* What it is that the project has accomplished.

* An example of what one teacher and/or group of children has done and what has been learned.

* Why what has been done is important.

* What you did that led to this success.

Use your imagination to think of a scenario for this exercise.

Among the responses were the following:

Project Manager	Developer	Teacher
Technology aids teachers	**The People's Internet**	**From last to first in just two years**
Three years ago a group of experts got together to help teachers make more use of the Web. They brought existing online lessons together in one place where any teacher could search for topics they wanted to teach and find useful material ready-made. The European Commission provided the funding for the work and are delighted with what's been achieved. Roman Klinkov, the EC project officer, said recently 'This will make all the difference to primary school teachers. The European Commission is very keen to see schools building on this important initiative … .'	Everyone is using the Internet these days. In fact there's so much stuff out there that it can be very confusing, especially for busy professionals like teachers. That's why leading experts in interoperability, including world renowned Professor Eva Brickova, were brought together three years ago to devise a new system for sharing material that teachers themselves develop. Software developers from Hungary, Latvia, Sweden and the UK worked together to solve some difficult problems, like how to reuse material created in different languages. Professor Brickova commented recently: 'this project has demonstrated that European software developers are among the best in the world … .'	Julia is ten years old now, a happy, outgoing young girl doing well at school. Who would think that two years ago she was at the bottom of the class and going nowhere? What made the difference? For one thing teachers who took a close interest. For another, technology that helped overcome her key problem – she was a thousand miles away from where she was born and learning in a foreign language. But a new system, launched just a year ago, meant her teachers could get hold of lessons in her native language. Putting these together with what she was learning in school, she regained interest, became motivated and now leads the pack. Ed Ifise, her form teacher, said: 'I don't think we could have helped her in the way we did without the new system. It's really made all the difference … .'

A brief analysis reveals:

- The management perspective is mainly about meeting the goals of the high-level policy makers (and future funders!) in the European Commission
- The developer perspective is about solving tricky technical problems and being ahead of the game among the worldwide developer community
- The teacher perspective is about changing the lives of children.

These are not incompatible objectives and can readily be held together in one project. However, unless these perspectives are brought to the surface early on, there is a danger that individual participants will pursue their own agendas at the cost of cohesion and with the loss of potential outcomes and impacts. A straightforward *History of the Future* exercise run at the start of the project, using simple forms of storytelling, helps to ensure that this does not happen.

Possible Extensions

It is possible to extend the *History of the Future* exercise in a number of different ways, for example, by:

- holding a press conference, putting one of the participants in front of a microphone and getting the others to ask questions about what's been achieved. It's important to ask questions that can't be answered by a simple 'Yes' or 'No' – so ask questions beginning 'Why … ?' or 'How … ?' or 'When … ?'
- bringing in neutral observers who can give feedback about the value of the outcomes being described.
- repeating the exercise part-way through a project so as to enable participants to explore any changes in their perceptions of desirable and feasible outcomes.

Appendix 3

'I, the Customer': Using Storytelling to Reach Understanding of Customer Experiences

Introduction

The method described in this appendix is one that was developed over a period of time in working with different groups of professionals in different organisational contexts, ranging from an international agency to local government. In essence, it encourages staff to put themselves in the shoes of their customers, but to do so by drawing on what they *know* of customers, not simply what they have imagined. In other words, the imaginative element is used to explain the significance of a customer encounter; they are not producing merely fictional descriptions. The example given at the end of this appendix comes from an international organisation.

Method

1. The method works best with small groups of between six and twelve staff, preferably occupying different roles, from one organisation. The aim is to gain understanding of service issues, and particularly of outcomes, from a customer perspective. Even numbers are best as they work for part of the time in pairs.

2. Participants begin by sharing descriptions of customer encounters, talking about these from their own experience. It may be that the encounter chosen is typical, or it may stand out because of a particular conversation or occurrence. It can refer to either external or internal customers – some excellent learning has taken place when the subject taken has been relationships between departments and whether people do treat each other as 'customers'. Descriptions begin 'I remember ... ' or 'I'll never forget ... ' and everyone in the group contributes, but in any order. It is OK for questions to be asked.

3. Participants are then given a simple briefing about storytelling, which emphasises two particular aspects: temporal structure, and cause and effect. They will be asked to ensure that they use these in the next step. In other words, their stories begin before the actual encounter, describe the encounter, and then describe

what happened after it. They are also encouraged to include elements which describe people's feelings and emotions as well as their actions.

4. Working in pairs, participants work on their own stories, each person sharing parts of their story, as it emerges, with their partner, asking questions and giving encouragement but making sure not to take over the story. They are asked to:

- work in the first person singular as if they were the customer. So all stories begin 'I ... ';
- write a short section describing what happened to the customer *before* the service encounter. For example, in a group of public library staff one story started, 'I knew my library books were overdue so I caught the bus into town ... ';
- tell of the service encounter in the words of the customer. Again, sentences begin 'I ... ' or 'My ...'. They should also include what the person providing the service said or did, using the third person: 'He said ... ', 'She seemed very unsympathetic ... ', and so on, and
- write another short section which tells what happened *after* the service encounter, again in the first person and again including emotional aspects. These should include a cause-and-effect relationship, so that they explain that *because* of the encounter something happened. For example, 'I was so upset I'm never going to borrow a book from there again ... ', 'I was so relieved that she found me the address of the care home ... '.

5. The group then gets together again and each of the participants reads their story. It is not unusual for each telling to be greeted with a round of applause! This part of the training session is then rounded off by a group discussion, which typically focuses on how realistic others feel the description was, explores customer experiences in more depth and reveals empathy between those involved (for example, 'I never realised that you had to do that ... ').

Outcomes

In most sessions there are found to be three outcomes:

- Participants comment that they found it useful to broaden out their thinking beyond the service encounter itself to think about what might have been happening in the life of the customer both before and afterwards.
- When participants come from different parts of the organisation, they find it a useful way to delve beneath the surface of statistics on services and increase their understanding of what other people in the organisation do.
- Most participants have commented that they have never used storytelling in this way before, found the experience enjoyable and gained both a new skill and a different way of thinking about their customers. Typical participant

feedback from these training days included the comment from one senior manager: 'very informative. I'm sure everyone gained from it.'

Example

'I grew up in one of the poorest parts of the city. I learned some English at school but my parents couldn't afford to let me stay on so I started working full time when I was 14 doing cleaning jobs. I was trying to improve my English all the time because I was sure that it would be necessary if I wanted to get a good job but it is very difficult when you are working and I couldn't afford lessons. Then my friend Maria told me that she had heard that you could apply to XXX [name of organisation] and that they had a programme for people like us that their government funded as part of the aid programme. I didn't know how to find out more about it and I was too scared just to go down there and ask them and anyway it probably wouldn't be for people like me. But then I lost my job and I thought, "Well, what is there to lose?" so I went down there and I said to the guard at the gate that I wanted to ask about learning English and he looked me up and down but eventually he let me in. There was someone at a desk in the entranceway and she said, "Can I help you?" and I explained why I had come. I thought she would laugh at me and tell me to go away but I was so surprised when she said "Yes, we have a programme like that. You have to fill out this form first. Let me help you." She spent half an hour helping me and then she said that I would hear from them in about two weeks. I went back home hardly daring to hope that they would take me on their programme but two weeks later a letter came and it said, "yes", I could join the course and well, to cut a long story short, that was five years ago and now I am the assistant to the Minister of Agriculture. It made all the difference to my life.'

Bibliography

Abbott, A. (1988), *The System of Professions: An Essay on the Division of Expert Labor* (London: University of Chicago Press).

Ackoff, R.L. (1989), 'From Data to Wisdom', *Journal of Applied Systems Analysis* 16(1): 3–9.

Ackroyd, P. (2002), *Dickens*, abridged edn (London: Vintage).

Adams, J. (2006), *Tacit Knowledge: making it explicit* (London: London School of Economics). <http://www.lse.ac.uk/collections/economicHistory/Research/facts/tacit.pdf>

Albrecht, T.L. and Adelman, M.B. (eds) (1987), *Communicating Social Support* (Beverley Hills, CA: Sage).

Andrews, M. et al. (eds) (2000), *Lines of Narrative* (London: Routledge).

Anon., 'The new oases', *The Economist*, 10 April 2008 <http://www.economist.co.uk/specialreports/displaystory.cfm?story_id=10950463> Accessed 21 October 2008.

Armstrong. K. (2006), *The Great Transformation: The World in the time of Buddha, Socrates, Confucius and Jeremiah* (London: Atlantic Books).

Ashmos, D and Duchon, D. (2000), 'Spirituality at work: a conceptualization and measure', *Journal of Management Inquiry* 9(2): 134–45.

Baek, E.-K. (2006), 'Stories: the way we inspire ourselves and each other', *Design Management Review* 17:3, 35–40.

Baker, D., Clay, J. and Fox, C. (eds) (1996), *Challenging Ways of Knowing in English, Maths and Science* (Sussex: Falmer).

Bamberg, M.G.W. (ed.) (1997), 'Oral Versions of Personal Experience: Three Decades of Narrative Analysis', *Journal of Narrative and Life History* 7:1–4 (Special Issue) <http://www.clarku.edu/~mbamberg/Pages_Journals/Pages_Contents/contentsv7.html>

Barry, D. and Elmes, M. (1997), 'Strategy Retold: "Toward a Narrative View of Strategic Discourse"', *The Academy of Management Review* 22:2, 429–52.

Barthes, R. (1966), *Introduction to the Structural Analysis of Narrative. A Roland Barthes Reader*, trans. S. Heath, ed. S. Sontag (London: Vintage).

—— (1967) *Elements of Semiology*, trans. A. Lavers and C. Smith (London: Jonathan Cape).

Basu, K. (2007), 'The Traveler's Dilemma', *Scientific American* [online journal] <http://www.sciam.com/article.cfm?id=7750A576-E7F2-99DF-3824E0B1C2540D47&page=5>, accessed 8 January 2008.

Becker, H.S. (1970), *Sociological Work: Method and Substance* (Harmondsworth: Allen Lane).

—— (1993) 'How I learned what a crock was', *Journal of Contemporary Ethnography* 22:1, 28–35.

Bednar, A. et al. (1993), 'Theory into practice: how do we link?', in T. Duffy and D. Jonassen (eds), *Constructivism and the technology of instruction* (Hillsdale, NJ: Lawrence Erlbaum Associates), 17–34.

Behn, R.D. (2003), 'Why Measure Performance? Different Purposes Require Different Measures', *Public Administration Review* 63:5, 586–606.

Belker, L.B. (1997), *The First-time Manager*, 4th edn (New York: American Management Association).

Bennis, W.G. and Thomas, R.J. (2002), *Geeks and Geezers: How Era, Values and Defining Moments Shape Leadership* (Boston, MA: Harvard Business School Press).

Berliner, D.C. and Calfee, R.C. (eds) (1996), *Handbook of Educational Psychology* (New York: Macmillan).

Birchard, B. (2002), 'Once upon a time', *Strategy + Business* [online journal] 27 (Second Quarter 2002) <http://www.strategy-business.com/press/article/18637?pg=0> accessed 31 May 2008.

Birdsall, W.F. (2008), 'The Chiasmus of Librarianship and Collaborative Research for Evidence Based Practice', *Evidence Based Library and Information Practice* 3:2, 65–75.

Bitner, M.J. et al. (1994), 'Critical service encounters: the employee's viewpoint', *Journal of Marketing* 58:4, 95–106.

Boje, D.M. (1995), 'Stories of the Storytelling Organization: A Postmodern Analysis of Disney as "Tamara-Land"', *The Academy of Management Journal* 38:4, 997–1035.

—— (2002), 'Using narrative and telling stories' in D. Holman and R. Thorpe (eds), *Management and Language: The Manager as a Practical Author* (London: Sage), 41–53.

Bowles, M.L. (1989), 'Myth, Meaning and Work Organization', *Organization Studies* 10:3, 405–21.

Branigan, E. (1992), *Narrative Comprehension and Film* (London: Routledge).

Bredin, H. (1982), 'The Displacement of Character in Narrative Theory', *British Journal of Aesthetics* 22:4, 291–300.

Brice, A. et al. (2005), 'Evidence Based Librarianship: A Case Study in the Social Sciences', *World Library & Information Congress: 71st IFLA General Conference and Council, August 14th–18th 2005, Oslo, Norway.* <http://www.ifla.org/IV/ifla71/papers/111e-Brice_Booth_Bexon.pdf> accessed 14 April 2008.

Brien, A. (1998), 'Professional Ethics and the Culture of Trust', *Journal of Business Ethics* 17:4, 391–409.

Brilhart, J. (1978), *Effective Group Discussion* (Dubuque, IA: W.C. Brown).

Brookfield, S.D. (1995), *Becoming a Critically Reflective Teacher* (San Francisco, CA: Jossey-Bass).

Brophy, P. (2001), 'Networked learning', *Journal of Documentation* 57:1, 130–56.

—— (2004), *The People's Network: Moving Forward* (London: Museums, Libraries and Archives Council).

—— (2006), *Measuring Library Performance: Principles and Techniques* (London: Facet Publishing).

—— and Coulling, K. (1996), *Quality Management for Library and Information Managers* (Aldershot: Gower).

Brown, J.S. et al. (1996), 'Situated cognition and the culture of learning', in D.P. Ely et al. (eds), *Classic Writings on Instructional Technology* (Westport, CT: Libraries Unlimited), 31–52.

—— (2005), *Storytelling in Organizations: Why Storytelling is Transforming 21st Century Organizations and Management* (Oxford: Elsevier Butterworth-Heinemann).

Brown, S. et al. (2003), 'Teaching Old Brands New Tricks: Retro Branding and the Revival of Brand Meaning', *Journal of Marketing* 67:3, 19–33.

Brown, S.L. and Eisenhardt, K.M. (1997), 'The Art of Continuous Change: Linking Complexity Theory and Time-Paced Evolution in Relentlessly Shifting Organizations', *Administrative Science Quarterly* 42:1, 1–34.

Bruner, J. (1990), *Acts of Meaning* (Cambridge, MA: Harvard University Press).

Bruns, A. (2007), 'Produsage: Towards a Broader Framework for User-Led Content Creation', in *Proceedings Creativity & Cognition 6*, Washington, DC. <http://eprints.qut.edu.au/archive/00006623/01/6623.pdf>

Buckland, M.K. (1991), 'Information as thing', *Journal of the American Society for Information Science* 42:5, 351–60.

Burton, L. (1996), 'Mathematics, and its learning, as narrative – a literacy for the twenty-first century', in D. Baker et al. (eds), *Challenging Ways of Knowing: in English, Mathematics and Science* (London: Routledge), 29–40.

Cameron, C. and Wang, M. (1999), 'Frog, Where Are You? Children's narrative expression over the telephone', *Discourse Processes* 28, 217–36.

Carr, D. et al. (2006), *Computer Games: Text, Narrative and Play* (Cambridge: Polity Press).

Chambers, P. (2003), 'Narrative and reflective practice: recording and understanding experience', *Educational Action Research* 11:3, 403–14.

Charles, C. et al. (1997), 'Shared decision-making in the medical encounter: what does it mean? (or it takes at least two to tango)', *Social Science and Medicine* 44:5, 681–92.

Charon, R. (2001), 'Narrative medicine: a model for empathy, reflection, profession, and trust', *Journal of the American Medical Association* [online journal] 286:15, 1897–902. <http://jama.ama-assn.org/cgi/content/full/286/15/1897>

Clark, B.R. (1972) 'The organizational saga in higher education', *Administrative Science Quarterly*, 17:2, 178–84.

Clarke, J.B. (1999), 'Evidence-based practice: a retrograde step? The importance of pluralism in evidence generation for the practice of health care', *Journal of Clinical Nursing*, 8:1, 89–94.

Coe, R. (1999), *A manifesto for evidence-based education* (Durham: University of Durham Curriculum, Evaluation and Management Centre), <http://www.notjustvalueadded.org/RenderPagePrint.asp?LinkID=30317000>.

Cohen, B.L. (2007), 'Notes from Educause 2007: On the subject of leadership', *Library Hi Tech News* 24:9/10, 6–7.

Cole, H.P. (1997), 'Stories to live by: a narrative approach to health behaviour research and injury prevention', in D.S. Gochman (ed.) *Handbook of Health Behavior Research IV* (New York: Plenum Press), 325–49.

Collins, J.C. and Porras, J.I. (1998), *Built to Last*, 2nd rev. edn (London: Random House Business Books).

Condon, J.C. and Yousef, F.S. (2002) 'Communication perspectives', in Little, S. et al. (eds), *Managing Knowledge: An Essential Reader* (London: Sage), 214–37.

Cornellissen, J.P. (2002), 'On the "Organizational Identity" metaphor', *British Journal of Management* 13:3, 259–68.

Cortazzi, M. and Jin, L. (2007), 'Narrative learning, EAL and metacognitive development', *Early Child Development and Care* 177:6, 645–60.

Crawford, C. (2002), *The Art of Interactive Design: A Euphonious and Illuminating Guide to Building Successful Software* (San Francisco, CA: No Starch Press).

Cronbach, L.J. (1988), 'Five perspectives on validity argument', in Wainer, H. and Braun, H.I. (eds) *Test Validity* (Hillsdale, NJ: Lawrence Erlbaum Associates), 3–17.

Csikszentmihalyi, M. (1990), *Flow: The Psychology of Optimal Performance* (New York: Cambridge University Press).

—— (1993), *The Evolving Self: A Psychology for the Third Millennium* (New York: Harper Perennial).

—— (1997), *Finding Flow: The Psychology of Engagement with Everyday Life* (New York: Basic Books).

Culler, J. (1997), *Literary Theory: A Very Short Introduction* (Oxford: Oxford University Press).

Currie, M. (1998), *Postmodern Narrative Theory* (London: Palgrave Macmillan).

Daniels, H. (ed.), *An Introduction to Vygotsky* (London: Routledge).

Davenport, T.H. and Prusak, L. (1998), *Working Knowledge: How Organisations Manage What they Know* (Cambridge, MA: Harvard Business School Press).

Davenport, T.H. et al. (1998), 'Successful knowledge management projects', *Sloan Management Review*, 39:2, 43–57.

Davis, M. and Travers, M. (2003), 'A Brief Overview of the Narrative Intelligence Reading Group', in M. Mateas and P. Sengers (eds), *Narrative Intelligence* (Amsterdam: John Benjamins Company), 27–38.

Denby, D. (2007), 'The New Disorder: adventures in film narrative', *The New Yorker* [online journal] <http://www.newyorker.com/arts/critics/atlarge/2007/03/05/070305crat_atlarge_denby> accessed 27 June 2008.

Deng, P.X. (2008), 'Update your profile from more websites' [website] <http://www.facebook.com/about.php> accessed 23 May 2008.

Denning, S. (2001), *The Springboard: How Storytelling Ignites Action in Knowledge-era Organizations* (Boston, MA: Butterworth-Heinemann).

—— (2007), *The Secret Language of Leadership: How Leaders Inspire Action through Narrative* (San Francisco, CA: Wiley).

Denzin, N.K. (2000), 'Narrative's moment', in M. Andrews et al. (eds) *Lines of Narrative* (London: Routledge), xi-xiii.

DeRose, K. (2005), *What Is Epistemology? A Brief Introduction to the Topic* [website] .<http://pantheon.yale.edu/%7Ekd47/What-Is-Epistemology.htm> accessed 30 March 2008.

Descartes, R. (1997), *Key Philosophical Writings*, trans. E. Haldane and G.R.T. Ross (Hertfordshire: Wordsworth Editions Limited).

Devlin, K. (2000), *The Math Gene: How Mathematical Thinking Evolved and How Numbers are Like Gossip* (New York: Basic Books).

Dewey, J. (1933), *How We Think. A Restatement of the Relation of Reflective Thinking to the Educative Process*, rev. edn (Boston, MA: D.C. Heath).

—— (1938), *Logic: A Theory of Inquiry* (Carbondale: Southern Illinois University Press).

Diekelmann, N. (2001), 'Narrative Pedagogy: Heideggerian Hermeneutical Analyses of Lived Experiences of Students, Teachers, and Clinicians', *Advances in Nursing Science* 23:3, 53–71.

Downing, S. (2005), 'The Social Construction of Entrepreneurship: Narrative and Dramatic Processes in the Coproduction of Organizations and Identities', *Entrepreneurship Theory and Practice* 29:2, 185–204.

Draper, S. (2006), *Narrative Pedagogy* [website] <http://www.psy.gla.ac.uk/~steve/nped.html> accessed 14 May 2008.

Driver, M.J. et al. (1993), *The Dynamic Decision Maker* (San Francisco, CA: Jossey-Bass).

Druss, B.G. and Marcus, S.C. (2005), 'Growth and decentralization of the medical literature: implications for evidence-based medicine', *Journal of the Medical Library Association,* 93:4, 499–501.

Duffy, T.M. and Jonassen, D.H. (eds) (1993), *Constructivism and the Technology of Instruction* (Hillsdale, NJ: Lawrence Erlbaum Associates).

—— (1993), 'Constructivism: new implications for instructional technology', in T.M. Duffy and D.H. Jonassen (eds) *Constructivism and the Technology of Instruction* (Hillsdale, NJ: Lawrence Erlbaum Associates), 1–16.

Dunning, M. and Needham, G. (eds) (1994), *But Will it Work Doctor?* (London: The Consumer Health Information Consortium).

Earl, M. (2001), 'Knowledge management strategies: toward a taxonomy', *Journal of Management Information Systems* 18:1, 215–33.

The Economist (2008), 'The new oases: nomadism changes buildings, cities and traffic' *The Economist* (10 April) [online journal] <http://www.economist.com/specialreports/displaystory.cfm?STORY_ID=10950463> accessed 28 June 2008.

Eldredge, J.D. (2002), 'Evidence-based Librarianship: what might we expect in the years ahead?', *Health Information Libraries Journal*, 19:2, 71–7.

Eliot, George (1856), 'A Natural History of German Life', *Westminster Review* 66 (July), 51–79, reprinted in N. Sheppard (ed.) *The Essays of "George Eliot." Complete* (New York: Funk & Wagnalls, 1883), 141–77.

Ely, D.P. et al. (eds) (1996), *Classic Writings on Instructional Technology* (Westport, CT: Libraries Unlimited).

Engestrom, Y. (1996), 'Non scolae sed vitae discimus: toward overcoming the encapsulation of school learning', in H. Daniels (ed.) *An Introduction to Vygotsky* (London: Routledge), 151–70.

Escalas, J.E. and Stern, B.B. (2007), 'Narrative structure: plot and emotional responses', in T.M. Lowrey (ed.) *Psycholinguistic phenomena in marketing communications* (Hillsdale, NJ: Lawrence Erlbaum Associates), 157–76.

Evans J. R. (1987), 'Toward a shared direction for health in Ontario', *Report of the Ontario Health Review Panel* (Toronto: Government of Ontario).

Feurer, R. and Chaharbaghi, K. (1995), 'Strategy formulation: a learning methodology', *Benchmarking for Quality Management & Technology* 2:1, 38–55.

Fineman, S. (ed.) (2000), *Emotion in Organizations*, 2nd edn (London: Sage).

Fineman, S. and Gabriel, Y. (1996), *Experiencing Organizations* (London: Sage).

Fitzpatrick, M. (2003) 'Mast madness', *The Lancet* 361:9367, 1484.

Flavell, J.H. (1976), 'Metacognitive Aspects of Problem Solving', in L.B. Resnick (ed.) *The Nature of Intelligence* (Hillsdale, NJ: Lawrence Erlbaum Associates),

Forbes, D.A. et al. (1999), 'Warrantable evidence in nursing science', *Journal of Advanced Nursing* 29:2, 373–9.

Forster, E.M. (1927), *Aspects of the Novel* (London: Edward Arnold).

Foucault, M. (1980), *Power/Knowledge: Selected Interviews and Other Writings, 1972–1977* (New York: Pantheon).

Fournier, V. (1999), 'The appeal to "professionalism" as a disciplinary mechanism', *Sociological Review* 47:2, 280–307.

Freeman, D. (1983), *Margaret Mead and Samoa: The Making and Unmaking of an Anthropological Myth* (Cambridge, MA: Harvard University Press).

—— (1999), *The Fateful Hoaxing of Margaret Mead: A Historical Analysis of her Samoan Research* (Boulder, CO: Westview Press).

Gabriel, Y. (1991), 'On Organizational Stories and Myths: Why it is easier to slay a dragon than to kill a myth', *International Sociology* 6(4): 427–42.

—— (2000), *Storytelling in Organizations: Facts, Fictions, and Fantasies* (Oxford, Oxford University Press).

—— (2004), *Myths, Stories, and Organizations: Premodern Narratives for Our Times* (Oxford: Oxford University Press).

Galves, A. (2004), *Discussion: Evidence-Based Practice in Children's Mental Health* [website] <http://www.rtc.pdx.edu/FeaturedDiscussions/pgFD12.php> accessed 12 June 2008.

Gambrill, E. (1999), 'Evidence-based clinical behavior analysis, evidence-based medicine and the Cochrane collaboration', *Journal of Behavior Therapy and Experimental Psychiatry*, 30:1, 1–14.

Gardner, W.L. and Martinko, M.J. (1988), 'Impression Management in Organizations', *Journal of Management* 14:2, 321–38.

Gargiulo, T.L. (2006), 'Power of stories', *The Journal for Quality and Participation* [online journal] 29:1, <http://www.asq.org/data/subscriptions/jqp_sub/2006/spring/jqp0406gargiulo.pdf>, accessed 31 May 2008.

Garvin, D. A. (1984), 'What does "product quality" really mean?', *Sloan Management Review*, Fall, 25–45.

Gay, P. (1966), *The Enlightenment: An Interpretation: The Rise of Modern Paganism* (New York: Alfred A. Knopf).

Gendlin, E.T. (1986), 'Process ethics and the political question', in A.-T. Tymieniecka (ed.) *Analecta Husserliana, vol. XX. The Moral Sense in the Communal Significance of Life* (Boston, MA: Reidel), 265–75.

Genette, G. (1988), *Narrative Discourse Revisited* (Ithaca, NY: Cornell University Press).

Gergen, K.J. and Gergen, M.M. (1986), 'Narrative form and the construction of psychological science', in T.R. Sarbin (ed.) *Narrative Psychology: The Storied Nature of Human Conduct* (New York: Praeger), 22–44.

Glanzberg, M. (2006), 'Truth', *Stanford Encyclopedia of Philosophy* [website] <http://plato.stanford.edu/entries/truth/> accessed 1 June 2008.

Goffman, E. (1959), *The Presentation of Self in Everyday Life* (New York: Doubleday).

Gortner, S.R. and Schultz, P.R. (1988,) 'Approaches to nursing science methods', *Image: Journal of Nursing Scholarship* 20(1): 22–4.

Graesser, A.C. et al. (1994), 'Constructing inferences during narrative text comprehension' *Psychological Review* 101, 371–95.

—— (2002), 'How does the mind construct and represent stories', in M.C. Green et al. *Narrative Impact: Social and Cognitive Foundations* (Mahwah, NJ: Lawrence Erlbaum Associates), 229–62.

Grant, R.M. (2002), 'The knowledge-based view of the firm', in C.W. Choo and N. Bontis (eds) *The Strategic Management of Intellectual Capital and Organizational Knowledge* (Oxford: Oxford University Press), 133–48.

Green, H. (2007), 'The Water Cooler Is Now On The Web', *Business Week* [online journal] 1 October <http://www.businessweek.com/magazine/content/07_40/b4052072.htm?chan=search> accessed 15 June 2008.

—— and Hannon, C. (2007), *Their space: education for a digital generation* (London: Demos) <http://www.demos.co.uk/files/Their%20space%20-%20web.pdf> accessed 21 October 2008.

Green, M.C. and Brock, T.C. (2000), 'The role of transportation in the persuasiveness of public narratives', *Journal of Personality and Social Psychology* 79:5, 701–21.

—— et al. (2002), *Narrative Impact : Social and Cognitive Foundations* (Mahwah, NJ: Lawrence Erlbaum Associates).

Greenhalgh, T. (1999), 'Narrative based medicine in an evidence based world', *British Medical Journal* 318:7179, 323–5.

—— (2006), *What Seems to Be the Trouble? Stories in Illness and Healthcare* (Abingdon: Radcliffe).

Greeno, J.G. et al. (1996), 'Cognition and learning', in D.C. Berliner and R.C. Calfee (eds), *Handbook of Educational Psychology* (New York: Macmillan), 15–46.

Grunebaum, H. (2006), 'On wisdom', *Family Process* 45:1, 117–32.

Guba, E.G. and Lincoln, Y.S. (1981), *Effective Evaluation: Improving the Usefulness of Evaluation Results through Responsive and Naturalistic Approaches* (San Francisco, CA: Jossey-Bass).

—— (1982), 'Epistemological and methodological bases of naturalistic inquiry', *Educational Communication and Technology Journal* 30:4, 233–52.

—— (1988), ''Naturalistic and rationalistic enquiry', in Keeves, J. (ed.), *Educational Research, Methodology, and Measurement: An International Handbook* (Oxford: Pergamon Press), 81–5.

Hall, S. (1996), 'Introduction: who needs identity', in Hall, S. and du Gay, P. (eds), *Questions of Cultural Identity* (London: Sage), 1–17.

—— and du Gay, P. (eds), *Questions of Cultural Identity* (London: Sage).

Hammersley, M. (1992), *What's Wrong with Ethnography?* (London: Routledge).

Hannabuss, S. (2000a), 'Telling tales at work: narrative insight into managers' actions', *Library Review* 49:5, 218–29.

—— (2000b), 'Narrative knowledge: eliciting organisational knowledge from storytelling', *Aslib Proceedings* 52:10, 402–13.

—— (2000c), 'Being there: ethnographic research and autobiography', *Library Management* 21:2, 99–106.

Hansen, T. (2003), 'The narrative approach to mediation', *Mediate.com* [website] <http://www.mediate.com/articles/hansenT.cfm> accessed 30 May 2008.

Hemmings, T. et al. (2002), 'Probing the Probes',. in *Proceedings of the Participation and Design Conference* 2002, 42–50. <http://www.mrl.nott. ac.uk/~axc/documents/papers/PDC02.pdf> accessed 1 April 2008.

Herz, J.C. (2002), 'Harnessing the Hive: How Online Games Drive Networked Innovation', Release 1.0 [online journal] 20:9 <http://www.oss.net/ dynamaster/file_archive/041017/96a13ea1954b4fa57ad78d790077637a/ J C % 2 0 H e r z % 2 0 o n % 2 0 H a r n e s s i n g % 2 0 t h e % 2 0 H i v e %20Via%20Online%20Games.pdf> accessed 23 May 2008.

Hewlin, P.F. (2003), 'And the award for best actor goes to … Facades of conformity in organizational settings', *Academy of Management Review* 28:4, 633–42.

Hicks, B.J. (2002), 'A framework for the requirements of capturing, storing and reusing information and knowledge in engineering design', *International Journal of Information Management* 22:4, 263–80.

Hinchman, L.P. and Hinchman, S.K. (eds) (1997), *Memory, Identity, Community: Idea of Narrative in the Human Sciences* (Albany: State University of New York Press).

Hodge, R.A. (2004), 'Tracking Progress toward Sustainability: Linking the Power of Measurement and Story', *Society for Mining, Metallurgy and Exploration (SME) Symposium: Sustainable Development from the Ground Up: Measuring Progress Toward Sustainable Development 25 February 2004* [website] <http:// anthonyhodge.ca/publications/Linking_the_Power_Measurement_Story.pdf>, accessed 31 March 2008.

Hodgson, D. (2002), 'Disciplining the Professional: the case of project management', *Journal of Management Studies* 39:6, 803–21.

Hogan, T.P. and Palmer, C.L. (2005), 'Information preferences and practices among people living with HIV/AIDS: results from a nationwide survey', *Journal of the Medical Library Association* 93:4, 431–9.

Holmes, D. et al. (2006), 'Deconstructing the evidence-based discourse in health sciences: truth, power and fascism', *International Journal of Evidence-Based Healthcare* 4:3, 180–86.

Hopkinson, G.C. (2003), 'Stories from the Front-line: How they Construct the Organization', *Journal of Management Studies* 40:8, 1943–69.

Ironside, P.M. (2006), 'Using narrative pedagogy: learning and practising interpretive thinking', *Journal of Advanced Nursing* 55:4, 478–86.

Jaatinen, M. and Lavikka, R. (2008), 'Common understanding as a basis for coordination', *Corporate Communications: An International Journal* 13:2, 147–67.

Jenkins, K. (1999), *Why History? Ethics and Postmodernity* (London: Routledge).

Joachim, H.H. (1906), *The Nature of Truth* (Oxford: Clarendon Press).

Keeves, J. (ed.) (1988), *Educational Research, Methodology, and Measurement: An International Handbook* (Oxford: Pergamon Press).

Keillor, G. (1989), *We Are Still Married* (London: Faber and Faber).

Kermode, F. (1981), 'Secrets and Narrative Sequence', in W.J.T. Mitchell (ed.) *On Narrative* (Chicago, IL: University of Chicago Press), 79–97.

Kerry, A.P. (1991), *Narrative and the Self* (Bloomington: Indiana University Press).

Klamma, R. et al. (2006), 'Virtual Entrepreneurship Lab 2.0: Sharing Entrepreneurial Knowledge by Non-Linear Story-Telling', *Journal of Universal Knowledge Management* 1:3, 174–98.

Kleiner, A. and Roth, G. (1997), 'How to make experience your company's best teacher', *Harvard Business Review* 75:5, 172–7.

Knights, D. and McCabe, D. (2000), 'Bewitched, bothered and bewildered: the meaning and experience of teamworking for employees in an automobile company', *Human Relations* 53:11, 1481–517.

Koro-Ljungberg, M. (2004), 'Impossibilities of Reconciliation: Validity in Mixed Theory Projects', *Qualitative Inquiry* 10:4, 601.

Kuhn, D. et al. (1997), 'Effects of Dyadic Interaction on Argumentive Reasoning', *Cognition and Instruction*, 15:3, 287–315.

Kunde, J. (2000), *Corporate Religion* (London: Prentice Hall).

Labov, W. and Waletzky, J. (1997), 'Narrative analysis: oral versions of personal experiences', in Bamberg, M.G.W. (ed.), <http://www.clarku.edu/~mbamberg/ LabovWaletzky.htm> accessed 2 July 2008.

Laing, R.D. (1967), *The Politics of Experience and The Birds of Paradise* (Harmondsworth: Penguin).

Laurillard, D. (2002), 'Rethinking university teaching in the digital age', *Forum Futures 2002* (Boulder, CO: Educause) <http://net.educause.edu/ir/library/pdf/ ffp0205s.pdf> accessed 21 June 2008.

Lauritzen, C. and Jaeger, M. (1997), *Integrating Learning through Story: The Narrative Curriculum* (London: Delmar Learning).

Lave, J. and Wenger, E. (1991). *Situated Learning: Legitimate Peripheral Participation* (Cambridge: Cambridge University Press).

Leitch, C. et al. (1996), 'Learning organizations: the measurement of company performance', *Journal of European Industrial Training*, 20:1, 31–44.

Leont'ev, A.N. (1978), *Activity, Consciousness, and Personality* (Englewood Cliffs, NJ: Prentice-Hall).

Lesser, E. and Prusak, L. (eds) (2004), *Creating Value with Knowledge: Insights from the IBM Institute for Business Value* (Oxford: Oxford University Press).

Levin, I.M. (2000), 'Vision Revisited: Telling the Story of the Future', *Journal of Applied Behavioral Science* 36(1): 91–107.

Lewis, J.S. and Geroy, G.D. (2000), 'Employee spirituality in the workplace: a cross-cultural view for the management of spiritual employees', *Journal of Management Education* 24:5, 682–94.

Lincoln, Y.S. and Guba, E.G. (1985), *Naturalistic Inquiry* (Beverly Hills, CA: Sage).

Linde, C. (2001), 'Narrative and social tacit knowledge', *Journal of Knowledge Management* 5:2, 160–70.

Lips-Wiersma, M. (2002), 'Analysing the career concerns of spiritually oriented people: lessons for contemporary organizations', *Career Development International* 7:7, 385–97.

Loomis, J.M. (1992), 'Distal attribution and presence', *Presence: Teleoperators and Visual Environments* [online journal] 1:1, 113–19. <http://www.psych. ucsb.edu/~loomis/loomis_presence.pdf>.

Loughran, J.J. (2002), 'Effective Reflective Practice: in search of meaning in learning about teaching', *Journal of Teacher Education* 53:1, 33–43.

Lupton, D. (1997), 'Doctors on the medical profession', *Sociology of Health and Illness,* 19:4, 480–97.

Lyotard, J.-F. (1984), *The Postmodern Condition: A Report on Knowledge* (Manchester: Manchester University Press).

—— (1988), *The Differend: Phrases in Dispute* (Manchester: Manchester University Press).

Malinowski, B. (1922), *Argonauts of the Western Pacific* (London: Routledge).

Marcusohn, L.M. (1995), 'The information explosion in organizations', *Swedish Library Research* 3:4, 25–41.

Markland, M. et al. (2007), 'The History of the Future: evaluating projects and service developments before they begin', *Performance Measurements and Metrics* 8:1, 34–40.

Martin, J. et al. (1983), 'The Uniqueness Paradox in Organizational Stories', *Administrative Science Quarterly* 28:3. 438–53.

Marzec, M. (2007), 'Telling the corporate story: vision into action', *Journal of Business Strategy* 28:1, 26–36.

Mateas, M. and Sengers, P. (eds), *Narrative Intelligence* (Amsterdam: John Benjamins Company).

May, C. and Fleming, C. (1997), 'The Professional Imagination: narrative and the symbolic boundaries between medicine and nursing', *Journal of Advanced Nursing* 25:5, 1094–100.

McAllister, D.J. (1995), 'Affect- and Cognition-Based Trust as Foundations for Interpersonal Cooperation in Organizations', *The Academy of Management Journal* 38:1, 24–59.

McKibbon, K.A. (1998), 'Evidence based practice', *Bulletin of the Medical Library Association* 86:3, 396–401.

McLoughlin, J.A. and Jordan, G.B. (1999), 'Logic models: a tool for telling your program's performance story', *Evaluation and Program Planning* 22:1, 65–72.

Mead, M. (1928), *Coming of Age in Samoa* (New York: Morrow).

Metz, C. (1974), *Film Language: A Semiotics of the Cinema* (Chicago, IL: University of Chicago Press).

Miles, M.B. and Huberman, A.M. (1994), *Qualitative Data Analysis: An Expanded Sourcebook* (Beverley Hills, CA: Sage).

Miller, G.A. (1956), 'The magical number seven, plus or minus two: some limits on our capacity for processing information', *Psychological Review*, 63, 81–97.

Miller, K.I. et al. (2007), '"Let me tell you about my job": exploring the terrain of emotion in the workplace', *Management Communication Quarterly* 20:3, 231–60.

Mintzberg, H. (1979), *The Structuring of Organizations: A Synthesis of Research* (Englewood Cliffs, NJ: Prentice-Hall).

—— (1992), 'Five Ps for Strategy', in H. Mintzberg and J.B. Quinn (eds) *The Strategy Process* (Englewood Cliffs, NJ: Prentice-Hall), 12–19.

Mintzberg, H. and Quinn, J.B. (eds) (1992), *The Strategy Process* (Englewood Cliffs, NJ: Prentice-Hall).

Mishler, E.G. (1985), *The Discourse of Medicine: dialectics of medical interviews* (Westport, CT: Greenwood Publishing).

Mitroff, I.I. and Kilmann, R.H. (1975), 'Stories managers tell: a new tool for organizational problem solving', *Management Review* 64:7, 18–28.

Monaco, S. (1984), *How to Read a Film: The Art, Technology, Language, History and Theory of Film and Media* (New York: Open University Press).

Monaghan, R. (1936), 'The Liability Claim Racket', *Law and Contemporary Problems*, 3:4, 491–504.

Moran, B. (2005), 'Continuity and Change: the Integration of Oxford University's Libraries', *Library Quarterly* 75:3, 262–94.

Moss, R. (1998), *Dreamgates: An Explorer's Guide to the Worlds of Soul, Imagination, and Life Beyond Death* (New York: Three Rivers Press).

Murphy, P. (ed.) (1999), *Learners, Learning and Assessment* (London: Paul Chapman).

Newell, A. and Simon, H.A. (1972), *Human Problem Solving* (Englewood Cliffs, NJ: Prentice-Hall).

Nonaka, I. and Konno, N. (1998), 'The concept of "ba": building a foundation for knowledge creation', *California Management Review* 40:3, 40–54.

—— and Takeuchi, H. (1995), *The Knowledge-Creating Company* (Oxford: Oxford University Press).

Nozick, R. (1989), *The Examined Life* (New York: Touchstone Press).

O'Neill, D. (2004), 'Narrative skills linked to mathematical achievement', *Literacy Today* [online journal] 41 <http://www.literacytrust.org.uk/pubs/oneill.html> accessed 28 June 2008.

O'Reilly, T. (2005), *What Is Web 2.0: Design Patterns and Business Models for the Next Generation of Software* [website] <http://www.oreillynet.com/pub/a/oreilly/tim/news/2005/09/30/what-is-web-20.html?page=1> accessed 1 June 2008.

Oakley, J.G. (2000), 'Gender-based Barriers to Senior Management Positions: Understanding the Scarcity of Female CEOs', *Journal of Business Ethics* 27, 321–34.

Pace, S. (2004), 'The roles of challenge and skill in the flow experiences of Web users', *Journal of Issues in Informing Science and Information Technology*, [online journal] 1, 341–58. <http://proceedings.informingscience.org/InSITE2004/056pace.pdf>.

Panda, A. and Gupta, R.K. (2001), 'Understanding Organizational Culture: A Perspective on Roles for Leaders', *Vikalpa: The Journal for Decision Makers* 26:4, 14–19.

Pask, G. (1975), *Conversation, Cognition, and Learning* (New York: Elsevier).

Pattyn, B. (2006), 'Voorwoord', *Terugblik op Wetenschap en Ethiek* (Leuven: Katholieke Universiteit Leuven) [website] <http://www.wetenschap-en-ethiek.be/page.php?LAN=N&FILE=subject&ID=352&PAGE=2> accessed 21 June 2008.

Pennington, N. and Hastie, R. (1986), 'Evidence evaluation in complex decision making', *Journal of Personality and Social Psychology* 51:2, 242–58.

—— (1988), Explanation-based decision making: the effects of memory structure on judgment, *Journal of Experimental Psychology: Learning, Memory, and Cognition* 14:3, 521–33.

Peters, T.J. and Waterman, R.H. (1982), *In Search of Excellence* (New York: Harper & Row).

Piaget, J. (1923), *The Language and Thought of the Child* (New York: Routledge & Kegan Paul).

—— (1932), *The Moral Judgment of the Child* (New York: Harcourt Brace).

Pilkington, R.M. and Walker, S.A. (2003), 'Facilitating debate in networked learning: Reflecting on online synchronous discussion in higher education', *Instructional Science* 31:1–2, 41–63.

Plato (369 BCE) *Theaetetus*. Cambridge, MA: Internet Classics Archive. [website] <http://classics.mit.edu/Plato/theatu.html> accessed 12 June 2008.

Pojman, L.P. (2003), *The Theory of Knowledge: Classic and Contemporary Readings* (Boston, MA: Wadsworth).

Polanyi, M. (1958), *Personal Knowledge: Towards a Post Critical Philosophy* (London: Routledge).

—— (1966), *The Tacit Dimension* (Garden City, NY: Doubleday).

Polichak, J.W. and Gerrig, R.J. (2002), '"Get up and win!"': participatory response to narrative', in M.C. Green et al. (eds), *Narrative Impact: Social and Cognitive Foundations* (Mahwah, NJ: Lawrence Erlbaum Associates), 71–95.

Polkinghorne, D.E. (1988), *Narrative Knowing and the Human Sciences* (New York: State University of New York Press).

Popper, K. (1963), *Conjectures and Refutations* (London: Routledge).

Porter, R. (1994), 'Dr Doubledose: a taste of one's own medicine', *British Medical Journal*, 309:6970, 1714–18.

Prensky, M. (2001), 'True Believers: digital game-based learning in the military' [website] <http://www.learningcircuits.org/2001/feb2001/prensky.html> accessed 2 July 2008.

Price, L. (2007), 'Narrative Mediation: a transformative approach to conflict resolution', *Mediate.com* [website] <http://www.mediate.com/articles/priceL1.cfm> accessed 23 April 2008.

Rabinow, P. and Sullivan, W. (1987a), 'The interpretive turn: emergence of an approach', in P. Rabinow and W. Sullivan (eds) *Interpretive Social Science: A Second Look* (Los Angeles: University of California Press).

—— (eds) (1987b), *Interpretive Social Science: A Second Look* (Los Angeles: University of California Press).

Rafieli, S. et al. (2005), 'Social cognition online', in Y. Amichai-Hamburger (ed.) *The Social Net: Understanding Human Behaviour in Cyberspace* (Oxford: Oxford University Press), 57–90.

Randazzo, S. (1993), *Mythmaking on Madison Avenue* (Chicago, IL: Probus Publishing).

Rawls, A.W. (2008), 'Harold Garfinkel, Ethnomethodology and Workplace Studies', *Organization Studies* 29:5, 701–32

Ray, E.B. (1987), 'Supportive relationships and occupational stress in the workplace', in T.L. Albrecht and M.B. Adelman (eds), *Communicating Social Support* (Beverley Hills, CA: Sage), 172–91.

Ray, N. (ed.) (2005), *Architecture and Its Ethical Dilemmas* (London: Taylor & Francis).

Rego, A. and Cunha, M.P. (2008), 'Workplace spirituality and organizational commitment: an empirical study', *Journal of Organizational Change Management* 21:1, 53–75.

Reissner, S.C. (2005), 'Learning and innovation: a narrative analysis', *Journal of Organizational Change Management* [online journal] 18:5, 482–94. <http://www.emeraldinsight.com/Insight/ViewContentServlet?Filename=Published/EmeraldFullTextArticle/Articles/0230180506.html#idb8%20b9> accessed 31 May 2008.

Resnick, L.B. (ed.) (1976), *The Nature of Intelligence* (Hillsdale, NJ: Lawrence Erlbaum Associates).

Resnicow, K. et al. (1999), 'Cultural sensitivity in public health: defined and demystified', *Ethnicity and Disease* 9:1, 10–21.

Reznitskaya, A. et al. (2001), 'Influence of oral discussion on written argument', *Discourse Processes*, 32:2–3, 155–75.

Richards, K.E. (1959), 'A New Concept of Performance Appraisal', *The Journal of Business* 32:3, 229–43.

Ricoeur, P. (1983), *On Interpretation* (Cambridge: Cambridge University Press).

—— (1984) *Time and Narrative*, Vol. 1 (Chicago, IL: University of Chicago Press).

Riedl, M.O. and Young, R.M. (2003), 'Character-focused narrative generation for execution in virtual worlds', in Balet, O. et al. (eds), *Virtual Storytelling: Using Virtual Reality Technologies for Storytelling* (London: Springer), 47–56.

Roazen, L. (2007), 'Why ear candling is not a good idea', *Quackwatch* [website] <http://www.quackwatch.com/01QuackeryRelatedTopics/candling.html> accessed 17 April 2008.

Robson, C. (2002), *Real World Research: A Resource for Social Scientists and Practitioner-Researchers* (Oxford: Blackwell Publishing).

Rowley, J. (2000), 'From learning organisation to knowledge entrepreneur', *Journal of Knowledge Management*, 4:1, 7–14.

—— (2006), 'Where is the wisdom that we have lost in knowledge?', *Journal of Documentation* 62:2, 251–70.

—— (2007), 'The wisdom hierarchy: representations of the DIKW hierarchy', *Journal of Information Science*, 33:2, 163–80.

Rowntree, B.S. (1901), *Poverty: A Study of Town Life* (London: Macmillan).

Ryan, S. (2007), 'Wisdom', *Stanford Encyclopedia of Philosophy* [website] <http://plato.stanford.edu/entries/wisdom/> accessed 16 June 2008.

Salter, M. (2008), 'Get away from statistics. Trust the doctor', *The Guardian*, 1 July: 6–7.

Sarantakos, S. (1998), *Social Research*, 2nd edn (London: Macmillan).

Saussure, F. (1974), *Course in General Linguistics*, trans. W. Baskin (Glasgow: Fontana).

Schank, R.C. (1990), *Tell Me a Story: A New Look at Real and Artificial Memory* (New York: Simon & Schuster).

—— and Abelson, R.P. (1995), 'Knowledge and memory: the real story', in R.S. Wyer (ed.) *Advances in Social Cognition* (Hillsdale, NJ: Lawrence Erlbaum Associates), 1–86.

—— and Berman, T.R. (2002), 'The pervasive role of stories in knowledge and action', in M.C. Green et al. (eds), *Narrative Impact: Social and Cognitive Foundations* (Hillsdale, NJ: Lawrence Erlbaum Associates), 287–313.

—— and Morson, G.S. (1995), *Tell Me a Story: Narrative and Intelligence* (Chicago, IL: Northwestern University Press).

Scheurich, J.J. (1993), 'The masks of validity: a deconstructive investigation', *International Journal of Qualitative Studies in Education* 9:11, 49–60.

Schlenker, B. (1980), *Impression Management* (Monterey, CA: Brooks/Cole).

Schreyögg, G. and Koch, J. (2005), 'Linking organizational narratives and knowledge management: an introduction', in Schreyögg and Koch (eds) *Knowledge Management and Narratives: Organizational Effectiveness through Storytelling* (Berlin: Erich Schmidt), 1–14.

—— (eds) (2005), *Knowledge Management and Narratives: Organizational Effectiveness through Storytelling* (Berlin: Erich Schmidt).

Schön, D. (1987), *Educating the Reflective Practitioner: Toward a New Design for Teaching and Learning in the Professions* (San Francisco, CA: Jossey-Bass).

Schultz, P.R. and Meleis, A.I. (1988), 'Nursing epistemology: traditions, insights, questions', *Image: Journal of Nursing Scholarship* 20, 217–21.

Shamir, B. and Eilam, G. (2005), 'What's your story? A life-stories approach to authentic leadership development', *The Leadership Quarterly* 16, 395–417.

Shannon, C.E. (1948), 'A Mathematical Theory of Communication', *Bell System Technical Journal* 27: 379–423, 623–56.

Sheldon, T. (1994), 'Not all health care is appropriate', in M. Dunning and G. Needham (eds) *But Will It Work Doctor?* (London: The Consumer Health Information Consortium).

Shell International Exploration and Production (2001), *Story-telling in Shell: Managing Knowledge through New Ways of Working* (Rijswijk: Shell International Exploration and Production B.V.).

Simanowski, R. (2001) 'The reader as author as figure as text', *Poetics of digital text* [website] <http://www.p0es1s.net/poetics/symposion2001/full_simanowski.html#_ftn4> accessed 12 June 2008.

Simmons, A. (2006), *The Story Factor: Secrets of Influence from the Art of Storytelling*, 2nd edn (London: Basic Books).

Simpson, R. and Galbo, J. (1986), 'Interaction and Learning: Theorizing on the art of teaching', *Interchange* 17(4): 37–51.

Skjørshammer, M. (2002), 'Understanding Conflicts between Health Professionals: A Narrative Approach', *Qualitative Health Research* 12:7, 915–31.

Slater, M.D. (2002), 'Education Entertainment and the Persuasive Impact of Narratives', in M.C. Green et al. (eds), *Narrative Impact: Social and Cognitive Foundations* (Mahwah, NJ: Lawrence Erlbaum Associates), 157–81.

Smith, D.W. (2002), 'Mathematical form in the world', *Philosophia Mathematica* 10:2, 102–29.

Smith, N.D. (1998), 'Wisdom', in E. Craig (ed.) *Routledge Encyclopedia of Philosophy* (London: Routledge), 752–4 <http://www.rep.routledge.com/>.

Snow, C.E. (1983), 'Literacy and Language: Relationships during the Preschool Years', *Harvard Educational Review* 53:2, 165–89.

Snowden, D.J. (2004), 'Narrative Patterns: the perils and possibilities of using story in organisations', in E. Lesser and L. Prusak, *Creating Value with Knowledge: Insights from the IBM Institute for Business Value* (Oxford: Oxford University Press), 201–16.

Solnet, D. and Kandampully, J. (2008), 'How some service firms have become part of "service excellence" folklore', *Managing Service Quality* 18:2, 179–93. <http://www.emeraldinsight.com/Insight/ViewContentServlet?Filename=Pub lished/EmeraldFullTextArticle/Articles/1080180205.html> accessed 22 May 2008.

Squire, C. (2005), 'Reading narratives', *Group Analysis* 38:1, 91–107.

Starr, C. (1969), 'Social Benefits versus Technological Risks', *Science*, 165:3899, 1232–8.

Stormer, F. and Devine, K. (2008), 'Acting at Work: Façades of Conformity in Academia', *Journal of Management Inquiry* 17:2, 112–34.

Stott, D. (2007), 'Learning the second way', *British Medical Journal* 335: 7633, 1318–19.

Stowe, H.B. (1853), *A Key to Uncle Tom's Cabin: presenting the original facts and documents upon which the story is founded, together with corroborative statements verifying the truth of the work*, reprinted 1998 (Bedford: Applewood Books).

Strange, J.J. (2002), 'How fictional tales wag real-world beliefs', in M.C.Green et al. (eds), *Narrative Impact: Social and Cognitive Foundations* (Mahwah, NJ: Lawrence Erlbaum Associates), 263–86.

Straus, S.E. et al. (2005), *Evidence-based Medicine: How to Practice and Teach EBM*, 3rd edn (Edinburgh: Churchill Livingstone).

Tait, J. (2003), 'A small boy's view of WW2', *WW2 People's War: An Archive of World War Two Memories*<http://www.bbc.co.uk/ww2peopleswar/stories/05/ a2014705.shtml> accessed 21 October 2008.

Tajfel, H. and Turner, J.C. (1986), 'The social identity theory of inter-group behavior', in S. Worchel and L.W. Austin (eds), *Psychology of Intergroup Relations* (Chicago, IL: Nelson-Hall), 7–24.

Tanenbaum, S. (2003), 'Evidence-based practice in mental health: practical weaknesses meet political strengths', *Journal of Evaluation in Clinical Practice* 9:2, 287–301.

Tanner, L.N. (1988), 'The Path Not Taken: Dewey's model of inquiry', *Curriculum Inquiry*, 18:4, 471–9.

Taylor, C. (1987), Interpretation and the sciences of man', in P. Rabinow and W. Sullivan (eds), *Interpretive Social Science: A Second Look* (Los Angeles: University of California Press), 33–81.

Thier, K. and Erlach, C. (2005), 'The transfer of tacit knowledge with the method "Story Telling"', in G. Schreyögg and J. Koch (eds), *Knowledge Management: Organizational Effectiveness through Storytelling* (Berlin: Erich Schmidt), 123–41.

Thomas, Z. (2005), 'It pays to be a good listener', *Sunday Times*, 6 March, 8–9.

Tichy, N.M. and Cohen, E.B. (1997), *The Leadership Engine: How Winning Companies build Leaders at Every Level* (London: HarperBusiness).

Toulmin, S.E. (1958), *The Uses of Argument* (Cambridge: Cambridge University Press).

Trinder, L. (2000), 'Introduction: The Context of Evidence-Based Practice', in L. Trinder and S. Reynolds (eds), *Evidence-Based Practice: A Critical Appraisal* (Oxford: Blackwell Science), 1–16.

Trinder, L. and Reynolds, S. (eds) (2000), *Evidence-Based Practice: A Critical aAppraisal* (Oxford: Blackwell Science).

Tymieniecka, A.-T. (ed.) *Analecta Husserliana. Vol. XX. The Moral Sense in the Communal Significance of Life* (Boston: Reidel).

Van Maanen, J. (1988), *Tales of the Field: On Writing Ethnography* (Chicago, IL: University of Chicago Press).

von Glasersfeld, E. (1999) 'How Do We Mean? A constructivist sketch of semantics', *Cybernetics and Human Knowing* 6:1, 9–16.

Vygotsky, L.S. (1978), *Mind in Society* (Cambridge, MA: Harvard University Press).

Wack, P. (1985), 'Scenarios: Shooting the Rapids: How Medium-Term Analysis Illuminated the Power of Scenarios for Shell Management', *Harvard Business Review* 63 (November–December), 139–50.

Wainer, H. and Braun, H.I. (eds) (1988), *Test Validity* (Hillsdale, NJ: Lawrence Erlbaum Associates).

Waldron, V.R. (2000), 'Relational experiences and emotion at work', in S. Fineman (ed.) *Emotion in Organizations*, 2nd edn (London: Sage), 64–82.

Wallace, M. and Wray, A. (2006), *Critical Reading and Writing for Postgraduates* (Thousand Oaks, CA: Sage).

Washington, O.G.M. and Moxley, D.P. (2008), 'Telling My Story: from narrative to exhibit in illuminating the lived experience of homelessness among older African American women', *Journal of Health Psychology* 13:2, 154–65.

Watson, J.B. (1930), *Behaviorism* (Chicago, IL: University of Chicago Press).

Watson, S. (2007), 'An extraordinary moment: the healing power of stories', *Canadian Family Physician* 53:8, 1283–7.

Weick, K.E. (1995), *Sensemaking in Organizations* (Thousand Oaks, CA: Sage).

Weil, S.A. et al. (2005), 'Assessing the Potential of Massive Multi-Player Games to be Tools for Military Training', *Proceedings of the Interservice/Industry Training, Simulation, and Education Conference (I/ITSEC) 2005* [website]

<http://openmap.bbn.com/~thussain/publications/2005_IITSEC_paper.pdf> accessed 1 June 2008.

Wenger, E. (1998), *Communities of Practice: Learning, Meaning, and Identity* (Cambridge: Cambridge University Press).

Whetten, D.A. and Godfrey, P.C. (eds) (1998), *Identity in Organizations: Building Theory through Conversations* (London: Sage).

White, S.J. (1997), 'Evidence-based practice and nursing: the new panacea?', *British Journal of Nursing* 6(3): 175–8.

Wilcox, D. (2008), 'Charles Leadbeater: How the web can create social innovation', *Designing for Civil Society* [website] <http://www.designingforcivilsociety. org/2008/03/charles-leadbea.html> accessed 13 April 2008.

Winterowd, W.R. (1975), *Contemporary Rhetoric: A Conceptual Background with Readings* (New York: Harcourt Brace Jovanovich).

Witmer, B.G. and Singer, M.J. (1998), 'Measuring presence in virtual environments: a presence questionnaire', *Presence: Teleoperators and Virtual Environments* 7(3), 225–40.

Wittgenstein, L. (1953), *Philosophical Investigations* (New York: Macmillan).

—— (1975), *On Certainty [Uber Gewissheit]* G.E.M. Anscombe and G.H. von Wright (eds), trans. D. Paul and G.E.M. Anscombe (Oxford: Basil Blackwell). [website] <http://budni.by.ru/oncertainty.html>.

Woodward, H. (1998), 'Reflective journals and portfolios: Learning through assessment', *Assessment and Evaluation in Higher Education* 23:4, 415–24.

World Bank (1999), *World Development Report 1998: knowledge for development* [website] <http://www-wds.worldbank.org/external/default/ WDSContentServer/IW3P/IB/1998/11/17/000178830_98111703550058/ Rendered/PDF/multi0page.pdf> accessed 12 May 2008.

Wyer, R.S. (ed.) (1995), *Advances in Social Cognition* (Hillsdale, NJ: Lawrence Erlbaum Associates).

—— et al. (1995), *Knowledge and Memory: The Real Story* (Hillsdale, NJ: Lawrence Erlbaum Associates).

Index